D0850778

SOVIET TRADE UNIONS

SOVIET AND EAST EUROPEAN STUDIES

Editorial Board

The National Association for Soviet and East European Studies exists for the purpose of promoting study and research on the social sciences as they relate to the Soviet Union and the countries of Eastern Europe. The Monograph Series is intended to promote the publication of works presenting substantial and original research in the economics, politics, sociology and modern history of the USSR and Eastern Europe.

SOVIET AND EAST EUROPEAN STUDIES

Books in the series

SOVIET TRADE UNIONS

THEIR DEVELOPMENT IN THE 1970s

BLAIR A. RUBLE

KENNAN INSTITUTE FOR ADVANCED RUSSIAN STUDIES
WOODROW WILSON INTERNATIONAL CENTER FOR SCHOLARS
WASHINGTON, D.C.

CAMBRIDGE UNIVERSITY PRESS

CAMBRIDGE
LONDON   NEW YORK   NEW ROCHELLE
MELBOURNE   SYDNEY

Published by the Press Syndicate of the University of Cambridge
The Pitt Building, Trumpington Street, Cambridge CB2 1RP
32 East 57th Street, New York, NY 10022, USA
296 Beaconsfield Parade, Middle Park, Melbourne 3206, Australia

First published 1981

Printed in the United States of America

Library of Congress Cataloging in Publication Data
Ruble, Blair A   1949–
Soviet trade unions.
(Soviet and East European studies)
Bibliography: p.
Includes index.
1. Trade-unions – Russia.   I. Title.   II. Series.
HD6732.R82   331.88'0947   80–29646
ISBN 0 521 23704 1

Sally:
С милой -рай,
и в шалаше!

Contents

Tables and figures

Tables

Figures

Acknowledgments

This book grew out of a more lengthy doctoral dissertation. Unfortunately, I am unable to thank all the individuals who have helped me during the preparation of the dissertation and its revision for publication. The institutions and scholars mentioned here represent but a small number of those who have assisted me at various stages during the project's long life. It goes without saying that I alone am responsible for the content of this book and accept any criticism that may arise.

In spite of the limited space available to me for acknowledgments, I cannot overlook my indebtedness to the International Research and Exchanges Board of New York and the Centre for Russian and East European Studies of the University of Toronto for providing generous financial assistance for dissertation research. In addition, I wish to thank H. Gordon Skilling and Peter H. Solomon, Jr., of the University of Toronto, both of whom led me through the dissertation process, and V. N. Smirnov of the Leningrad State University, who supervised my work while I was an exchange scholar at that institution. I want to thank once again the staffs of the University of Toronto Library system, the Toronto Public Library, the Leningrad Public Library, the Academy of Sciences Library in Leningrad, the Library of the Leningrad State University Juridical Faculty, the Lenin Library, the Library of Congress, and the Library of the Woodrow Wilson International Center for Scholars for their patience with my pleas for bibliographic assistance.

In revising this manuscript for publication I benefited enormously from the constant encouragement and good advice of S. Frederick Starr. There is no doubt that there would not have been a book without his counseling throughout the revision process. Many other individuals have commented on one or more sections of the manuscript at various stages of its preparation, but I hope that they will understand why I cannot list them here and will find that their frequently sharp criticisms have had beneficial impact upon the final product.

Finally, I would like to make special mention of my great debt to Arcadius Kahan of the University of Chicago. In an academic world too often marred by petty squabbles, Professor Kahan has demonstrated time and time again that it is possible to be at once a gentleman and a scholar.

I gratefully acknowledge permission of the following publishers for using portions of my previously published work:

"Dual Functioning Trade Unions in the USSR," *British Journal of Industrial Relations*, Summer 1979, Vol. 17, No. 2, pp. 235–41.

"Full Employment Legislation in the USSR," *Comparative Labor Law*, Fall 1977, Vol. 2, No. 3, pp. 176–85.

"The Soviet American Comparison: A High Risk Adventure," *Comparative Labor Law*, Winter 1977, Vol. 2, No. 4, pp. 247–59.

"The Changes in Soviet Trade Unions," *New Leader*, 23 April 1979, pp. 12–14.

"Factory Unions and Workers Rights," Chapter 4 in Arcadius Kahan and Blair A. Ruble (eds.), *Industrial Labor and the USSR* (Elmsford, N.Y.: Pergamon Press, 1979), pp. 59–84.

BLAIR A. RUBLE

Washington, D.C.
March 1981

Abbreviations

AATUF	All-African Trade Union Federation
AFL	American Federation of Labor
ATUC	African Trade Union Conference
AUCCTU	All-Union Central Council of Trade Unions
CGIL	Italian General Confederation of Labor
CIO	Congress of Industrial Organizations
CPSU	Communist Party of the Soviet Union
CPUSTAL	Permanent Committee for Labor Unity in Latin America
FZMK	Factory Trade Union Committee
Gosplan	State Planning Committee
ICATU	International Confederation of Arab Trade Unions
ICFTU	International Confederation of Free Trade Unions
IFCTU	International Federation of Christian Trade Unions
IFTU	International Federation of Trade Unions
ILO	International Labour Organisation
ITS	International Trade Secretariats
Komsomol	Young Communist League
KTS	Commission on Labor Disputes
LAFCTU	Latin American Federation of Christian Trade Unions
Narkomtrud	People's Commissariat of Labor
NEP	New Economic Policy
NTO	Scientific-Technical Society
OATUU	Organization of African Trade Unity
Profintern	Red International of Labor Unions

RKK	Union–management Dispute Commission
RSFSR	Russian Soviet Federated Socialist Republic
SMOT	Free Interprofessional Association of Workers
TI	Trade International
TUC	Trade Union Congress (British)
UAW	United Auto Workers
VKP(b)	All-Union Communist Party (Bolshevik)
VOIR	All-Union Society of Innovators and Rationalizers
VRSPS	All-Russian Council of Trade Unions
VSNKh	Supreme Council of the National Economy
WCL	World Confederation of Labor
WFTU	World Federation of Trade Unions

Introduction

It is axiomatic in the field of Soviet studies that one is never right; he is only wrong with varying degrees of vulnerability.
  – Raymond A. Bauer, *The New Man in Soviet Psychology*, 1952

Throughout much of Soviet history, industrial labor remained the subject of hotly contested political battles. Legitimated by its claims of proletarian power, the Soviet state could not ignore basic issues of worker living standards, nor could it fail to define an essential place for workers within Soviet society. Yet the pull of industrialization created powerful counter pressures, forces rewarding the specialist and the bureaucrat over the worker. It was only during the 1960s and 1970s that the labor question was solved – defused through a broad consensus on the optimal nature of Soviet labor policies. That concurrence was based upon inattention to manpower supply problems, reduction of monetary wage differentials, and moderation in dealing with labor discipline violations.

In spite of the public complaints concerning labor shortages resulting from World War II, Soviet economic development during much of the postwar period has been more or less predicated on an abundant and relatively cheap supply of labor. Such an assumption may no longer be warranted. With the exception of the Central Asian republics, the rate of population growth (largely through births) has declined and, again with the exception of Central Asia, rural population reserves have been expended. Moreover, the contemporary Soviet population is older and better paid than Soviet populations of the past. As in North America and Europe, a smaller proportion of the population must support services for a larger proportion, and, as elsewhere, this pressure can only be reduced by increased labor productivity.

1

Yet some Soviet economists have noted that Soviet wage policies are incompatible with the need to increase productivity. Major wage reforms from 1956 to 1960 and in 1968 increased the minimum wage significantly, as they did middle salaries, while upper-level monetary incomes were frozen. As a result, some Soviet political leaders and economic planners have come to argue that wage differentials need to expand rather than contract.

Finally, turning peasants into workers is always difficult. The Soviets have had no better luck than anyone else in this regard. During the 1930s, the Soviets dealt with the resulting labor indiscipline through the enactment of severe criminal sanctions. However, as early as 1951 such policies began to change, and in 1956 all such sanctions were lifted. Since then, trade union job protection rights have been expanded so that, by the late 1960s, Soviet workers were beyond the reach not only of the judicial system for labor discipline violations but of their managers as well. This "freedom not to work hard," as some observers have called it, flies in the face of the growing need to improve productivity. At the same time, sociological investigations began to present indiscipline as the product of mismanagement. The emphasis in labor discipline policies and practices shifted dramatically from punishment to education.

Given the need to improve productivity and a general consensus regarding the broad lines of a labor policy that is perceived by many in the Soviet Union as thwarting that goal, one should not be surprised by the growing evidence that Soviet labor policy can no longer remain outside the larger political arena. Even more important, the labor question is becoming political precisely at a time when a major leadership succession is about to take place.

This book does not examine Soviet policies toward industrial labor in their entirety. Rather it focuses upon an institution – the trade unions – whose reemergence was closely tied to the consensus of the 1960s and 1970s. After all, Soviet trade unionists claim to represent 98 percent of their country's total work force. About 128 million union members belong to some 31 industrial unions, 170 regional councils, 700,000 "primary organizations," 500,000 shop committees, and 2.5 million trade union groups.[1] In return for 1 percent of their monthly salaries, union members receive housing, medical, welfare, and wage benefits unavailable to nonunion workers. According to some estimates, nearly two-thirds of the union cardholders work in industrial enterprises. They are the primary subject of this inquiry.[2]

The facts on trade union representation fail to impress many Western observers.[3] Western knowledge of Soviet trade union operations is usually confined to relentless attempts to gain control over international labor forums and brutish efforts to suppress labor unrest. The Russian Revolution immediately polarized the international labor community. Both the Amsterdam-based International Federation of Trade Unions and the new League of Nations' International Labour Organisation in Geneva bitterly opposed the goals and tactics of Bolshevism. In response to continued hostility, Soviet union officials moved in 1920 to create the Red International of Labor Unions (Profintern). Considerable enmity soon developed between Bolshevik and anti-Bolshevik union groups, a conflict which even their shared fear of Hitler's Germany could not overcome. World War II and the formation of the World Federation of Trade Unions in 1945 provided yet another opportunity for Soviet, British, and some U.S. unionists to work together. Their efforts quickly disintegrated under the pressures of the Cold War and the various ideological diatribes and institutional vendettas that lasted well into the 1970s.

The aggressiveness of Soviet union officials in suppressing the legitimate demands of Soviet workers has only reinforced this polarization of the international labor community. One need not turn the clock back to the days of Stalin to find flagrant violations of basic human rights by the state. Even during 1980, Amnesty International reported that the Soviet Union had initiated yet another major crackdown on dissidents with "an increase in the number of arrests and trials."[4]

Apart from the general Soviet disregard for human dignity and civil rights, there are several recent instances of Soviet trade union officials responding to worker demands with anything but sympathy. In 1978 Vladimir Klebanov, the prime mover in the formation of an independent worker organization – the Free Trade Union Association – was confined to the Donetsk Psychiatric Hospital. A year later several organizers of a similar group – the Free Interprofessional Association of Workers (SMOT) – faced arrest, trial, and/or confinement to mental institutions.[5] Knowledge of such actions is fundamental to an understanding of the Soviet labor scene. The consistency with which such official behavior has occurred throughout Soviet history only reinforces the image of repression. Yet it is equally important for the Western observer to place the issue of labor dissent and the suppression of that discord within the broader context of changes that have taken place in Soviet union behavior over the past quarter-century.

During much of Stalin's rule, Soviet workers could not leave their jobs for fear of criminal prosecution. The income structure of the Soviet work force was strikingly inequitable. Despite wartime losses the population of able-bodied citizens grew rapidly, with still sizable reserves of potential industrial labor in the countryside, the army, and the prison camps. Although a corps of young, educated, and ambitious managers nominally ran the economy, this elite group was made to feel insecure by unrealistic production targets, ministerial decrees, Party interference, and police scrutiny.[6]

A quarter of a century later, Soviet workers can leave their jobs – and they do so with a frequency that threatens the very stability of Soviet economic life. The income structure has become so equitable that many Western and Soviet economists suggest that it could greatly retard economic growth. The economy absorbs nearly all labor reserves and now faces severe manpower shortages. The political, economic, and social dimensions of the contemporary Soviet labor scene, although derived from the policies of the past, cannot be compared with those of Stalin's time. The Soviet Union is not the country it was in 1953, nor is the world of the Soviet worker unchanged.[7]

Some changes, such as those affecting manpower allocation, occurred independently of government policies. Others, such as those influencing labor–management relations, resulted as much from a maturing economy as from conscious planning. Still others, such as the alteration of the wage structure, were consequences of decisions reached by senior officials of the government and the Party.

Deliberate or not, these changes have been influenced by political decisions that lie at the core of Soviet labor policies.

Immediately after Stalin's death, previously covert opposition to the use of indiscriminate terror burst into the open. Initially, Nikita Khrushchev and other members of the Party's Presidium engineered a coup against secret police chieftain L. P. Beria. As time passed, deeper and more fundamental shifts in policy began to occur. The state granted amnesties for various groups of prisoners, and legal scholars discussed the need to erect barriers against the abuses of the 1930s and 1940s.[8] Such movements gained strength after Khrushchev's 1956 denunciation of Stalin.

In order to dismantle a system rooted in terror, Party leaders sought alternative supports for compliance with civil authority. Could one base compliance upon a sense of mutual trust between manager and worker? Despite the fervent desires of some, no one has found a way to generate such trust within Soviet society, and the Soviet Communist Party has shown no keen desire to alter the status quo, even if such means should be devised. What Khrushchev and Brezhnev sought, each in his own way, was to end the excesses of Stalinism without dismantling the system that gave rise to them. To do so they were willing to pay off blue collar workers with more money as long as greater income did not mean greater power. As a result, post-Stalinist generations of political and economic managers have found themselves in the unenviable position of being unable either to revert to the use of terror or to introduce systematic change.

At the time of Stalin's death, conventional wisdom in the Soviet Union held that violations of labor discipline were almost solely the acts of malicious individuals working against the best interests of the state. Responsibility for violation of labor rules lay either with the individual worker or with the union and management officials who permitted a violation to occur in the first place. In 1954, for example, the chairman of the All-Union Central Council of Trade Unions (AUCCTU), Nikolai Shvernik, declared that truancy, absenteeism, and other violations of discipline could not be tolerated and had to be stopped by any means possible.[9] Soviet union leaders viewed such violations as willful acts against the state and defined truancy and absenteeism as criminal offenses.

The Party, union, and government had begun to reduce some

of the harsher disciplinary methods before the death of Stalin. Administrative and judicial directives of July 1951, releasing factory officials from the legal requirement of considering attendance records when distributing social welfare benefits, proved to be the first step toward less repressive employment legislation. However, an immediate increase in violations of labor discipline inhibited any further thaw. Finally, on 25 April 1956, the Presidium of the USSR Supreme Soviet decriminalized industrial absenteeism. Since that time labor legislation has generally protected the worker's right to change jobs at will.[10]

Meanwhile, the growing shortage of skilled labor has combined with centralized control over wages to prod factory managers into competition with one another over personnel. Although the Communist Party, the Soviet government, and the trade unions removed terror from the worker–manager relationship and replaced it with fringe benefits, the new system of positive rewards diminished managerial control over the behavior of workers. By the late 1960s, several Soviet legal scholars had begun to explore the motivation underlying compliance and noncompliance with norms of labor discipline. As a result of these efforts, political leaders and the popular press no longer portray violations of labor discipline as "bourgeois wrecking." Instead, they contend that tardiness, absenteeism, and slacking off are understandable responses to inadequacies in the services available to workers. Spokesmen for this new approach claim that improved working conditions are an essential step toward improved productivity.[11]

Union officials do not implement national labor policy in isolation; they must cooperate with managerial and Party colleagues at the plant. Together, these officers form the so-called troika governing every Soviet factory. Each member of this team must deal with the other two as well as with immediate supervisors outside the plant. These complex formal and informal relationships determine the effectiveness of centrally established policies. For example, Party and union officials may choose to cooperate with one another by organizing a political lecture series; union and management by organizing so-called socialist competitions. The practical significance of national policies for industrial workers will be determined by the extent to which cooperation takes place.

In theory Soviet workers enjoy a wide range of formal, legal, and social rights. Local union officials remain the primary guarantors of these rights through their control of grievance procedures. To understand the true character of these "socialist" human rights, one must assess the actual performance of trade union officials in hundreds of thousands of factories, stores, and offices throughout the Soviet Union.

The 1977 constitution guarantees Soviet citizens the right to participate in economic management.[12] This right is as old as the Soviet Union itself and theoretically is exercised through the involvement of union representatives in various conferences, forums, and planning sessions. Having been elected by the workers of a given shop or factory, these union officers supposedly represent the viewpoints of a plant's entire work force. This approach begs several important questions: What institutions, if any, exist for workers and managers to sit down together and talk? If the unions really do participate in managerial decision making, do the factory directors necessarily consider the opinions of on-line workers? If not, why not?

Once the role of Soviet unions in domestic affairs is understood, the Western observer can evaluate their policies and behavior in the international arena and can ask: How has the involvement of Soviet labor in international affairs been altered over time? Is there any connection between these changes and the development of more sophisticated approaches to internal policies? Are there any differences between the international posture of the AUCCTU and that of the Soviet Ministry of Foreign Affairs? How serious are Soviet union officials about using international labor forums as something other than a "bully pulpit" for Marxist-Leninist propaganda?

Whether one discusses the role of the AUCCTU in the International Labour Organisation (ILO) or that of a disputes commission in a local metalworks, no single image of Soviet labor relations emerges as totally valid. Critics of the Soviet system find ample evidence of union failings; admirers find much evidence of success. Both base their arguments upon "facts" that they claim to have unearthed.

Soviet reality is much more complex than either the critics or the admirers of Soviet trade unions are willing to admit. The question one should ask is not whether Soviet trade unions represent workers, but when, where, and how. And when, where, and how do they fail to do so? Is it possible to discern patterns of behavior within the union record? Can an environment be posited in which unions are most (or least) likely to meet their legal obligations? These are the truly interesting questions to be raised in any study of Soviet unions.

Ultimately, Western observers must relate the lessons of Soviet labor development to those of their own society. To do so they must first understand how Soviet institutions function within their own environment. It is not sufficient, for example, to compare Soviet and Western collective agreements simply because they share a similar nomenclature. Soviet agreements legitimize decisions already taken by factory union and managerial officials, whereas U.S. and European contracts establish mutually agreed-upon norms for a single plant or an entire industry. The first task of any cross-cultural comparison, then, must be to understand what is being compared on its own terms.

A further complication is that far more people know something about Soviet trade unions than know them well. Many Western observers know one or two ingredients but not the entire recipe. They know that the Soviet Union sabotaged the World Federation of Trade Unions or that the AUCCTU turned its back on the dissident Klebanov. They recognize that Stalin's unions helped to imprison scores of workers and that Brezhnev's Soviet Union regularly violates many cherished human rights, or that Soviet reality frequently falls short of Soviet ideology. The purpose of this study is to build upon this base in order to construct a complete portrait of Soviet union activity in all its varied forms (both positive and negative) so that appropriate comparisons can be made in the future between Western trade unions and their Soviet counterparts.

1

Soviet trade union development: 1917–1956

Unlike their Western counterparts, Soviet trade union leaders perceive the interests of the assembly-line worker and those of the Soviet state (and, through that state, factory management) as identical.[1] Now that the workers own the means of production, trade union leaders argue, any increase in national wealth through higher productivity will be to the direct benefit of the new owners – the workers themselves. As a result, Soviet union officials view higher productivity as a preeminent goal. They also recognize, however, that individual managers may seek short-term gain at the expense of workers by introducing illegitimate managerial practices. They admit that simple administrative inefficiency may cheat some workers out of their rightful benefits. Therefore, Soviet unions acknowledge that they must defend their membership against the "bureaucratism" of management. In other words, a factory union leader in the Soviet Union must both mobilize workers behind production goals and defend those same workers against unscrupulous administrators.

This concept of dual-functioning trade unions emerged from the turmoil of the revolutions of 1917.[2] As is well known, V. I. Lenin and the Bolsheviks staged a successful coup d'état in that year, deposing the Provisional Government of A. Kerensky. In order to gain control, however, Lenin's party needed to broaden its support while appearing to remain loyal to the self-proclaimed goal of creating a workers' state. Meanwhile, cumbersome trade union organizations in operation since the Revolution of 1905 found themselves on the verge of losing whatever support they had to factory workers' councils. Union leaders needed outside help to maintain their authority within the increasingly turbulent factories. Thus union leaders and Bolsheviks alike came to rely upon each other; neither paid much attention to the terms of their alliance.

Once the Civil War ended, however, the Bolsheviks and trade unionists reevaluated their relationship. A bitter debate ensued within Party and union ranks over the appropriate role of unions within a Communist Party–dominated workers' state. Various options were discussed that, although compatible with the notion of Party dictatorship, offered greater and lesser degrees of union autonomy. This debate reached its zenith at the Tenth Party Congress in March 1921, at which scores of propositions were distilled into three contending proposals.

The first suggestion, put forth by A. Shlyapnikov and A. Kollontai under the title Workers' Opposition, emphasized trade union independence from Party and state supervision.[3] This proposal supported a syndicalist approach by which trade unions would manage major sectors of the economy. A single All-Russian Producers Council would replace the Supreme Council of the National Economy (VSNKh), the People's Commissariat of Labor (Narkomtrud), and the All-Russian Council of Trade Unions (VRSPS). Subordinate trade union and state organizations would then administer policies established by the new agency. In addition, Shlyapnikov and Kollontai suggested several supplemental programs, including a number of free services for workers and an accompanying phasing out of the currency system.

Directly contradicting this syndicalist position, the second recommendation, that of Leon Trotsky and Nikolai Bukharin, urged the complete subjugation of the unions to Party and state authority. According to their proposals, the unions would manage compulsory labor programs, improve productivity, and enforce labor discipline. They believed such a configuration to be the logical evolution of Bolshevik authority from a period of war communism to one of proletarian dictatorship. Trotsky and Bukharin, then, hoped to prevent trade union operations from becoming either independent of or supraordinate to the Communist Party and the workers' state.

The third proposition, that of the Group of Ten (which included both Lenin and trade union leader Mikhail Tomsky), allowed for some union independence, but only within the strict confines of broader Party and government policies. This position, which with Lenin's support carried the day, represented a compromise between the resolution of the Workers' Opposition, on the one hand, and that of Trotsky and Bukharin, on the other.

Like many compromises it lacked internal consistency. By offering an alternative to opponents on both his left and his right, Lenin conceded that unions should help raise productivity, but on condition that they guarantee workers' legitimate rights against infringements by management. Moreover, according to Lenin, the unions could not use coercive measures against laborers as Bukharin and Trotsky had suggested. Instead union leaders would serve as a "school of administration, a school of economic management, and a school of communism" for members of a new communist society. Out of this compromise position emerged the concept of dual-functioning trade unions.

Some observers consider the defeat of the Workers' Opposition to have been a deathblow to independent Russian unionism.[4] Certainly union policies have been subordinate to those of the Communist Party ever since, yet the role of trade unions within the Soviet political and economic system has not remained static. The 1921 debate became important to subsequent union development because Vladimir Ilich Lenin himself proposed a solution to the troublesome union question, which a Party congress then ratified. As Lenin became canonized, any discussion of the role of unions in Soviet political and economic life had to take Lenin's 1921 position into account. Those forms of labor organization outside the perimeters of that position – such as autonomous factory workers' councils – became inconceivable.

The events of 1921 were not inevitable. Past policy discussions preconditioned but did not predetermine the future course of events. It can be argued, for example, that had sailors at Kronstadt not been in open revolt and had the country's industrial plant not deteriorated into shambles, the Workers' Opposition might well have emerged victorious. The Russia of March 1921 could ill afford an experiment with syndicalism.[5] If the young Soviet state had been able to achieve a modicum of stability, would the Workers' Opposition have had a greater impact? It must be remembered that the Tenth Party Congress did not refute syndicalism so much as it responded to an appeal for absolute Party unity at a time of acute political and economic crises, and that this appeal took the form of a personal summons from no less a personage than Lenin himself.

During the spring of 1921, the Soviet leadership approved a policy combining features of a socialist economy with those of small capitalist ventures. The promulgation of the New Economic Policy, or NEP (1921–9), failed to spark a renewed discussion of the trade union question. Within months an article drafted by Lenin appeared in *Pravda* spelling out trade union functions under the new mixed economy. This article declared the underlying principles of union activity to be those endorsed by the Tenth Party Congress. The unions, Lenin concluded, must serve as "the transmission belt from the Communist Party to the masses."[6]

The NEP severed all formal linkages between the unions and the state. The Russian Soviet Federated Socialist Republic (RSFSR) People's Commissariat of Labor and the RSFSR People's Commissariat of Social Welfare (both became USSR commissariats after 1922) gained control of state social insurance programs, disputes procedures, and safety regulations – all of which previously had been administered by the unions. The state withdrew financial subsidies for union programs as union membership became voluntary. Most significantly, the unions could now organize strikes in government enterprises.[7]

Initially these reforms led to a marked decline in union membership. This reduction combined with diminishing union revenues to undermine union assistance to beleaguered industrial workers. Union responsibilities, which were well defined in the private sector, remained obscure in the public sector. Many local and national union leaders proved indecisive, ineffectual, or incompetent.[8]

By 1925 this bleak situation began to improve. Membership grew to its pre-NEP high while several union officials adapted traditional Western methods of labor relations – such as collective bargaining – to the NEP environment. The latter half of the 1920s became a kind of golden age. In 1927, on the eve of the tenth anniversary of the October Revolution of 1917, the Soviet government proposed step toward a thirty-five-hour work week. This announcement led union chief Mikhail Tomsky to declare that Soviet trade unions had succeeded in defending the economic interests of workers where countless other unions had failed. *"Workers' wages, work time,"* Tomsky cried, "these are the chief indicators of the achievements of our unions."[9]

In 1929, Stalin's success in reorienting Party policies toward a dramatic acceleration of industrialization undermined union efforts, ineffectual though they may have been, and halted any further evolution of the unions toward the defense of workers' rights. Instead, the leading slogan of the period exhorted union officials to "turn their faces towards production."

Following 1928, Soviet trade union officers came to pay less and less attention to the workers, while both national and local Party and government officials became more and more unconcerned about unions. Unable to gain the support of prominent political leaders, local union leaders had little choice but to support Party-approved production plans. At the same time, the Party began to tighten its political control over union organization, severely limiting independent union activities.[10]

During the NEP, Party members gradually gained a monopoly over central union leadership positions.[11] Nevertheless Party membership among regional and local union officers remained markedly low. During L. M. Kaganovich's tenure as the Party's untitled regent over the unions in 1929 and 1930, as well as under the new AUCCTU Chairman Nikolai Shvernik, relative newcomers to the union movement were recruited into leadership positions. In general, this new generation replaced those who had participated in the uprisings of 1905 and 1917. As late as October 1928, 28 percent of the holders of sixty top union posts had previous political affiliations with parties other than the communist All-Union Communist Party (Bolshevik) (VKP(b)). By October 1930, that figure had dropped to 3 percent.[12]

The stridently callous attitude of the new leadership group toward the worker may be seen in several accounts published during the period by the Berlin-based Menshevik newspaper *Sotsialisticheskii vestnik.* For example, at one construction site, union and management officials forced laborers to work "not less than" ten to twelve hours a day, and in Stalingrad the city trade union council agreed that outdoor workers could labor in − 20°C temperatures without even provision for special clothing.[13]

In 1933 the Soviet government abolished the People's Commissariat of Labor. Shortly thereafter Party leaders moved to break up large and powerful unions into much smaller units. They suggested that this decentralization process would improve relations between central and local union officials, thereby improving contacts between leaders and workers. In practice their actions, which were followed by a decision to abolish regional inter–trade union councils, further weakened the unions and shattered the last remnants of a national power base.[14]

The erosion of national and local trade union power resulting from the Party assault on union institutions became manifest in a number of labor policies throughout the 1930s. First, union officials failed to meet their obligations to defend workers' rights to work in a safe environment, to strike, and to formulate comprehensive collective agreements. Second, a growing number of union administrative norms governing wages and production management, as well as unemployment and social insurance programs, became distinctively proproduction in orientation.

Labor protection and safety

Among the administrative duties transferred from the unions to the People's Commissariat of Labor at the beginning of the NEP, those governing labor protection, labor safety, and overtime regulations were the most important.[15] During the NEP, the unions exerted considerable influence over the formation and regulation of safety standards. In the beginning of the period, working conditions had become intolerable. The AUCCTU, citing alarming accident rates, lobbied for and obtained an agreement with the Supreme Council of the National Economy raising the national budgetary allocation for the improvement of factory conditions to 37 million rubles in 1926 and to 43 million in 1927. As a result of growing pressure, economic managers became increasingly sensitive to the problem of industrial safety.[16] However, the decision to accelerate the process of industrialization reversed this trend.

In 1933 the Soviet state dismantled the People's Commissariat of Labor, forcing the trade unions to establish a People's

Inspectorate of Safety.[17] Elected factory inspectors were to seek strict enforcement of safety norms with the assistance of regional and central union organizations. During the Second Five-Year Plan (1933–7), trade union leaders made one last-ditch effort to salvage safety norms. Between December 1934 and May 1935 the unions carried on a debate in *Trud* and *Za industrializatsiiu* over the unhealthy conditions in factories. Reversing their response to earlier attempts in the mid-1920s, Party leaders now rejected union demands, and by 1936 the AUCCTU disbanded its own labor inspectorate.[18] In the spring of 1937, trade union spokesmen spoke out for greater adherence to safety standards, once again to no avail.[19] As the Soviet economy geared up for war, the trade unions grew increasingly powerless against deteriorating working conditions and the widespread use of overtime labor.

Strikes and disputes resolution

Although less successful, strikes had become more serious as the 1920s progressed. By 1926, management had gained the right to initiate binding arbitration for disputes arising out of collective bargaining. Finally, by 1929, Party leaders had declared strike actions to be antiproletarian and counterproductive.[20]

Union leaders retained their ambivalent attitude toward the strike mechanism throughout the 1920s, believing other forums, such as joint union–management dispute commissions (RKK) established under a 1922 decree drafted by Lenin, to be more effective. Under the 1922 law, once collective bargaining broke down, either labor (i.e. union) or management representatives could turn to local officers of the People's Commissariat of Labor for conciliation or arbitration. Individuals had obtained the right to bring their complaints before the joint union–management factory disputes commissions or before the people's courts. When these efforts failed to alleviate pressures for strikes, regional offices of the People's Commissariat of Labor began to organize conciliation and arbitration tribunals.

Although the actual performance of the union commissions varied widely from factory to factory, workers consistently perceived these bodies as having a distinctively managerial predisposition. The courts had proved themselves to be more prolabor yet significantly slower in deliberation. In August 1928, a new law further clarified the position of the factory disputes commission vis-à-vis management by limiting the number of disputes entering the formal judicial system. This act proved to be the last of its type for nearly three decades.

The slightly promanagement bent of disputes resolution procedures during the NEP was magnified during the First Five-Year Plan as unions began to abrogate their duties as defenders of workers' rights. By 1933, the factory commissions emerged as management-dominated bodies seeking increased labor productivity. The conciliation and arbitration boards of the People's Commissariat of Labor fared even worse during this period. After their initial transfer in 1933 to the inter–trade union councils, they ceased to exist. The 1937 resolutions disbanding regional union councils failed to provide for the continuation of conciliation and arbitration efforts beyond the industrial enterprise.

Collective agreements

Western-style collective bargaining appeared in the Soviet Union during the first years of the NEP,[21] but early on union leaders found bargaining unsuited to Soviet conditions and abandoned it. In its place a new approach to the formulation of collective agreements arose, one which proved somewhat beneficial to the workers from about 1925 through 1928. Previously, under the early NEP, regional committees of individual unions had negotiated with industrial trusts, whereas central committees of individual unions had negotiated with commissariats to determine wage, safety, and hygiene norms. The system of agreements covering industrial workers that developed from these negotiations was only moderately successful.

After the period 1924–5, under a new approach to collective agreements, either centralized planning bureaucracies or state arbitrators could establish wages; as a result pay scales became increasingly unimportant to the core of union–management agreements, and traditional Western methods of collective bargaining became restricted. Subsequent contracts negotiated by factory union committees focused primarily on issues of safety, cultural services, and production norms. The collective agreement gradually evolved into a bilateral document through which unions sought decent working conditions and management sought higher levels of worker productivity.

The Communist Party decision to accelerate industrialization brought about further changes in the Soviet collective agreement. From 1929 until 1934, central union agencies launched several campaigns designed to increase the use of collective agreements as instruments for improving productivity. The use of the agreements, never an effective means of raising production, declined, until by 1935 they had quietly passed out of existence.[22]

Except for the period from 1937 to 1938, this situation remained unchanged until after World War II. In the period 1937–8 the question of the desirability of reintroducing the agreements came to the fore. In April 1937, two articles appeared in the official AUCCTU monthly, *Voprosy profdvizheniia*, openly debating the merits of a system of agreements negotiated at the enterprise level.[23] The first stated that such constraints would only duplicate previously existing norms and were therefore unnecessary; the second argued that the agreements would ensure both safe working conditions and high levels of productivity and therefore were desirable. In May 1937, the AUCCTU granted local union organizations the right to reintroduce the agreements during the following year. By August a new editorial board had denounced the "narrow democratism" of "counterrevolutionary elements" among enterprise-level union activists.[24] When the time finally came for the first documents to be negotiated, the union monthly (now entitled *Profsoiuzy SSSR*) noted that a sound wage policy had become a precondition for the agreements. Such a policy, however, could not be achieved until a "Trotskyite-Bukharinist gang" opposing the linkage of wages to productivity "had been eliminated."[25] By May 1939, new course outlines for trade union volunteers failed to make any mention of the collective agreements.[26]

Wages

The extent to which wages were to be differentiated according to professions remained a dominant issue in Soviet labor politics throughout the 1920s and 1930s. Abram Bergson has identified two complete cycles of wage inequality during the period, a dramatic equalization of wages following the Revolution, and a reversal of this equalization during the first years of the NEP.[27] A second cycle in the period 1926–31 began with a marked decrease in wage inequality, but the differentiation of wages grew substantially between 1931 and 1934. Overall, the wage structure of the Soviet Union in 1934 remained more equal than that of tsarist Russia on the eve of World War I.

In the 1920s, the trade unions generally had supported the abolition of payment of wages in kind but had opposed both increased wage inequality and the linkage of wages solely to production.[28] Nationally, the AUCCTU had struggled with the Supreme Council of the National Economy for Party support of this position, while local, regional, and trust trade union bodies had attempted to establish wage rates through collective bargaining.

Trade union opposition to wage policies ended with the NEP. By 1931, union leaders were openly supporting Stalin's call for increased wage differentiation despite the 50 percent reduction in real industrial wages that took place during the First Five-Year Plan (1928–32). Although real wages improved slightly during the Second Five-Year Plan, they dropped off once more as the build-up for a wartime economy began in the late 1930s.[29]

Participation in production management

As the NEP developed, monthly production conferences involving representatives from factory union, management, and Party organizations emerged as a primary mechanism for the inclusion of union officers in production management. Initially Party leaders perceived these bodies to be another means of raising productivity. From the very beginning, national trade union leaders were ambivalent toward the conferences. They rightfully foresaw that the development of such assemblies would undermine union partnership with management.[30]

By the end of the NEP, Party and management officials had transformed the production conference into organizing bodies for socialist emulation.[31] The organization of socialist competition (one form of such emulation) allowed brigades of workers to compete for bonuses of various forms. Such programs became the cornerstone for the activities of union production management, and the Shock Worker Movement (another form of emulation) demanded increasing attention from local union officers.[32] By the end of the First Five-Year Plan the Shock Worker Movement had also run its course. The Stakhanovite Movement – perhaps the ultimate form of socialist competition – carried union preoccupation with production to new heights. Launched in August 1935, when a Donbass coal miner named A. G. Stakhanov filled his quota by 1400 percent, this movement eventually affected every Soviet citizen and combined with war preparations to further increase the union obsession with productivity.[33]

Despite abuses, socialist emulation remained a system of positive rewards which was used to reinforce high levels of productivity. As such, it could not solve crucial manpower problems, such as turnover, truancy, and absentceism. When, by the end of the First Five-Year Plan in 1932, existing sanctions had failed to limit such offenses, Party leaders had to choose between sacrificing increased industrial growth and enacting more stringent labor laws. They chose the latter.[34]

In 1932, for the first time since the beginning of the NEP, government officials reintroduced the internal passport system. Truancy, now more narrowly defined, carried with it the risk of losing union food rationing, housing, employment, and social welfare benefits. As a result of these steps, the price for one lost day of work became the loss of access to most goods and services. Although these measures proved initially successful, management and union officials frequently were loath to enforce them.[35]

Even more stringent revisions of the labor code approved in December 1938 placed the industrial worker almost entirely under the command of management and the Soviet state, for leaving one's job became tantamount to a criminal offense. Regulations effective January 1939 defined twenty minutes' tardiness as unjustifiable absence and subjected the tardy employee to unyielding criminal prosecution. When management, Party, union, medical, and judicial officials failed to enforce these regulations, a 1940 state decree made these officials equally liable to criminal sanction.[36]

As bad as conditions had become within the civilian economy, life in penal colonies was clearly worse. Writing in 1937 for the *Moscow Daily News,* E. Genkin noted that "pioneers in mastering the Soviet Arctic" were constructing rail lines in −50°C temperatures and blinding snow storms, and that settlements "and a hospital with a surgical department" grew up "where formerly human foot had never stepped." Comrade Genkin could scarcely find the words to express the importance of these projects to the Soviet economy:

During the Stalinist Five-Year plans the Party entrusted the workers of NKVD (People's Commissariat of Home Affairs) with a number of gigantic construction undertakings which were of tremendous national economic importance. . . .

Under the leadership of Yezhov, the Stalinist People's Commissar, permanent cadres have been acquired for construction jobs. Hundreds of the best Bolsheviks have now been sent to the most important construction jobs being carried out by men of the NKVD. They have brought a live Bolshevik atmosphere there, and they have already achieved no small success in labor productivity.

Relentlessly exposing the enemies of the people, the Trotskyite-Bukharinite Japano-German spies, smoking them out of all their holes, protecting the integrity and inviolability of the Soviet frontiers, the glorious workers of the People's Commissariat of Home Affairs are, at the same time, carrying on tremendous work in industry.[37]

One need not even turn to Aleksandr Solzhenitsyn to understand that, as the 1930s drew to a close, the unions served as agents of state and Party control over the Soviet population. When factory administrators refused to increase production quotas, assiduous union organizations moved to have them punished. When workers failed to meet higher production quotas, vigilant factory union officers took severe disciplinary action. Thus, over the course of the early five-year plans, the Communist Party and the Soviet government imbued union participation in management with state control of the unions.

Unemployment and social insurance programs

Throughout the NEP, unemployment remained the most acute labor problem confronting Soviet society.[38] Not surprisingly, unemployment insurance had emerged as a primary issue for bureaucratic competition between the trade unions and the People's Commissariat of Labor. By February 1921, only the commissariat's Department of Labor (later Labor Exchange) had gained the right to distribute benefits, thereby compelling the unemployed to accept employment before they could receive benefits. Party and government leaders had altered the program on several occasions, but it remained inadequate at best and on 1 January 1925 was abolished.

The free labor market lasted less than two years. In 1926 the Soviet government reinstituted a system of labor exchanges. The unions considered this move a victory because they had been struggling to protect their membership against job losses to nonunion workers. The situation continued to deteriorate throughout the 1920s, with union members being only marginally better off than their nonunion colleagues. Once the rapid industrialization program began, however, more jobs became available. In October 1930 both the exchanges and unemployment benefits ended. Since that time there has been no officially recognized unemployment in the Soviet Union and, hence, no unemployment benefits.[39]

In the realm of social insurance, the NEP brought about slow but perceptible improvement in services as the government transformed the generous 1917–18 program ever so slowly into a reality.[40] At the beginning of the period, the People's Commissariat of Labor and, to a lesser extent, the People's Commissariat of Social Welfare had reduced the number of eligible persons and had improved the government's ability to meet payment schedules to those remaining on the eligibility list. The commissariats initiated a pension program at this time, and in February 1925 the People's Commissariat of Labor established the Council of Social Insurance. This body, which consisted of representatives from the labor commissariat, the AUCCTU, and the Supreme Council of the National Economy, administered nearly all industrial social insurance programs. Social insurance coverage gradually expanded to include a wider array of citizens while under the direction of this body.

Three fundamental changes during the early five-year plans undermined existing social welfare programs. First, the unions accepted responsibility for the distribution of benefits upon the dissolution of the People's Commissariat of Labor. Second, the Commissariat of Social Welfare linked social insurance payments to productivity. Third, the unions remodeled all social insurance programs in December 1938 to serve as instruments against labor turnover. By 1940, union officers were using social benefits both as a reward for high levels of productivity and as punishments for poor production performance.[41]

E. H. Carr has observed that Soviet labor relations theory is marked by a desire to integrate the unions and the worker's state:

The Russian unions had no effective prerevolutionary organization or experience. They were part of the revolutionary movement. Once the revolution had triumphed, some people wondered ... whether they would survive. . . . They did survive – they were strong enough for that – but at the logical cost of their integration in the state machine. The organs of the workers and the organs of the workers' state could not go their separate way.[42]

During the NEP, "not going their separate way" still meant that union representatives could seek retribution from managers who had ignored the rights of workers. Once the Communist Party and the Soviet government had decided to accelerate the pace of industrialization, though, this goal was forgotten.

The abnormal pressures on the unions resulting from World War II compounded even further this imbalance among union obligations. In 1941, events forced the AUCCTU to dispatch supervisors across the Soviet Union to coordinate home front efforts. By 1942 trade union organizations had virtually ceased to function in most parts of the country. By the end of the war, the union hierarchy needed a top-to-bottom reorganization. This task of internal union "normalization," as American political scientist Edwin Morrell has labeled it, fell to V. V. Kuznetsov in 1944.[43]

Under Kuznetsov, the AUCCTU began systematically to reconstruct the trade union bureaucracy. The central committees of several branch trade unions were reamalgamated and relocated in Moscow, and the unions reestablished regional interunion councils as well. Union publications such as *V pomoshch' FZMK/profsoiuznomu aktivu* and *Professional'nye soiuzy* began to promote production conferences, general meetings, and trade union elections at the factory level.[44] Meanwhile the AUCCTU reintroduced enterprise collective agreements.[45]

The national union leadership soon went beyond the reconstruction of bureaucratic structures and embarked upon an ambitious program designed to improve the performance of union officers within those structures. Trade union staffs were reduced. The AUCCTU fined several top-level officials for incompetency; and several leading union spokesmen began to speak out openly about the substandard quality of many of their subordinates' performance. In December 1947 AUCCTU Secretary N. V. Popova told that body that there continued to be a great need for knowledgeable, competent trade union personnel.[46] Citing earlier AUCCTU resolutions, Popova indicated that existing training programs prepared union officials inadequately for their duties. Accompanying commentary reinforced her notion that central, regional, and local union personnel were so incompetent that they unwittingly prevented the fulfillment of many trade union obligations.

Kuznetsov and the senior AUCCTU leaders evidently realized that a knowledgeable activist union leadership constituted a necessary condition for the normalization of union operations. Once the level of leadership improved, illegal managerial practices could no longer be ignored. A point of no return was fast upon the union leadership: Either normalization would continue, with the unions regaining some of their lost authority, or the process must screech to a halt. It was precisely at this crucial moment that the Tenth Trade Union Congress convened in 1949.

In 1938, preparations for this tenth national assembly of union representatives had been underway when, without explanation, the AUCCTU canceled the meeting, and more than a decade passed before the tenth congress finally met. As local and regional union organizations began to follow procedural norms, for the first time since the 1930s union leaders found it necessary to convene regional, republic, and finally all-union conferences and congresses. Hence, by the time the delegates gathered in Moscow, virtually every level of trade union organization had been restored to at least its meager prewar activities.[47]

The delegates to the Tenth Trade Union Congress participated in surprisingly open discussion of union failures over the period. Although concerns with productivity clearly dominated many of the sessions, numerous speakers managed to air complaints concerning union officials' neglect of membership needs. Several major articles expressing similar opinions appeared in the union press during the period preceding and immediately following the meeting. Although the congress did not alter the basic nature of Soviet union obligation functions, it did mark one of the few moments during the 1940s when the union leadership publicly discussed some of its more glaring failures.

The tenth congress represented both a culmination of the normalization policy and a beginning of still other efforts toward improving union performance. Following the congress, union publications incorporated an active defense of workers' rights as defined by Soviet law into a new model for union performance. The next step in the reestablishment of union efforts at protecting the workers from management's abuse came in July 1951, when judicial directives annulled the 1938 requirements forcing factory trade union and management officials to consider attendance and production records in the distribution of welfare benefits. However, an immediate and dramatic increase in labor discipline violations temporarily ended further liberalization measures.[48]

In addition to these actions, the AUCCTU demanded that local union administrators become more responsive to the requests of union members. Two editorials in *Professional'nye soiuzy* concerning the significance of the Nineteenth Party Congress and the November 1952 AUCCTU plenum were particularly forceful on this point. The first appeared in December 1952, before Nikolai Shvernik replaced Kuznetsov as AUCCTU chairman; the second appeared in June 1953, following the changes in Party and union leadership precipitated by Stalin's death.[49]

The December editorial proclaimed the importance of socialist competition and criminal and administrative regulations to union work. The editors also urged local trade union organizations to increase their demands upon economic managers and to guarantee the fulfillment of factory social and cultural plans. The journal acknowledged the failure of unions to meet the demands of local union constituencies. Trade union officers at all levels, the editorial suggested, should attempt to make union meetings more lively and serious.

The editorial of June 1953 went further yet in demanding

that trade union officials improve their leadership of union organizations. The editors placed even greater emphasis upon the need for factory and shop union officials to become more responsive to local needs. The journal suggested that mere formal compliance to union rules was no longer sufficient and urged central union agencies to demand complete adherence to all existing union regulations.

An ever increasing concern over formalism in union affairs continued to dominate union publications and AUCCTU decrees throughout the period immediately following Stalin's death. Discussions in the union press and at union convocations leading up to, during, and following the Eleventh Trade Union Congress of June 1954 underscored the desires of union leaders for something more than pro forma adherence to union rules and regulations.[50] These latest discussions began during local, regional, and central meetings held to select delegates for the Eleventh Trade Union Congress and continued throughout the gathering itself.

Some but certainly not all of the articles appearing in *Sovetskie profsoiuzy* during the period encouraged union groups to discuss their problems more openly and admonished lower union officials for failing to handle members' complaints more expeditiously. Several unidentified authors advocated collective leadership and "collegialism" (*kollektivnost'*). The editorial policy of the journal, as established by the AUCCTU, began to define union democracy as "centralism" without "bureaucratism." Although rhetorical condemnations of "bureaucratism" had appeared before, the proponents of this latest campaign went beyond the old Stalinist formulas to advocate "frank and business-like discussions" among the rank-and-file membership. By 1955, attempts to force compliance to central union decrees had expanded to include greater adherence to rules governing working and living conditions of all union members.[51]

By 1956, then, the general consensus urged the adoption of what can only be considered less coercive methods to improve labor productivity. This shift toward encouragement, education, innovation, and improved managerial techniques found official union endorsement following the Twentieth Party Congress during the March 1956 AUCCTU meeting, at which Party and union spokesmen demanded the rejuvenation of factory trade union offices.[52] The USSR Supreme Soviet Presidium decrees of 25 April 1956, decriminalizing industrial absenteeism and truancy would soon end labor's dependence on management. The inequitable relationship between employer and employee that had developed during the 1930s was beginning to change.

2

Soviet trade union development: 1957–1980

Not everyone welcomed the reemergence of Soviet unions during the 1950s, and the viewpoints in favor of increased union responsibilities did not gain immediate acceptance. Union revitalization remained merely one of several political, social, and economic issues to emerge following I. V. Stalin's death. Indeed, since Communist Party support for union reform did not appear certain until after N. S. Khrushchev had gained control of the Central Committee, there could well have been a link between the two events. Although definitive statements about the interrelationship between Khrushchev's rise to power and union revitalization require more substantial documentation than is currently available, one can argue vigorously that the events surrounding Khrushchev's defeat of the so-called Anti-Party Group played an important role in the further development of the unions.

Even though Party First Secretary Khrushchev had emerged as first among equals at the Twentieth Party Congress in February 1956, more than half of his fellow Presidium members turned against him sixteen months later. This unstable situation in the Soviet Union's most powerful political council provided an otherwise rare opportunity for politically weak institutions such as the trade unions to exert influence over the policy-making process. The AUCCTU, now chaired by Khrushchev protégé V. V. Grishin, took fullest advantage of this opportunity by forestalling Party-supported union reorganization and by gaining Party backing for union-initiated reform efforts.[1]

In December 1956, the Communist Party's Central Committee backed proposals made by Khrushchev's opponents to increase the authority of the State Economic Commission. However, the

Central Committee did not implement that decision since Khrushchev's supporters regained the upper hand in February 1957. Dominant once again, Khrushchev now warned economic managers of the evils of "departmentalism" and proposed that regional economic councils replace central economic ministries. At the same time, Khrushchev indicated that the trade union bureaucracy would undergo a similar reorganization.

The Soviet press did not report Khrushchev's proposals until 30 March 1957, when every leading Soviet newspaper published the complete text of Khrushchev's February address. The papers urged their readers to forward comments on the reorganization of economic management. The very next day a well-controlled national discussion of the Khrushchev proposals began, and it continued until early May, when the USSR Supreme Soviet ratified a new economic order.[2]

Union publications, especially the daily paper *Trud* and the monthly journal *Sovetskie profsoiuzy*, used the forum provided by the discussion of the "Khrushchev theses" to air demands for trade union reform. Although a few factory trade union committee members attacked union central committees, this debate decidedly opposed Khrushchev's call for the abolition of all union central committees.

From 31 March to 7 May 1957, *Trud* published 117 letters concerning union questions in complete or abbreviated form and 118 other letters concerning the more general ramifications of economic reorganization, many of which dealt with the proposed boundaries of specific economic regions, the impact of changes on socialist competition, and the importance of economic reorganization for innovation.[3] The 117 discussing the restructuring of union work fell into three distinct groups: the first letters generally favored Khrushchev's policies on all issues (31 March–8 April); next, some union spokesmen questioned the wisdom of replacing intra-union central committees with interunion territorial councils (9–24 April);[4] and the last letters generally opposed any reorganization of the unions (25 April–7 May). Disagreeing with the Khrushchev proposals to abolish branch union central committees, this last group expressed discontent over the linkage of the unions' fate to that of the economic ministries. A similar trend is evident in the debate's coverage found in the AUCCTU monthly *Sovetskie profsoiuzy*.

On the eve of the discussions over the "Khrushchev theses," *Sovetskie profsoiuzy* published an editorial about the February 1957 Central Committee meetings stressing the need for technological innovation and improved labor productivity.[5] This article suggested that regional economic councils could better manage in an increasingly complex economy than could narrowly specialized ministries. Such a reorganization, the editors pointed out, would demand a similar change in union operations. By the time that the April issue appeared, the tone of the journal's editorials had undergone a subtle yet distinct transformation. The editors compressed their discussion of economic reorganization into eight articles submitted by various central, regional, and local union officers.[6] An introductory editorial discussed solely union concerns and stressed the desirability of strengthening local union institutions. It was left to several subsequent contributors to confront the issue of union reorganization directly, but only the first recommended replacing the intraunion industrywide central committees with interunion regional councils. Editorials appearing in May and in June echoed these positions.[7]

Only *Pravda* among the nonunion press made mention of union concerns. As early as 2 April, the Party daily published a major article by Grishin supporting the reorganization of economic management along territorial lines. Grishin justified this proposal on the grounds that it could improve local union performance. Even so, Grishin remained surprisingly vague on the issue of union reorganization. In one key passage, he observed:

The new structure of the trade unions is to be set in conformity with the organization of administration in industry and construction. However, it is already possible to say that which is obvious, that there will take place a strengthening of the trade unions. This will reduce through merger the larger number of currently existing republic and regional committees, which will make possible a strengthening of local union organs.[8]

This statement would appear to indicate that the reorganization of the unions should resemble that taking place in the economy at large, yet there is no clear notion of what such changes would mean in practice. Would the central committees be abolished? The union chairman did not say.

The Grishin statement is out of step with other articles in *Pravda* during this period concerning the unions. Most *Pravda* articles, to the extent that they dealt with unions at all, strongly supported the abolition of individual union central committees.[9] For example, F. Siumakov, an official of the Novosibirsk Regional Trade Union Council, suggested that branch production departments modeled after the State Planning Committee (Gosplan) replace individual union central committees.[10]

If any doubts remained as to Khrushchev's and Grishin's attitudes concerning union reorganization proposals, they were quickly dispelled at the USSR Supreme Soviet meeting convened 7–10 May 1957.[11] That session ratified most of Khrushchev's plans, abolishing nearly all of the ministries and creating 105 regional economic councils (the sovnarkhozy) in their place. In his address to that meeting Khrushchev stated that the unions faced a similar fate. In response, Grishin asserted that the public debate over the "Khrushchev theses" directed union attention toward general issues of internal organization and overall performance. The AUCCTU, having received numerous suggestions, would have to give them all full hearing at its next scheduled meeting.

The ability of the unions to forestall reorganization provided one indication that, although Khrushchev had won an important battle, he was still amidst a great war. During the remainder of May, *Trud* only occasionally would run an article concerning union reorganization. The political struggle between Khrushchev and his opponents moved out of a semipublic forum back into closed Party councils, and once out of public view it moved rapidly toward resolution.

In early June, while Khrushchev and Premier N. A. Bulganin were making a state visit to Finland – returning to Moscow on 14 June – Khrushchev's opponents met to arrange his demotion.[12] The Presidium of the Central Committee met from 18 to 21 June and voted to demote Khrushchev to minister of agriculture, raising Molotov to first secretary. During the early stages it appears that seven of the eleven full Presidium members stood in opposition to Khrushchev: V. M. Molotov, G. M. Malenkov, L. M. Kaganovich, R. E. Voroshilov, N. A. Bulganin,

M. G. Pervukhin, and A. N. Saburov. Khrushchev, however, was able to argue that only the full Central Committee had elected him first secretary and thus only the full Central Committee could remove him from that post. Following the three-day closed session of the Presidium, the full Central Committee met from 22 June until 29 June (also in secret session).

Meanwhile, Marshal G. K. Zhukov, a candidate member of the Presidium, worked to gain support for Khrushchev. Zhukov threw the weight of the armed forces behind the first secretary and used his influence to win Voroshilov, Bulganin, Pervukhin, and Saburov over to Khrushchev's side. It has been reported that he arranged for military planes to transport Khrushchev's Central Committee supporters to Moscow. In any event, the full Central Committee reversed the earlier decision of the Presidium, and when the Central Committee plenum closed on 29 June Khrushchev had retained his position as first secretary of the Communist Party.

On 4 July 1957, the Soviet press announced dramatic changes in the ruling Presidium. Malenkov, Kaganovich, and Molotov left both the Presidium and the Central Committee; Saburov left the Presidium. Pervukhin lost his position as candidate member of the Presidium; D. T. Shepilov lost his place on the Secretariat, his candidate status on the Presidium, and his full membership in the Central Committee. Zhukov rose to full membership in the Presidium.

The unions found themselves in the midst of this chaotic situation as the AUCCTU gathered to discuss the significance of reorganization for the unions. The next scheduled meeting of the AUCCTU following the Supreme Soviet meeting of 7–10 May convened on 11–15 June,[13] precisely the moment when Khrushchev's fortunes had sunk to their lowest ebb.

During a rather lengthy address at that session, AUCCTU Chairman Grishin enunciated an agenda for union reform that included a greater union role in economic management, wide rights for regional and local union agencies, as well as further development of production conferences, worker meetings, and technical societies. He portrayed the factory committee as the linchpin of the new union structure, with enterprise collective agreements providing a juridical base for that committee's actions. Over the course of a year, nearly every item outlined in this speech would gain Party endorsement.

On the crucial topic of territorial reorganization, Grishin spoke for the retention of union central committees in conjunction with a general improvement in the work of regional interunion councils. Some central committees could be eliminated, but it would be through a merger of the existing forty-seven central union committees into twenty-three by late 1957 rather than through total elimination of all existing committees. By establishing a role for central committees as well as factory committees and regional councils, Grishin carefully differentiated between internal union administration (carried out by the committees) and external ties with the regional economic councils (conducted through the councils).

The full names and titles of several speakers were published in *Trud* accounts of that June meeting. Six of eight speakers advocating severe limitation or the complete liquidation of branch union central committees were not reelected at the Twelfth Trade Union Congress in March 1959. The most outspoken proponent of regional councils, S. V. Martynov, retained his AUCCTU membership. Meanwhile, the congress did not reelect three of the fourteen speakers who had supported Grishin. One might conclude, then, that a stance against the retention of the central committees had a decidedly negative influence on a union career – and certainly a greater influence than would be expected in view of the position of the Communist Party's titular head on this issue. The AUCCTU voted (although not unanimously as was the custom) to accept the proposed merger of several union central committees. On 17 June, a *Pravda* editorial praised union leaders for the extent to which they had moved to improve their work at all levels.[14] Significantly, the Party's newspaper failed to mention the planned merger of the central committees, thereby ignoring the single most important substantive result of the meeting.

Khrushchev won a major victory in June 1957. He retained his position as party first secretary, and his proposals for economic reorganization were realized. Yet this victory was not total. Many of his opponents were not even dismissed from the Party's Central Committee. Khrushchev was forced to seek support wherever he could win it. This situation gave the unions a unique opportunity to avoid policies with which they disagreed. It also afforded an opportunity to gain Party support for policies of which they approved. Although hardly conclusive, the available evidence suggests that the AUCCTU leadership may well have made optimal use of these circumstances. At a minimum one might conclude that the unions found themselves in a uniquely favorable position vis-à-vis the new Party leadership. Immediately following the events surrounding the defeat of the Anti-Party Group, several union and some Party leaders openly promoted general principles of union reform. Moreover, Khrushchev himself spoke out on the need for union officials to improve their efforts on behalf of the workers. By the summer of 1957 some kind of union reform had become inevitable.

The question of how reform might be carried out remained unanswered. Previous discussions in the union press had focused on a handful of issues, which constituted a loose agenda for union reform. All the elements of that agenda were evident in Grishin's June address: a revitalization of mechanisms to ensure workers' legal rights; a reorientation of union activities around the industrial enterprise; and a restructuring of unwieldy union bureaucracy. In December 1957 the agenda became official Party policy when the Central Committee reaffirmed the concept of dual-functioning unions.[15] Any connection between the December resolution and any other of that year's events may have been coincidental. In the absence of complete documentation it appears that some connection does exist between the December resolution and the other events of that year.

The December 1957 Central Committee resolution on the trade unions primarily restated a growing list of acknowledged union failures. It did nothing either to undermine the central place of productivity within the hierarchy of union obligations or to undermine the unions' subordinate position to the Communist Party. Nevertheless, the plenum demanded increased worker involvement in production administration both through the quasiparliamentary councils of workers' deputies and through the trade union structure itself. Moreover, the Central Committee promoted the education, safety, and welfare of the Soviet workers.

Hardly a revolutionary document, the December resolution eventually had greater psychological than juridical impact on subsequent union policies. For the first time in decades, the Party's Central Committee had proclaimed an official policy that recognized the unions as important participants in managerial decision making. It urged other Party institutions to guarantee a sympathetic hearing for union proposals by factory directors. In sum, then, the December resolution signified a new covenant between the trade unions and the Communist Party insofar as union officials could now seek Party support when raising issues of workers' rights before factory administration.

References to union participation in management and, through that partnership, to defense of workers' rights recur throughout the December 1957 resolution. Party leaders singled out three primary agents through which such participation could take place: the factory trade union committee (FZMK); the production conference; and the enterprise collective agreement. Factory trade union committees could give advice and, in the case of dismissals, could exercise veto power over managerial decisions affecting the daily operation of the plant. They could serve on production conferences. Finally, the Party leadership once again labeled the collective agreement as the juridical foundation for all trade union activity at the enterprise level. Following the December plenum, newly encouraged union leaders initiated systematic procedures for review of these agreements and labor safety norms.

Between 1957 and 1974, the status of senior trade union officers within the Communist Party rose steadily. At the time of Stalin's death, union leaders were not major participants in the Soviet political system but played only marginal roles in the determination of economic and social policies and minimal ones in the conduct of foreign policy. By the mid-1970s, the AUCCTU chairman was a major contender for party leadership; the unions were key actors in the establishment of economic and social policies and were coming to play an increasingly important role in Soviet relations with African and Asian nations. These changes point toward a truly substantial impact by new Party policies upon union authority.

There have been few subsequent declarations of Party policy

as important as that of December 1957. This is not to suggest that Party policy has remained static. Senior Party leaders frequently reconfirm the basic tenants of the 1957 resolution by stressing the preeminent position of the factory trade union committees and the increased significance of union participation in management.[16] In so doing, they no longer portray the unions as a building block of some future communist society, as had been the case under Khrushchev, but the more pragmatic approach of the Brezhnev era allows the unions to exercise greater control over managerial indiscretions. As is apparent in decrees such as the 1967 Central Committee resolution concerning the Perm Party organization's leadership of local trade union work,[17] formal Party support for union efforts to improve living and working conditions continued throughout the 1960s and into the 1970s.

There is considerable evidence to suggest that the AUCCTU leadership was generally pleased with the new policy but dismayed at the inability of local union institutions to live up to their new responsibilities. In one speech before an AUCCTU meeting in April 1966, Chairman Grishin spoke of increased factory trade union responsibility for wages, working conditions, and consumer services.[18] However, he also noted that union officials do not always fulfill their responsibilities. Grishin's successor, A. N. Shelepin, similarly moved to press union organizations to act more effectively on behalf of workers. In several blistering attacks on union failures, Shelepin reproached union representatives who had failed to protect workers' interests.[19]

The personal prestige of N. M. Shvernik, Grishin, and Shelepin can explain to some extent the improved position of union officials within the Communist Party. Grishin's appointment as AUCCTU chairman immediately following the Twentieth Party Congress in 1956 represented an attempt by Khrushchev to gain influence over the union bureaucracy through the nomination of a friendly administrator. As the course of the 1957 debate over economic and trade union decentralization indicated, Grishin acted as a spokesman for union causes even when union positions may have been at odds with those of his mentor, Khrushchev.

Grishin's influence continued to grow throughout the

Khrushchev period. In January 1961, the AUCCTU chairman
gained candidate status on the Central Committee's Presidium.
This improved personal standing no doubt enhanced the ability
of both central and local union officials to deal with their Party
and ministerial counterparts.

Grishin's successor, Aleksandr N. Shelepin, was the first
AUCCTU chairman to hold full membership in the Politburo
in thirty-eight years. He already held that position at the time
of his appointment and evidently realized that the unions –
with their mass membership, their ability to address socioeco-
nomic and foreign affairs issues, and their wide-ranging facilities
for propaganda – offered an effective stepping stone to the
Party leadership. He openly pursued an activist union role in
the decision-making process at every level of Soviet society. As
important as the personal concern of a Grishin or a Shelepin
over union performance may have been, its significance can be
fully understood only within the context of the unions' institutional relationships with other Soviet policy-making bodies.
Here, American political scientist Jerry Hough has pointed to
three major institutions directly involved in labor policy making:
the State Committee on Labor and Social Questions, the Central
Committee of the Communist Party of the Soviet Union (CPSU),
and the All-Union Central Council of Trade Unions.[20]

The USSR Council of Ministers established the State Committee on Labor and Social Questions in 1955 as the State
Committee on Labor and Wages in order to coordinate Soviet
wage policies. The scope of the committee's work has expanded
to cover manpower issues, social security administration, scientific organization of labor, working conditions, and vocational
education, in addition to wages. The committee manages several
divisions covering each of these policy concerns as well as
divisions organized in accordance with branches of the national
economy, such as metallurgy, transportation, and agriculture.
Finally, the committee operates the Scientific-Research Institute
of Labor, which conducts policy-oriented academic research.

The state committee, with its wide-ranging authority over
several bureaucratic spheres, remains the central locale of many
policy discussions concerning labor, but there could well be
differences within the committee itself concerning the future

direction of Soviet policy. For example, Hough has suggested that administrators from the social security division may disagree with representatives from the wage department over pension policies. Moreover, officials from the committee's heavy industrial divisions may join their union counterparts at the AUCCTU and in individual heavy industrial unions to advocate specific policy options. As a result, complex relationships emerge which make it difficult to generalize in discussions of policy positions taken either by the committee or by the AUCCTU.

The role of the Central Committee of the CPSU is even more difficult to define. Several Central Committee departments, such as the Heavy Industry Department, deal with labor problems. Central Committee officials undoubtedly exert considerable influence over both the course of policy discussions and the policy itself. Without doubt the Central Committee's Politburo is the final arbiter of policy decisions. Yet others probably formulate the issues and options well before they reach the senior leadership ranks of the CPSU. Precisely because the Politburo and the Central Committee have final decision-making authority, lower-ranking institutions such as the State Committee on Labor and Social Questions, or events themselves, often define and clarify policy issues.

In addition to the state committee and the Central Committee, the AUCCTU exerts considerable influence over the course of Soviet labor policy. As the supreme union agency, this body includes representatives from each of some thirty-one unions and selects its own chairman, deputy chairman, and secretaries. Each senior AUCCTU officer assumes responsibility for one or more policy areas, and the AUCCTU as a whole maintains two dozen departments and divisions and operates two institutions of higher learning and one research institute. As the unions entered the 1980s senior ranks among AUCCTU administrative officers were remarkably stable. Nearly half of the secretaries and more than a third of the department division chiefs had held their positions for a decade or more. Taking into account the fact that one-third of the division chiefs at the State Committee on Labor and Social Questions also had decade-long tenures, one could well imagine that many important decisions were made through informal working relationships built up

Table 2.1. *Central Committee CPSU status of AUCCTU secretaries,*
1956–1976

	1956^a	1961^b	1966^c	1971^d	1976^e
Total number of AUCCTU secretaries	6	6	7	7	10
Number of AUCCTU secretaries elected full members of CC CPSU	0	2	1	1	3
Number of AUCCTU secretaries elected candidate members of CC CPSU	2	1	3	3	2
Percentage of AUCCTU secretaries with CC CPSU status	33	50	57	57	50

[a] As elected following the Twentieth Party Congress in February 1956
(*Pravda*, 26 February 1956, p. 1).
[b] As elected following the Twenty-Second Party Congress in October
1961 (*Pravda*, 1 November 1961, p. 2).
[c] As elected following the Twenty-Third Party Congress in April 1966
(*Pravda*, 9 April 1966, p. 2).
[d] As elected following the Twenty-Fourth Party Congress in April 1971
(*Pravda*, 10 April 1971, p. 2).
[e] As elected following the Twenty-Fifth Party Congress in March 1976
(*Pravda*, 6 March 1976, p. 2).

over years of contact. Moreover, senior AUCCTU officials
interact with their colleagues from various state institutions
through shared status in the Communist Party.

The Central Committee elected by the Twentieth Party Congress included only two AUCCTU secretaries (see Table 2.1).
Both L. N. Solov'ev and N. V. Popova obtained candidate status
in the Central Committee at that time; both had been members
of the AUCCTU Secretariat for over a decade, and Solov'ev
had actually been in charge of daily union administration since
late 1953.[21] It can be argued that, aside from Chairman
Shvernik, union representation on the Central Committee
should have included at least these two individuals, and yet they
obtained only candidate status.

Three out of six AUCCTU secretaries obtained Central
Committee status at the Twenty-Second Party Congress in 1961
(see Table 2.1). Interestingly, two of these three, A. A. Bulgakov

(a candidate member of the Central Committee) and T. N. Nikolaeva (a full member), had been elected to the AUCCTU Secretariat a scant two years earlier. Their selection demonstrated the already increasing prestige of union officials within the Party.

The late 1960s and early 1970s mark a high point for union presence on the Central Committee. As noted above, Chairman Grishin obtained candidate status on the Party's Presidium, and his successor, A. Shelepin, was already a full member of the Politburo when he became AUCCTU director. Moreover, four of the seven AUCCTU secretaries were elected to candidate and full membership on the Party's Central Committee, the highest proportion of the AUCCTU Secretariat ever to do so (see Table 2.1).

In February 1976, a period during which the AUCCTU had no chairman, the Twenty-Fifth Party Congress elected more full members from among AUCCTU secretaries (three) and more combined candidate and full members (five) than at any other time during the postwar era (see Table 2.1). Despite the relatively small number of officials involved, such a development suggests that the unions had gained increased stature within the Party during the previous two decades. Personnel changes following the Sixteenth Trade Union Congress in March 1977 did not significantly alter this growth.[22]

One should always remember that the increased representation of AUCCTU secretaries on the Central Committee does not indicate strengthened institutional status for all union bodies. The recent increase in overall membership of the Central Committee somewhat diminishes the ultimate significance of the union gains, as do the relatively small numbers involved. Moreover, status and prestige do not in themselves confer power. The mere presence of AUCCTU secretaries on the Party's Central Committee does not necessarily mean that the union "point of view" has either been represented or heeded within Party circles.

Nevertheless, the increasing number of AUCCTU secretaries having some status on the Central Committee is noteworthy in its own right. At a minimum, such prestige reinforces the self-confidence of union officials. The psychological significance of such perceptions should not be underestimated. Favorable self-images can and have precipitated bolder action on the part of subordinate union leaders in defense of workers' rights.

Two important questions regarding the increased prestige of certain AUCCTU secretaries remain unanswered. How could the secretaries use their new status to improve union performance at the enterprise level? Did they in fact do so?

One might well assume that the Central Committee status conferred on some AUCCTU secretaries helped lend greater substance to their appeals for improved union performance. First, local union officials, many of whom are also Party members, are more motivated by requests from a Central Committee member to improve performances than they would be from a nonmember. Second, lower managerial and Party officials are more inclined to accept the validity of directives from Central Committee members than from mere AUCCTU secretaries.

Considerable evidence suggests that the secretaries have attempted to use their positions to improve the performance of local union agencies. In one report before an October 1968 AUCCTU meeting, Secretary N. N. Romanov berated trade union central committees for their inability to meet norms established by affirmative action–type programs.[23] He noted that although women comprised 70 percent of all factory trade union committee chairmen in trade, 73 percent in health care, and 60.1 percent in textiles, only 28.8 percent of the chairmen in food production and 14.7 percent in agriculture were women, despite the fact that women dominated these sectors of the economy. Moreover, there were regions and even entire republics where no full-time trade union chairwomen were to be found in many industries. In another report a half-year later, Romanov indicated that far too many factory managers dismissed workers without prior union approval.[24] He reported that approximately 60 percent of all dismissals by management throughout the entire Soviet Union took place without union approval, and the figures for Uzbekistan (77.4 percent), Georgia (73.3 percent), and the Altai Region (69 percent) were even higher.

Statements and resolutions by high-ranking trade union officials and groups underline any existing skepticism concerning the ability of Soviet unions to live up to their self-ascribed standards.[25] Certainly, if these reports have any validity, a significant number of factory trade union officials do not meet their most basic obligations, yet such statements ironically confirm that Soviet trade union officials actually are concerned about poor union performance. After all, a Grishin, a Shelepin, and a Romanov not only highlight the failures of lower-ranking union officials but also condemn them.

Thus far the discussion has suggested that the unions play at least a pro forma role in the formulation of national labor policy. Although precisely what happens in senior policy councils is unknown, existing shreds of evidence indicate that the union role is something more than advisory. Interviews with Soviet union officials and legal specialists help to unravel the mystery. One legal scholar complains that members of the AUCCTU legal department wrote major sections of the 1970 Fundamental Principles of Labor Legislation. An AUCCTU administrator boasts that when strongman Shelepin was union boss he could deal with ministries as if they were children. A leading officer at the AUCCTU's Higher School of the Trade Union Movement brags about his days as a union liaison officer with the State Planning Committee, Gosplan. An AUCCTU safety inspector notes that he enforced rules established jointly by ministries and the central committees of their corresponding unions. The director of Scientific Research of the Institute of Labor of the State Committee on Labor and Social Questions tosses a twenty-page union critique of a proposed five-year economic plan at political scientist Jerry Hough and decries union obstinance on housing and social welfare issues.[26]

Ultimately, such anecdotal evidence is not sufficient to prove that the unions actually influence labor policy. Perhaps all that can be said is that the AUCCTU and its departments and staff are one of several important political institutions involved in the formulation of Soviet labor policy.

In addition to the State Committee on Labor and Social Questions, the Central Committee, and the AUCCTU, a myriad of additional state and Party agencies help to establish labor policies. The USSR State Planning Committee (Gosplan) determines the investment in social programs as well as total industrywide wage packages, a fact confirmed by the appearance of Gosplan Deputy Director V. Ia. Isaev at the November 1979 AUCCTU plenum.[27] Moreover, the Ministry of Finance frequently joins Gosplan in establishing policies reconciling conflicting claims on limited Soviet economic resources. The Supreme Soviet and its legislative committees promulgate various labor laws, while union republic ministries of social welfare and health administration direct both union and nonunion welfare and health programs.[28] The Young Communist League (Komsomol), the State Committee on Vocational and Technical Education, and the Ministry of Higher and Specialized Secondary Education all make decisions affecting manpower training and allocation. Finally, every ministry maintains authority to establish labor safety and wage norms. And all of these institutions interact within the context of previously mentioned personal relationships at the pinnacle of the Soviet political system.

In spring 1975, Shelepin was removed from his union post.[29] Although this discharge, like his earlier appointment, came as a result of a personal struggle with L. I. Brezhnev for control of the CPSU, one must recognize that in Shelepin the unions had an effective chief administrator. He fought to expand union influence, if for no other reason than that such a gain would also increase his own power.

Following Shelepin's removal, the AUCCTU chairmanship remained vacant for almost one and a half years. During this period, veteran AUCCTU Secretary V. I. Prokhorov fulfilled the administrative duties of the chairman.[30] In November 1976 the AUCCTU elected A. I. Shibaev, formerly Party first secretary of the Saratov Region, as its chairman. As was the case with every other AUCCTU chairman since Tomsky, Shibaev had had no previous union experience.[31]

Over the course of the post-Shelepin era, Party and union resolutions have come slowly but perceptively to favor a production orientation in the execution of union duties. Although the unions appear on the surface to have become more subordinate to the Party than at any other time in recent history, it is unlikely that such changes represent a well-planned movement away from the principal policies of the postwar era. No evidence suggests that the Communist Party would like to have union organizations abandon their defense of workers' legal rights. Furthermore, even though AUCCTU decrees betray increasing concern over production, labor discipline, and labor turnovers, editors of union journals have continued to publish a significant number of articles concerning the defense of workers' rights. Just as one is willing to accept the possibility of a more restricted union role, a crack appears in even more recent policy statements.

In November 1978, A. Viktorov, one of ten AUCCTU secretaries, told a meeting of the USSR Supreme Soviet that the social needs of Soviet citizens should not be ignored in an effort to improve national economic performance.[32] Following some largely pro forma statements concerning industrial productivity and technological innovation, Viktorov directed the attention of his audience to several failures on the social front. First, he indicated that some ministries had failed to spend the funds available to them for the improvement of factory housing and child care facilities. Viktorov pointed out that, during the first ten months of 1978, the Ministry of Machine Tool Production spent only 26 percent of funds provided for housing construction and 17 percent of those earmarked for construction of child care facilities; the Ministry of Coal Production had spent only 44 percent and 16 percent on these programs, respectively. Moreover, Viktorov noted with some dismay that capital funds set aside to improve factory cafeterias similarly went unspent. Perhaps most important of all, the Viktorov speech contained the most overt union references to date to wide disparity in social services available to workers in heavy industry as opposed to light. By questioning existing allocation procedures, Viktorov raised potentially embarrassing questions concerning the nature of the distribution of privilege in the Soviet Union.

It is in just such a context that the Viktorov speech assumes special meaning. The AUCCTU secretary made his remarks in response to a major economic address by Brezhnev. In that address, the Party's general secretary criticized economic managers for failing to come to grips with declining growth rates, declining labor supply, and declining natural resources. In short, Brezhnev told his audience that they must tighten their belts. Viktorov took this opportunity to remind the Supreme Soviet that any effort at economic rationalization that might undermine basic living standards could prove counterproductive. While never contradicting the view offered by Brezhnev,

Viktorov added a new dimension to the discussion concerning the future path of Soviet economic development – a social dimension.

Much of the discussion thus far has focused on attitudes about and perceptions of what the Soviet unions ought to be doing. The conflict and change apparent in nearly every period of Soviet history suggest that differences exist between theory and reality. Knowledge of the myth – the Leninist concept of dual-functioning trade unionism – represents a necessary first step to any study of Soviet trade union operations. One also needs to go further and try to understand precisely what union officials do or do not do every working day. The time has come to turn from the AUCCTU and the Politburo to the factory floor.

3

Union–management–Party relations at the plant

Few Soviet workers, let alone Western observers, are privy to the wheeling and dealing that takes place during closed meetings among factory managers, Party officials, and union chairmen. Nevertheless, the Western observer has an advantage that a Soviet worker does not: He can ask about such practices during an interview. Although responses to his queries may not be entirely candid, an anecdote told by a factory manager in conjunction with a tale told by a union official and a legal case summarized by a labor lawyer frequently create strong impressions as to what actually takes place behind closed office doors.

After several such interviews, it becomes possible to imagine a meeting among factory managers, union chairmen, and Party officials. Following the resignation of a trusted senior worker, for example, a union chairman might come to see a factory director and suggest that the plant must improve its recreation facilities if there is to be any hope of retaining its best workers. Such an event provides an opportunity for the union chairman to raise general issues concerning working and living conditions at the plant. In an effort to avoid further expenditures, the plant director might suggest that productivity is too low and that the factory cannot afford the costs of the necessary improvements, at which point the factory union chairman might link productivity to the overall work environment. If the union representative is successful in establishing such a causal relationship between poor conditions and poor performance, these two officials might call in a Party representative to discuss how to raise productivity while enhancing the quality of life for the factory work force. The Party officer, in turn, would be hard put to oppose any plan to improve recreational, living, and working conditions and might be trapped into lobbying for increased funding for the plant from regional economic planners.

Whether or not such events actually transpire might depend more on the personalities involved than on the workers' actual needs. Is a factory director predisposed to worrying about the quality of life enjoyed by enterprise employees? How well does the Party chairman relate to the director and the union chief? Eavesdropping at such a meeting would probably confirm that lofty ideals are put into action by officials who agree or disagree on the basis of personality and career aspirations.[1] Any statement about Soviet labor relations must take into account the factory "triangle" (*treugolnik*), or troika of management, Party, and union leaders. Nevertheless, none of these officials acts in isolation. Each faces multiple constituencies. A union chairman, for example, not only deals with the Communist Party, management, and Young Communist League colleagues but must also work within the trade union bureaucracy.

Unlike their North American counterparts, Soviet unions are organized according to the so-called production principle. In other words, every employee in a single branch of the economy becomes a member of the same union, regardless of profession.[2] Thus our fictional factory manager, union chairman, and Party leader would all be members of the same trade union. Contemporary Soviet union officials favor such an arrangement because they believe that, theoretically, problems within a specific enterprise (such as a shortage of places at a children's camp) are best resolved when factory managers have to deal with only a single union.

Unions are organized according to another principle in addition to the production principle – democratic centralism. This concept is shared by all Soviet institutions and prescribes democratically conceived but centrally enforced policies.[3] Soviet theorists explain that union decisions are democratic in that rank-and-file union members may suggest policy alternatives to their elected leadership and centralist insofar as central institutions dictate what their subordinates must do.

In attempting to create a hierarchical system on the basis of these two principles, Soviet union leaders have devised an extraordinarily complex organizational matrix in which intra-union committees and interunion councils operate on several administrative levels (see Figure 3.1).[4] Thus, in theory all union officials find themselves subject to a dual chain of union command: first, to the individual trade union (Figure 3.1); and, second, to the interunion councils. As if this were not enough, factory union chairmen must also respond to the demands of the rank-and-file membership who elected them in the first place.

Soviet trade union elections differ from those in the West.[5] First, an auditing commission of leading union and Party officials establishes a list of candidates, usually drawn from the voluntary union activists, known collectively as the *aktiv*, as well as from lower union officials, and offers it to the workers for approval. Then, after discussion at a general factory meeting, an open voice vote accepts the list of candidates in its entirety. During the subsequent secret ballot workers have an opportunity to vote "for" or "against" the individual candidates on the list. If the nominees receive a simple majority affirmative vote, they are elected to the union shop or factory committee. Should a candidate fail to gain such approval (not a frequent occurrence but known to happen in unusual situations), the meeting would immediately nominate new candidates for that position. Following such an election meeting, the newly elected council convenes to select its officers.

The auditing commission dominates this election process by determining the list of candidates to be presented to the workers for approval. Soviet officials suggest that the supervisory role of the commission protects the workers from their own mistakes. A Soviet labor relations specialist once explained the guardian function of the commission with a question: "What would happen if the workers elected a comrade whose greatest capacity lay in the area of vodka consumption?" And yet, this body clearly does more than prevent the election of drunkards to union posts.

The system of auditing commissions combines with the unions' *nomenklatura* personnel structure to predetermine the outcome of any union election. All salaried union officers enter the *nomenklatura* – or list – of a specified superior union agency.[6] That agency, in turn, maintains right of confirmation for all personnel actions within its *nomenklatura*. No one can be removed from or selected for any given *nomenklatura* position without

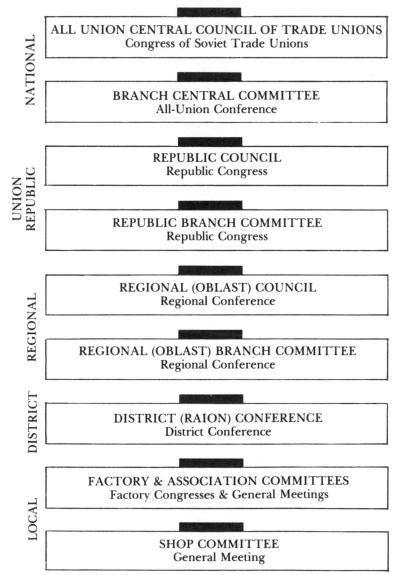

Figure 3.1. Soviet trade union organization.

the prior knowledge and consent of the appropriate *nomenkla-tura* agency. Moreover, each union position is assigned to a union agency according to the relative importance of each. Under the *nomenklatura* system, for example, a union's central committee selects union officials at an enterprise of national significance prior to their actual election, whereas a union's regional committee selects union officers at an enterprise of regional significance. In this manner, factory union chairmen become accountable to higher institutions of the union. The chairman most likely will be a Party member, and occasionally he will come in from another factory.[7] The future career of the chairman depends more on the evaluation of his union superiors than upon that of the workers he is elected to represent. Higher union institutions obtain a chairman's nomination to office and have sole authority to remove him from that position.

It would be naive and simplistic to suggest that an effective Soviet factory union chairman can ignore workers' wishes entirely. After all, a worker may vote with his feet by resigning from his job even when he cannot vote with his ballot. Such a display of discontent is common in the seller's labor market created by manpower shortages. Aside from pleasing union superiors above and workers below, chairmen must also work with the other members of their committees (see Figure 3.1), many of whom are or have been production line workers.

In 1975, the factory union chairman at Moscow Watch Factory No. 2 presided over a committee of thirty-five members, each elected for a one-year term.[8] The committee (80 percent of whom came from blue collar professions) met once a month, and a twelve-member presidium, or executive board, met every other week to discuss more pressing concerns. In the interim, the daily work of the union within the plant became the responsibility of thirteen commissions: production (15 members); social insurance (15 members); organizational (15 members); pension (15 members); labor protection (13 members); cultural (13–15 members); family and school (15 members); youth (15 members); housing (15 members); election (7 members); labor disputes (13 members); consumer services (15 members); and women's (15 members). Volunteer activists manned all these groups, which were chaired by a full member of the factory committee. Frequently the commissions of a factory union committee have significant responsibilities. For example, during the fiscal year 1974, the plant union committee and its commissions administered a social insurance budget of about 1.5 million rubles.

In addition to responding to the union committee as a whole, the factory union chairman must report to supervisors at the regional trade union committee (Figure 3.1). N. I. Zinov'ev, the chairman of one such committee in Leningrad, presides over a staff of 26 full-time employees who are responsible for the activities of union committees in 111 machine construction plants employing 215,000 workers throughout the greater Leningrad region.[9] Factory union chairmen may report either to Zinov'ev directly or, if a specific policy area is at issue, to him through one of the regional committee's departments. The committee, which includes departments specializing in wage and production policies, labor protection, social insurance, accounting, organizational concerns, cultural and housing facilities, and sports clubs, finances regional operations from 7.7 percent of the total wage fund of the enterprises within its supervision. Zinov'ev also serves on the Leningrad Regional (Inter–)Trade Union Council and reports to the machine construction workers' central committee in Moscow.

The Leningrad Regional Council (Figure 3.1) includes representatives of each trade union operating in Leningrad and is organized into eleven departments,[10] of which the Social Insurance Department employs fourteen persons who administer a social insurance budget of more than 95 million rubles, supervise the work of factory medical facilities, and operate vacation and health-care facilities for Leningrad workers. By 1975, L. Vinogradova, the head of the department, had been at her job for more than five years, having previously served as chairman of the Leningrad Regional Trade Union Committee of Medical Workers. A physician by training, Vinogradova took particular interest in efforts to improve industrial hygiene. Her current post required her to report both to the Leningrad Regional Council and through the weak republic-level inter–trade union council to the Social Insurance Department of the All-Union Central Council of Trade Unions in Moscow.

Subordinate only to the AUCCTU, the central committees of branch trade unions (Figure 3.1) retain responsibility for the

implementation of all national union policies and labor legislation as they apply to a specific industry. Both the elected
members of a union central committee and that body's employed
staff meet regularly with representatives of their corresponding
ministry to resolve conflicts over interpretation of industrywide
rules and regulations. For example, in 1979 the Forestry, Paper
and Wood-Processing Workers' Central Committee included
123 full and 39 candidate members who had been elected by a
national congress that convenes every five years. The committee
governs a union organization made up of some 70,000 local
organizations.[11] A majority of the 162 committee members are
drawn from the industry's best workers and have been involved
in daily union administration at the local and regional level.
Most participate in the work of the committee's three commissions: the Economic Commission (which developed new and
improved methods of labor organization and remuneration);
the Commission on Labor Safety (which established industrywide safety norms); and the Commission on Female Labor
(which cooperated with national commissions on the problems
of women workers). Each group works closely with the USSR
Forestry Ministry and reports directly to the AUCCTU.

The AUCCTU, which serves as the Soviet Union's supreme
trade union council (Figure 3.1) and is elected by trade union
congresses convened every five years, in turn elects a presidium
and secretariat charged with the supervision of union administration, the establishment of the broad trade union policies,
and the implementation of those guidelines. The secretariat,
consisting of some ten members, supervises the work of fifteen
departments covering every aspect of daily union administration. The Legal Department, for example, prepares legal briefs
for union agencies, supervises the work of factory comrade's
courts and disputes commissions, and generally seeks to enforce
labor legislation.[12] In addition, the department drafts legislative
proposals presented by the AUCCTU to the Supreme Soviet
for consideration.

Iurii Kositsyn, deputy director of the Legal Department, is
far removed from the world of factory union chairmen. Nevertheless, both Kositsyn and a factory union chairman are ultimately held accountable to the AUCCTU, its secretariat, its
presidium, and its chairman, A. I. Shibaev. Both, by virtue of

their place within the bureaucratic matrix governing Soviet
trade union activities, represent multiple constituencies, which
exist both outside and inside of Soviet factories. Within every
industrial enterprise, trade union chairmen must work closely
with their Party, management, and Young Communist League
counterparts in order to meet the unions' legal obligations to
their members and to their superiors (Figure 3.2). The union
chairman shares responsibility with the factory director for the
management of the labor force.[13] Soviet law requires that both

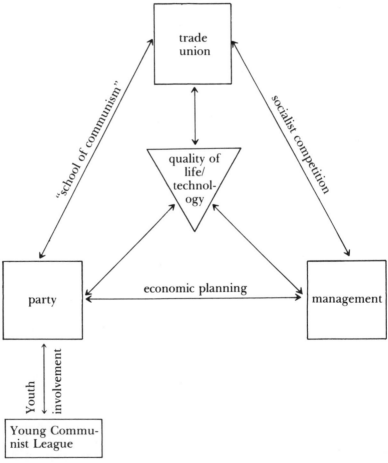

Figure 3.2. The troika.

declare their mutual obligations in the annual collective agreement.[14]

When a trade union chairman negotiates a collective agreement, he finds himself staring at a factory director who must also please various constituencies. A Soviet industrial enterprise is an autonomous juridical and financial unit at the bottom of a tightly organized hierarchical economic structure made up of enterprises (*predpriiatiia*), trusts (*tresty*), combines (*kombiny*), associations (*ob"edineniia*), chief administrations (*glavki*), and ministries (*ministerstva*).[15] The director and his staff at an individual enterprise seek to maximize output and minimize costs.

The rigidity of the national industrial framework is reflected within the enterprise itself in that the plant director serves as chief of yet another large and complex managerial pyramid. Along with a director, deputy directors, chief engineers, shop chiefs, section chiefs, and foremen, many Soviet industrial enterprises maintain planning departments, production and repair shops, design departments, power and energy offices, personnel departments, accounting and financial offices, technical information centers, and quality control sections. The planning process holds together this myriad of bureaucratic structures, reinforcing whatever tendencies may have existed toward managerial inertia.[16]

Any discussion of economic planning in the Soviet Union must begin by differentiating among a variety of interconnected plans varying in function, degree of aggregation, and period of implementation. At the outset of each planning period (traditionally five years), the national State Planning Committee (Gosplan) prepares a schedule of long-term goals and recommendations, which are distributed in turn to every industrial enterprise throughout the Soviet Union.[17] Each enterprise then reviews the proposals and prepares its own draft plan, which it sends back up the administrative ladder to the next highest level. At that level, officials review and coordinate the proposed plans of each enterprise under their supervision, consolidating them into a new united plan that is forwarded upward through the republic and national ministries to the national planning agency in Moscow. Gosplan then prepares a final aggregate five-year plan, which is presented to a Communist Party congress for approval and to the USSR Supreme Soviet for ratifi-

cation into law; annual and quarter-annual plans merely form
constituent parts of the overall national plan. Once ratified by
the Supreme Soviet, the economic plan becomes law, placing
managers who fail to meet its goals in violation of national
statutes.

The annual technical, industrial, and financial plans generated
by this process become the basis for all enterprise activity.[18]
The factory plan, which, in theory, has been drawn up in final
form by higher officials on the basis of recommendations from
enterprise administrators, establishes the nature of production,
supply, and finance for the entire plant. Although the specific
format varies from industry to industry, most factory plans
include a production schedule, a technical development outline
for technological innovation, quality control, cost reduction
goals, a supply schedule, a labor plan, capital construction
targets, and financial targets covering income and expenditures.
Soviet plant directors bear full responsibility for the fulfillment
of these goals.

Because the plan is formulated and finalized at the national
level and implemented primarily at the local level, officials who
intensify planning targets are not always responsible for plan
fulfillment. Not surprisingly, the system is permanently infused
with the potential for conflict among various bureaucratic
strata.[19] American economist David Granick has observed that
a primary test of any Soviet leadership must be its ability to
reconcile the interests of industrial enterprises with those of the
national economy as a whole.[20] According to Granick, defining
managerial success solely in terms of increased productivity
relative to plan targets can only compound bureaucratic tension.
Within this context of perpetual conflict the relationship between the factory director and the third partner in the factory
troika – the Party chairman – is played out and the concept of
one-man-rule (*edinonachalie*) takes on its significance.

The concept of one-man rule underlies much of Soviet
managerial thought and underscores the unlimited authority
that Soviet factory managers theoretically exercise over plant
operations. However, as American political scientist Jerry Hough
has noted, the principle of one-man rule is limited to hour-to-
hour and day-to-day administrative decision making of a fairly
routine nature.[21] Hough has pointed out that one-man rule

requires Party organizations to exert influence over managerial performance "through" and not "apart from" governmental agencies. The theory also urges employees to obey all instructions from their superiors. Workers may protest illegal directives once the task has been fulfilled.

Hough has suggested that any question pertaining to policy is not subject to one-man rule. As a result, Party officials are frequently required to participate in the managerial process. The lack of any clear distinction between "administration" and "policy" provides ample opportunity for Party–managerial conflict. While Hough suggests that policy issues may be thought of as those questions over which two technically qualified persons may disagree, the distinctions so clear to an American student of Soviet affairs do not necessarily reflect those of Soviet Party operatives and factory directors.

The principle of one-man rule for managers, then, comes into direct tension with the equally sacred principle of the Communist Party's "right of control," through which the enterprise Party organization has the right to check, verify, and inspect the work of management and to enforce laws and plan norms. Hough maintains that the Party organization frequently serves as a beneficial assistant for the plant director in a number of areas, including ideological work and partnership with the unions. Yet a broad interpretation of the right of control – a process made possible by a singular lack of precise rules and regulations concerning such questions – frequently leads to conflict between Party organizations and managers. Irresoluble disputes can be settled only when a factory Party official appeals to his superiors within the Party's hierarchy and the plant manager approaches his ministerial superiors. Thus, the resolution of a conflict involving Party chairmen and plant managers can bring about the daily intervention of outside forces into factory life. Therefore, even though the concept of one-man rule may suggest that Soviet factory directors are responsible for everything that happens to take place within the plant, it should be clear that the Party's right of control does not allow the director to control all the forces affecting plant operations, the most obvious being manpower allocation.

By Western standards, Soviet industrial enterprises are commonly overmanned.[22] Most plants hire a strikingly large number of auxiliary workers for jobs not directly related to production. Many of these people maintain factory equipment; others oversee the movement of supplies from shop to shop or supervise quality control. Facing a scarcity of numerous resources, the Soviet factory director is nonetheless under great pressure to meet production plans. Sometimes he must fulfill an entire month's production quota during the last week or ten days of a period simply because another plant has not shipped needed supplies.[23] In such a situation, factory managers often ignore overtime regulations, thereby raising the possibility of a union appeal to the courts. Soviet administrators must be flexible in their use of this supplemental work force in order to manage their plan effectively. Such flexibility is impossible under labor legislation, which gives union committees the right to review most personnel actions. At some point, labor shortages dictate that a manager must break the law. When he does, the unions must decide whether or not to bring the case to court.

A Soviet factory manager has several options. He may cooperate with the unions wholeheartedly, hoping that high worker morale will increase productivity, and this relatively sophisticated approach is gaining vocal support within the Soviet Union, particularly from legal scholars and sociologists.[24] Or, a factory manager may choose to cooperate with the unions in the hope of co-opting the union chairman. David Granick has suggested that Soviet factory officials may break the law in order to meet production goals, only to close ranks and form a "family circle" whereby one official protects another in return for protection at a later time of travail.[25] Such practices may draw in Party, union, and management officials within a single enterprise, or, in many instances, they may include a group of factory directors, a group of Party officials, or a group of union officials. When such an alliance exists between union and management, it is the worker who loses the most. Finally, a factory manager may ride roughshod over the unions. In this case, the manager calculates that sanctions against ignoring the unions are less severe than those against failure to meet production quotas.[26]

Ultimately, the third partner in any given troika will decide the resolution of this drama. Will the Party chairman side with management, thereby ensuring its power to do all that is necessary to raise production? Or will he side with the unions, thereby increasing Party control over factory management? The answers to these questions may depend largely on the personalities involved in each plant.

Over the past decade, senior Party officials have reiterated that local Party officials must support the unions.[27] The fact that such demands occur so frequently indicates that the reality must be rather different. For those Western skeptics who doubt the strength of Soviet unions, perhaps here is one possible answer to why the unions are allowed to gain increased power. By strengthening union institutions, the Party strengthens its own control over the managers. Both Party and management officials share responsibility for fulfillment of the enterprise's annual production plan. Although union officials may participate in these decisions, they are not held formally accountable for enterprise production. Management officials and, to a lesser degree, Party officials are. Moreover, all members of the troika cooperate to maintain what the Soviet officials identify as a high cultural level at the factory.[28] Finally, although they approach the question of technological innovation from differing perspectives, each has an obligation to ensure that the newest production techniques are used.[29]

The dynamics of these triangular relationships vary from enterprise to enterprise. In one plant, Party and union may join together to make sure that management lives up to the letter of safety regulations; at another, Party and management officials may take steps to overfulfill production quotas regardless of the human cost. Many such relationships find expression in the enterprise collective agreements, which, even when closely modeled upon central decrees, reflect the individual character of their authors.

Union and administration representatives begin consultation at Moscow Watch Factory No. 2 in October for the next year's collective agreement.[30] A joint union–management commission assesses the performance of factory officials in meeting the previous agreement and invites the recommendations of individual workers, trade union groups, and shop brigades. The commission reviews each proposal until January, when it prepares a draft agreement. For the next few weeks, union representatives present the draft to enterprise employees, and then, in early February, a factory conference convenes to discuss the agreement. If approved by a majority of those present, the new agreement goes into effect immediately. Quarter-annual factory conferences convene to evaluate compliance to the agreement.

If, as in the case at Leningrad Bus Depot No. 1, enterprise management does not meet its contractual obligations, the factory trade union committee may invite regional union officials to audit factory records.[31] In the Leningrad case, regional officials ruled that adequate funding was not available for management to meet its obligations under the collective agreement. The regional union committee criticized factory union officials for accepting an agreement that management could never fulfill.

As a result of this negotiation process, individual agreements may be lengthy and complex. The 1974 agreement of the Kamsk Cable Factory[32] contained seven sections and ten supplements in a printed booklet of seventy-eight pages. The seven sections delineate union and managerial agreements concerning plant production, workers' wages, employee participation in factory management, safety and social insurance, living conditions, and youth programs, as well as the status of female employees; the ten supplements elaborate upon these general obligations. For example, one supplement includes a schedule for the introduction of new machinery on a shop-by-shop basis; another lists professions eligible for daily rations of one-half liter of milk and one-fifth liter of apple juice.

The specific provisions found in the supplements may be inconsistent. A lathe operator (*tokar*) in Kamsk Cable Shop No. 4 is to receive one-half liter of milk each day, whereas a lathe operator in shop no. 18 is to receive one-fifth liter of apple juice. A metal worker (*slesar'*) in shop no. 12 is to receive a monthly ration of 400 grams of soap, whereas a metal worker in shop no. 11 does not. Such incongruities typify negotiation and compromise.

Once approved, the unions must enforce the collective agreement. Several Soviet union officials acknowledge that many factory directors attempt to shirk their responsibilities under the agreement. One particularly favored circumvention is for management to claim that the agreement has been broken by union officers who have failed to meet their obligations. Legal textbooks used at both Moscow and Leningrad universities warn future labor lawyers against accepting such a ploy and state quite plainly that union noncompliance can never justify managerial violation of these complex agreements. For example, one Leningrad manual notes that the obligations contained within a collective agreement of the administration are legal but those of the trade union organization and of the workers themselves are of a moral-political nature.[33]

Even though a Soviet collective agreement requires considerable attention to detail, fine legal and negotiating points unfortunately may be lost on unsophisticated union officials. Trade union bungling more than managerial duplicity may underlie much noncompliance.[34] Although generalizing about Soviet experience on the basis of East European experience is always dangerous, the observations on factory life offered by the Hungarian Marxist dissident Miklós Haraszti probably ring true to many Soviet workers. Haraszti concluded a discussion of Hungarian collective agreements by noting:

It consists of some 150 pages, largely covered with tongue-twisting abbreviations, incomprehensible clauses and paragraphs, numbered in a way that's impossible to follow. Even when text emerges out of this jungle, it consists only of a framework of regulations, reiterated in unimaginable bureaucratic-legalistic jargon, as off-putting as possible. Areas of responsibility are very vaguely indicated; lines are drawn sharply only when the interests of the company demand it.[35]

There are, of course, numerous other reasons for the failure to achieve many of the desired goals of Soviet collective agreements. If these causes were either purely legal or purely attitudinal, perhaps one could more easily remedy inconsistencies in enforcement. Instead, Soviet administrators on both sides of the conference table often must choose from among several undesirable options. As one Leningrad housing administrator has exclaimed: "You want more space. The law says that you should have more space. We want you to have more space. But there is no space to give you."

Varying conditions among different factories, industries, and regions make for a disparate pattern of compliance to collective agreements. Soviet spokesmen note that the performance of factory officials has improved steadily over recent years. Western critics charge that the agreements remain meaningless prose.[36] Both have little difficulty finding living examples to illustrate their claims. This disagreement over the true nature of Soviet collective agreements resembles a philosophical debate over whether a glass is half full or half empty. Neither appears willing to acknowledge that, given the total failure of the agreements during the 1930s,[37] the fact that there is an agreement – a glass if you will – to argue over is in itself remarkable, regardless of whether it is half full with milk or half empty with apple juice.

In examining the Soviet press for areas of cooperation among various troika members, one is overwhelmed by references to socialist competition.[38] At the most basic level, these competitions would appear to be a rather contrived substitution for piece-rate wage schedules. Yet their function does not stop there because these contests also provide important mechanisms for integrating workers into the life of the factory. At a practical level, they frequently center on the efforts of individual workers and groups of workers to meet their "self-proclaimed socialist obligations." More often than not, these obligations are set forth in the enterprise collective agreement.

In the 1974 Kamsk Cable agreement, union and management officials enumerated factory production goals,[39] projecting total annual output of various categories of cable by completion dates ranging anywhere from 1 September to 20 December. Assuming achievement of those targets, any additional production following those dates would exceed centrally planned norms. If the workers live up to their socialist obligations and meet these production targets, the enterprise receives 2 million rubles in profits, part of which employees share according to the results of the competition. In order to encourage the contest, factory union committees are to organize monthly meetings at which they praise the most productive workers. In addition, the competition's winners will be asked to give a public demonstration of their skills. The Kamsk Cable trade union committee, for example, organized field trips (*komandirovki*) to other plants in the Perm region to observe new production techniques.

Despite such programs, socialist competition has not markedly increased Soviet industrial productivity.[40] Many of the reasons for this failure lie beyond the scope of the competition itself. Consumer goods shortages limit the incentive of bonus payments. Moreover, many union and management officials claim that workers have come to expect annual bonus payments regardless of enterprise performance. One particularly candid Leningrad union official has noted that cancellation of the so-called thirteenth month wage is the only guaranteed provocation for riot. Finally, there is little evidence that union officials themselves take the program seriously. Many prefer to characterize it as a necessary concession for other desired ends, such as improved working conditions and expanded factory social services.

While union and management negotiate collective agreements and administer socialist competition, Party officials work with their union peers to improve workers' "cultural" level. The Party tends to dominate this relationship through broad policy guidelines rather than crude interference in union affairs. As one Soviet union official was heard to note, "The Party does not bother with small change."[41] Party membership, then, requires all Party cardholders to implement Party policies.[42] Those union officials who happen to be Party members are obliged to do so. Few contemporary union officers question such hegemony, merely accepting it as a precondition of Soviet industrial life. The Party becomes just one more constituency to please. In theory, it monitors nearly every aspect of union life. In practice, Party officials appear to be most directly concerned with union educational and cultural activities.

The Party asks the unions to help raise each new generation of *homo Sovieticus*.[43] During the 1960s, trade union and Party investment in educational work grew significantly. As one Soviet author observed: "The task of the trade unions is the education of a new man, a member of communist society; a man harmoniously combining in himself spiritual wealth, moral purity and physical perfection."[44]

Such obligations gained added significance when, in 1968, a new five-day work week provided Soviet workers with two days away from their jobs.[45] The unions soon expanded their efforts to plan leisure activities so that by 1977 they were operating over 22,000 clubs, 21,000 libraries, and 325,000 factory reading and recreation rooms.[46] In 1978, more than 25 million union members participated in amateur artistic performances.[47] Factory trade union organizations arranged special tours of local museums and historical sites, produced plays, sponsored sporting events, instigated antireligious campaigns, and offered technical and general training to union members.

In spite of these varied activities, Party officials remain most interested in political education. Such programs may consist of organized discussions concerning current world events at which a rapporteur directs deliberations in order to demonstrate the ultimate superiority of Marxism-Leninism. It is not unusual for such meetings to follow guidelines issued by regional Party and union committees. One such report, distributed by the Leningrad City and Regional Party Committees in May 1974, reviewed an array of topical events, passages discussing the prospects for a European security conference being of greatest historical significance:

A group of jurists and international relations specialists representing the interest of several European capitalist states has attempted to call into question the principles of non-intervention of one European nation in the affairs of another. This proposal alleges the existence of violations of human rights in several European nations. In our opinion, this proposal is fully irreconcilable with the doctrine of non-interference. We can never agree with this; its enactment would represent a form of tyranny.[48]

Leningrad workers listening to the lecture also found out that a new stage in the development of U.S.–Soviet relations was to be ushered in by President Richard M. Nixon's June visit to Moscow. They would never have known from the guidelines prepared by the Leningrad Party Committee that the U.S. President was in political difficulty. (He resigned less than three months later.)

As the discussion of one-man rule indicated, Party guidance over factory management, like that of Party over union, is no simple affair. Party officials do not concern themselves with detailed examination of the minutiae of managerial decision making. Instead, they generally review administrative successes and failures. As a textbook for Party activists explains:

Free from petty tutelage over the relationship of state agencies with economic agencies, free from direct interference in the industrial-managerial responsibilities of these agencies, Party organizations and their senior officials have the ability to concentrate their undivided attention and strength upon those fundamental and principal issues which have a decisive impact upon the development of the economy.[49]

Party officials may participate in decisions affecting technological innovation. In accordance with Party directives favoring mechanization and rationalization of the production process, many factory Party officials cooperate with factory directors and with the trade union–sponsored All-Union Society of Innovators and Rationalizers (VOIR) and Scientific-Technical Societies (NTO) to encourage the introduction of new work techniques. Here again, multiple constituencies are at work, and Party, management, and union officials must all answer to various superiors.

This chapter began with a fictional account of enterprise officials attempting to resolve mutual differences. A trade union chairman sought improving enterprise social services; a factory director sought increasing production. Meanwhile a Party chairman wanted both. None of the three arguments was based on noble motives or pristine ideals. In fact, each wanted to do just what was necessary in order to stay in the good graces of their many constituencies. They compromised and took relatively marginal measures to improve both the performance of their factory and the living standards of their workers. Yet their story demonstrates that change can occur within Soviet industrial enterprises. More often than not, such change is a result of real-life factory directors and union and Party chairmen sitting down and discussing problems such as those mentioned here. The success or the failure of union programs, including the protection of a Soviet worker's legal and social rights, depends on this triangular relationship and on the relationships of each of these groups to other constituencies.

4

The legal and social rights of Soviet workers

The discussion at the beginning of this book stressed the growing importance of the legal and social rights of workers to Soviet union organizations. Yet the lack of a precise definition of those rights has caused continuing conflict both within the unions themselves and between union and management. Some factory officials view increased productivity as the sole aim of plant operations, whereas others acknowledge broader issues of worker welfare. The degree to which union officials are able to protect their membership from managerial "bureaucratism" frequently hinges on such definitional conflict, as the story of Valerii Vecherenko illustrates.

A little more than ten years ago, Valerii Vecherenko joined a construction team near Norilsk. During a 1976 trade union meeting, he rose to speak out against the poor working and living conditions at various work sites operated by the Moscow Gas Line Construction Association. Much to his surprise, the hall exploded in applause, and within a few months Vecherenko found himself serving as the chairman of his construction unit's trade union committee.

As union chairman, he decided to tour every construction site within his jurisdiction and discovered, to his dismay, that management frequently violated safety regulations. Vecherenko took his evidence of legal transgressions directly to the supervisors involved, including Aleksandr Grigorevich Shcherbukha of the Building and Assembly Administration. The supervisors steadfastly refused to correct any of the violations. Vecherenko then organized a workers' meeting to discuss the situation further, and, as a result, the union committee requested that a local procurator bring criminal charges against one particularly negligent shop administrator, N. Masleia.

At this point in the story, the chairman of the entire association's trade union committee, A. Karpov, entered the scene in hopes of soothing increasingly hot tempers. He had little success, and by late 1977 many of the best workers were leaving the site for better conditions elsewhere. Following a failure to meet 1977 production targets, Karpov's superiors instructed him to return again to review the problems identified by Vecherenko. Karpov did so but reported that nothing appeared to be wrong except for a growing personal animosity between Vecherenko and Shcherbukha.

A serious accident took place at one of the construction sites under investigation shortly after Karpov filed his report. Dispatched to investigate the accident, V. Zenkov, a special correspondent from *Trud*, reported that Karpov should be reprimanded. Disputing the findings of the previous investigation, Zenkov wrote: "The reason for the conflict which developed between Shcherbukha and Vecherenko – between administration and union – has a far deeper basis than personal likes and dislikes. Two views of the role of union consultation in management have collided."[1] Unfortunately, no follow-up stories appeared in *Trud* to indicate the outcome of the conflict. A close reading of *Trud* does suggest, however, that such friction is not unusual in a system of labor relations governed by divergent goals. How these conflicts are resolved determines the extent to which a Soviet worker may gain at least some of the rights promised to him by law.

The 1970 Fundamental Principles of Labor Legislation represents the single most important legislative act regulating labor relations in the Soviet Union. The result of more than a decade of discussion, this act replaced an obsolete labor code nearly fifty years old. Yet the 1970 act is not in itself legally binding upon factory managers. Fifteen separate union republic labor codes, each closely modeled after the provisions of the 1970 labor legislation, give legal force to the new measures.[2] According to the 1970 act, Soviet workers enjoy the right to appropriate employment, safe working conditions, and adequate compensation. Trade unions protect these rights through a complex procedure for resolving conflict.

The 1974 Supreme Soviet resolution governing that media-
tion process specifies that any disagreement between labor and
management must receive two hearings within a given factory.[3]
Significantly, the first review now should take place before a
shop dispute commission (consisting of union and managerial
representatives at the smallest unit closest to the work site), and
a second hearing goes before a shop trade union committee.[4]
If the argument has factorywide implications, the case proceeds
to the factorywide Commission on Labor Disputes (KTS) (consisting of union and managerial representatives from more than
one work site) or to a factory trade union committee (FZMK).
The legislation further requires that the disputes commissions,
which consist of an equal number of union and managerial
representatives, must reach a unanimous decision. Otherwise
the case automatically goes before the entire shop or factory
trade union committee. Both the worker and manager have the
right of appeal once the entire factory trade union committee
has passed judgment on a dispute.

Theory and practice diverge mainly after the decision of the
factory committee. Both workers and manager may appeal to
a people's court, which generally upholds a decision of a union
committee that supports the position of the worker.

Should the trade union committee support management, a
worker still has several options. The most widely selected option
is to appeal the case to the next higher union agency, usually
an intraunion regional committee or an interunion regional
council. Either of these bodies, if it agrees with the worker, may
request ministerial officials to press factory management to
correct that situation. If the ministerial officials do not respond,
regional union officials may ask their Party counterparts to
pressure ministerial and factory officials. Indeed, Leningrad
regional trade union officials prefer such informal procedures
because they increase the probability of appropriate and flexible
managerial remedies being accepted.

Should the regional union body fail to agree with the worker,
the aggrieved worker may turn directly to a local procurator in
order to establish whether or not there has been a violation of
law. If the finding is in the worker's favor, the prosecutor may
bring criminal and/or civil charges against factory management,
as was the case in 1967 in the Donets region when the regional

procuracy initiated 490 protests, 453 representations, 108 disciplinary proceedings, and 14 criminal proceedings against managerial personnel, as well as 23 civil actions, the total cost of which was 1,099 rubles. District procuracy representatives throughout the region brought an additional 88 civil actions costing 5,671 rubles.[5]

If the procuracy rejects the worker's case, he can still hire legal counsel, but the courts discourage this action: not only are the dockets already filled, but once the procurator sides with management the worker has little hope of a favorable result. Should he lose in the first court, the worker still has a right to another hearing before an appellate court. Yet the function of such an appeals procedure is somewhat different from similar processes under Anglo-American law.

The role of judicial review in the Soviet legal system is not well defined, either by law or by tradition. In part, this confusion results from a long history of political involvement in the operation of the Soviet courts. The uneven development of case law, however, is more directly related to the influence of continental legal systems on nineteenth-century Russian practice and subsequent twentieth-century Soviet practice.

Primarily the product of a Roman system of law, the Soviet legal structure provides little room for judicial review. In order to standardize judicial practice, the young Soviet state established a system of appellate courts in 1922. The decisions of these courts alter only the outcome of the specific case under review; they do not establish legal precedent.

These procedures for the resolution of disputes between labor and management protect a worker's right to a job, a healthy work environment, and a legal wage. The unions and the courts have defended Soviet workers most strongly, however, in the area of employment rights.

Vasilii Dzhelomanov of the Organization Department at the All-Union Central Council of Trade Unions has noted that any worker can leave his job whenever he likes as long as he has given two-week notice (a limit raised in 1979 to one month). The administration cannot dismiss workers unless they present a serious labor discipline problem or have serious personal problems affecting their work. In either case, factory trade union officials must examine all the circumstances surrounding a proposed dismissal and reserve the right to veto management's decision.

Although factory administration may appeal a union committee's decision to a people's court, it is likely to agree with the union committee. In 1967, one of the few years for which data have appeared, Soviet people's courts found illegalities in dismissals and ruled that management reinstate employees in slightly more than one-half of all cases. The reinstatement rates have been significantly higher in Uzbekistan, Georgia, Tadzhikistan, Azerbaidzhan, and Kazakhstan.[6]

Furthermore, the USSR Supreme Court has issued guidelines for lower courts in the disposition of cases involving the dismissal of workers on several occasions following the promulgation of the 1970 Fundamental Principles of Labor Legislation.[7] Each time the court has emphasized the inviolability of the work contract and maintained that management may dismiss workers only with the prior approval of a majority of the factory union committee. Management must undertake all possible disciplinary measures before it seeks the committee's approval. In several instances when management has not met these guidelines, the Supreme Court has ruled that lower courts should reinstate the worker with full back pay. If this action proves impossible, either because the factory involved is closed down or the force is generally reduced (*sokhrashchenie shtatov*), back wages up to three months must be paid.

In 1977, the Supreme Court of the USSR undertook yet another review of judicial behavior on questions of worker dismissals.[8] Working with representatives of the supreme courts of the union republics as well as those of several regional tribunals, the court examined approximately four thousand cases adjudicated during 1975, and found that lower judicial bodies moved to reinstate workers to their positions in 54.9 percent of all cases. Regional variations from this national pattern were significant, however, violations of the law being most frequent in Uzbekistan, Armenia, Kirgiziia, Kazakhstan, Georgia, and Azerbaidzhan. More than 60 percent of the workers won their cases in these latter regions (more than 70 percent in Uzbekistan). Soviet judges upheld the complaints of workers in 61 percent of all cases involving dismissal for labor discipline violations and in 64 percent of all cases involving the reduction of the overall factory work force. (Both categories accounted for more than two-thirds of all cases relating to dismissals and transfers reaching the court system.) In short, workers bringing their cases before a Soviet judicial tribunal had a reasonable chance of winning back a job.

By the late 1970s, the USSR Supreme Court had moved to reduce the number of cases reaching the courts by improving the performance of factory officials involved in dismissals. For its part, the USSR Supreme Court urged lower courts to publicize illegal labor dismissals more widely, noting with some disappointment that the percentage of such cases tried before mass audiences had declined between 1971 and 1975 from 9.2 to 8.6 percent. Furthermore, the Soviet Union's highest court urged local judicial officials to work more closely with their colleagues in the procuracy, managers, and union committees to ensure that disputes were properly resolved before they ever reached the trial stage.

In 1978, the RSFSR Supreme Court undertook a similar review of the performance of tribunals under its jurisdiction.[9] In general, the justices found that the enforcement of those statutes protecting a worker's right to a job had improved. Court performance, however, had remained uneven throughout the republic, particularly in cases involving Article 215 of the RSFSR Labor Code.

According to Article 215, responsible managerial officials are liable for up to three months of a worker's back pay should a worker be dismissed or transferred to another position in violation of existing statutes. M. P. Naumov, chairman of the Vladimir Regional Court, reported to a March 1978 plenum of the RSFSR Supreme Court that the implementation of this measure had proven particularly effective in reducing illegal transfers and dismissals in his region. Z. I. Kornev, deputy chairman of the Moscow City Court, stated that his court worked closely with the Moscow City Council of Trade Unions to involve union officials systematically in the monitoring of such cases to good effect. Naumov's and Kornev's views were not shared by all present; some maintained that managerial officials should be liable only under the most egregious circumstances. The session closed with the republic's supreme court issuing a decree defining appropriate judicial behavior in dismissal cases.[10]

The March 1978 decree of the RSFSR Supreme Court began by noting that judicial officials had enforced Article 215 in a "majority" of instances and as a result the number of violations and court cases involving illegal dismissal had dropped off significantly. The justices further noted that clarification was necessary in order to ensure more consistent behavior throughout the republic. The court recommended that local courts increase preventative actions – including educational and monitoring efforts undertaken with the assistance of the procuracy and the unions – and that they use appropriate provisions of the republic's civil and criminal codes to prevent illegal actions on the part of Soviet managers. The justices maintained, however, that personal fines be levied against managers following only the most flagrant violation of the law. The meeting closed by calling for more attention to procedural norms in the adjudication of such cases. Similar suggestions were offered by the RSFSR Supreme Court in November 1978, following another review of judicial behavior, and in 1979.

A June 1979 decree of the RSFSR Supreme Court proposed specific guidelines to be used by the republic's courts in determining whether or not legal norms had been violated in the dismissal or transfer of a worker.[11] This decree considers a violation of the law to occur if: (1) the dismissal or transfer is not presented to the factory trade union committee for review; (2) trade union approval amounts to an abrogation of a legal and valid labor contract; (3) the proper disciplinary actions have not been taken or a proper amount of time has not been provided for those actions to have an effect; (4) a two-thirds quorum of trade union committee members is not present when the union reaches its decision; (5) a majority of union committee members present and voting do not approve the dismissal or transfer; (6) union approval is voted after the dismissal or transfer has already occurred; (7) shop or association and regional union bodies have not been consulted when appropriate; and (8) various commissions of the factory trade union committee, such as the commission on youth affairs, have not been consulted when appropriate.

Guidelines such as these require managerial officials to follow exceedingly complex procedures in order to remove a worker. In one 1973 case reaching the Supreme Court of the Russian

Republic, the highway patrol had suspended the license of a truck driver, Tokarev, who had requested permission to continue work as a metalworker until he could drive again.[12] Management had denied his request and fired him. The court ruled that Tokarev's dismissal would be valid only if a lower court could certify that the trucking firm had no position for the driver to fill. Tokarev returned to the firm's payroll pending the outcome of such an investigation.

In an earlier model case in 1971, the Kostromsk Vodka Factory had transferred a worker, Viktorov, from his job on the assembly line to the container assembly shop while his regular work site underwent repair.[13] Viktorov had a physical disability and could not meet his new obligations. The plant's management, citing prolonged absence from work, moved to dismiss him. The factory trade union committee concurred with this decision. The Russian Republic's Supreme Court did not and ruled that the dismissal was illegal as management fired the worker for medical reasons (his inability to assemble shipping containers), whereas the factory union committee had granted permission to dismiss him on disciplinary grounds. Once again, the court ordered reinstatement of the worker. More recently, the Civil Division of the RSFSR Supreme Court ruled in April 1979 that a retail clerk in the Stavropol' Region should be reinstated to her position because the factory trade union committee had failed to take into account during its review of the case the fact that the necessary documents had been signed by someone other than the official who had legal authority to hire, transfer, or fire.[14]

Court decisions such as these three suggest that Soviet labor legislation not only guarantees citizens the right to work but also a seemingly inflexible right to their present jobs. This right remains secure even when a dismissal of an employee may prove economically beneficial to the plant as a whole.

The recent film *Afonia* further illustrates this point. Afonia is a thoroughly despicable plumber who is a braggart, a drunkard, and a speculator – a totally degenerate and corrupt human being. Afonia systematically extracts large bribes from customers, but he cannot be fired. During one of several meetings called to discuss his behavior, a fellow worker suggests that Afonia be dismissed. The trade union spokesman intercedes to argue that it would be better to apply social pressure. The meeting votes yet another meaningless sanction, and Afonia continues to trample on the rights of management, his fellow workers, and his customers until he finally decides to leave town. This film underscores both the successes and failures of union efforts to improve the defense of workers' right to work. On the one hand, the hero cannot be fired; on the other, the rights of everyone else in the plant have been sacrificed.

Nonetheless, many Soviet labor relations specialists and union officials express the belief that negative sanctions will not improve the discipline or the turnover problems typified by *Afonia*. As AUCCTU Chairman Shibaev himself indicated in a major 1978 address, only the creation of a "healthy moral-psychological climate" can ultimately increase industrial productivity.[15]

The emphasis placed by Shibaev on psychological and social factors affecting working conditions further reflects the interest among Soviet union officials and labor relations specialists in less punitive approaches to labor discipline. This interest is in part a result of the efforts of legal experts to apply sociological methodologies in their examination of labor law violations.[16] Their findings suggest that undisciplined behavior has social causes and can be ameliorated only by the creation and main- tenance of a healthy work environment. Hence, the scholars argue, any expenditure for improved "moral psychological climates" at a plant may be offset by better worker morale and increased productivity.

The popular press has given considerable support to this view. For example, an article in the Leningrad evening news- paper *Vechernii Leningrad* concluded that the city's poor public transportation system and the plant's inadequate dining facilities were among the primary causes for tardiness at one local factory.[17] The article indicated that many tardy employees cannot even make their way through crowded cafeteria lines before the end of the lunch hours and, moreover, that many workers live far from the factory and must leave work twenty to thirty minutes early simply to make bus connections. Instead of imposing further sanctions against tardiness, the paper urged the factory management to reconstruct existing cafeteria facilities.

A 1974 novel by Stalin Prize winner Vladimir Popov, *And You*

Call It Doldrums, similarly hinted that a more enlightened approach to the work force is preferable.[18] The primary tension in this voluminous work arises from events surrounding the replacement of a sensitive, intelligent, and innovative manager of the new type with an old-line, boorish, and corrupt factory director. As events unfold at a metallurgy plant somewhere in the South, it becomes obvious that the villainous old-timer places his own career above the interests of the collective. Eventually, vigorous worker protests to this situation disrupt a factory meeting, which only the miraculous return from India of the younger, more erudite manager can bring to order.

Viewpoints such as these, which have gained wider acceptance in recent years, help to support union efforts to upgrade working conditions. One 1978 AUCCTU meeting that examined poor attendance records and a high incidence of petty theft in the heavy machine construction industry concluded by urging that the "socio-living conditions" of the industry's workers be improved.[19]

Numerous senior Party leaders have openly supported better working conditions rather than severe negative sanctions as the most effective approach to increasing industrial productivity. L. I. Brezhnev, for example, reminded several Party and trade union convocations that factory trade union officials must protect workers against abusive managerial practices as part of their general effort to increase labor productivity.[20] Furthermore, the Party's Central Committee instructed factory Party officials to side with unions and workers and not with managers in disputes over conditions. Armenian legal scholar I. A. Arabian explicitly discussed this Soviet-style "human relations" approach to labor–management relations in a 1978 article examining labor discipline violations in his native republic.[21] Arabian argued that the poor organization of municipal services significantly contributed to absenteeism. In the course of one day, he noted, a local district passport office served about three hundred persons, of whom two-thirds were away from their jobs and thus created a total loss of more than five hundred man-hours. Similarly he found that poor management within a factory could lead to labor discipline violations. Arabian concluded that only a "favorable psychological atmosphere" could improve productivity and that only improved dining facilities, transportation services, housing, and the like could help to foster a proper *sotsial'nyi klimat* (social climate). These concerns are also evident in a major decree of December 1979 on labor discipline and labor turnover.[22]

The December 1979 decree of the Central Committee of the CPSU, the Presidium of the USSR Supreme Soviet, the USSR Council of Ministers, and the AUCCTU "On the Further Strengthening of Labor Discipline and the Reduction of Labor Turnover in the National Economy" did not give Soviet workers a propitious start on the new decade. Citing the tremendous costs to the Soviet economy of the unproductive behavior among Soviet workers, the decree initially calls to mind the repressive labor policies of the past. Certainly, the decision to lengthen the required waiting period for leaving one's job following the submission of written notice from two weeks to one month can hardly be considered a liberalizing gesture.

Closer examination of the decree suggests that the trends of the 1960s and 1970s have left their unmistakable mark. Aside from the tightening of the regulations governing the submission of written notice, the measures taken or recommended by the Central Committee, the Supreme Soviet, the Council of Ministers, and the AUCCTU focus on rewards for good performance rather than punishment for bad. For instance, factory housing will be provided to workers having work tenure of not less than five years, or two years for young workers; up to three supplemental vacation days will be offered to workers with three to seven years of uninterrupted service; and 10–20 percent increases in old-age pensions will be made to make workers having twenty-five years of uninterrupted tenure and to female workers with children having twenty years of uninterrupted serivce.

Even more in line with the emergent "human relations" approach, economic managers, Party and union officials, and municipal governments are chided for contributing to the poor performance of Soviet workers. As a result of the December 1979 decree, social organizations can no longer organize nonwork activities during work time; working conditions are to be improved by technological innovation, which is expected to reduce hazardous and manual labor; factory housing is to be located closer to the place of work; factory-organized and municipal transportation and personnel placement services are to be upgraded; and the hours of consumer and municipal services are to be extended to allow Soviet citizens to run errands after, not during, the work day.

Finally, propaganda campaigns should glorify good work habits and contribute to an environment conducive to labor discipline. (The editors of all newspapers, journals, and publishing houses, as well as the leaders of all cultural organizations, are required to demonstrate the "economic, moral, and social significance of disciplined labor.") Perhaps most striking of all is the provision instructing the USSR State Committee on Labor and Social Questions and the AUCCTU to join with research institutes of the USSR Academy of Sciences to encourage the systematic study and analysis of the effectiveness of various economic, social, and legal measures that may be employed to strengthen labor discipline. It is precisely such study that led to more sophisticated approaches to labor discipline problems in the first place, as well as to full appreciation that union officials must be in a position to enforce labor safety norms in order to foster a proper social climate if productivity is ever to be increased.

Soviet labor legislation requires that factories use the most up-to-date safety techniques available.[23] Furthermore, the law states that factory trade union officials should be allowed to participate in all decisions affecting the general work environment through the enterprise collective agreement and through the organization of enterprise labor safety inspections.

The Kamsk Cable Factory's 1974 collective agreement[24] required factory management to eliminate all known causes of industrial accidents and to improve the quality of workers' protective clothing. Over the course of that year, the plant allocated nearly 300,000 rubles for improvements in the work environment, particularly for the needs of female employees. Workers, managerial personnel, and members of the factory engineering staff review the terms of collective agreements such as that at Kamsk every quarter. Should union officials become dissatisfied with the progress made toward meeting that agreement, they may request the removal of ineffectual administrators. For example, V. Isatov, supervisor of a motor pool at the Central Sanitary Technical Assembly Trust, lost his job after union investigators uncovered irregularities in his handling of salary funds.[25] At the national level, AUCCTU Secretary A. I. Shibaev reports that such measures led to the removal of over ten thousand factory administrators in 1977 alone, which, if accurate, is a truly astounding figure.[26] Meanwhile, in 1980, AUCCTU Deputy Chairman V. Prokhorov reported, "Just last year a total of 6,174 economic managers who violated labour protection standards or failed to ensure observance of the collective agreement were called to account along administrative lines. At the request of trade unions 146 of them were removed from their posts."[27] In November 1980, the Soviet press agency TASS reported that the director of a Vilnius gas equipment works had been removed at trade union request for failing to meet planned housing construction targets. According to Algirdas Ferensas, chairman of the Lithuanian SSR Republic Trade Union Council, this action was only one of twenty conflicts between union and management in the first ten months of 1980 alone resolved in the unions' favor by the republic council.[28]

In interviews, Soviet trade union administrators and legal specialists frequently assert that most factories fulfill the provisions of such collective agreements. One need only to consult the union daily newspaper *Trud* to find ample evidence to the contrary.[29] A group of workers at Factory No. 34 of the Onega Saw Mill and Wood Processing Combine writes that the air in and around their plant is saturated with sawdust, but factory management consistently refuses to improve the ventilation system. Another typical letter from forestry workers six thousand miles away in Komsomol'sk-on-Amur complains that inadequate housing and working conditions lead half of their plant's work force to leave each year. Meanwhile, a group of workers at a procurement shop in Minsk suffer from paint fumes while factory managers await the arrival of new equipment to ameliorate the spray-painting process at the plant.

This last example is perhaps most noteworthy, for it typifies a dilemma shared by many Soviet administrators. Although they may be fully aware of safety hazards and often quite willing to alleviate these dangers, many factory managers lack adequate funding to do so. Try as they might to live up to the ideals of labor legislation, many Soviet industrial officials simply cannot meet their obligations. This is as true of managerial officials struggling to meet the demands of safety inspectors as it is of those trying to live up to their own collective agreements.

Both intra–trade union regional committees and inter–trade union councils support a staff of permanent safety inspectors certified at the completion of an established curriculum. Their inspections carry the full weight of criminal sanctions. In addition, the AUCCTU works closely with the USSR State Planning Committee (Gosplan) and with the State Committee on Science and Technology to develop improved safety programs. During the past five-year plan (1976–80), these three agencies should have spent more than 42 million rubles for safety-related research carried out at over two hundred scientific research establishments and union republic ministries.[30]

The director and a section chief at the All-Union Scientific Research Institute for Labor Safety have reported that their institute has developed several experimental ventilation systems.[31] A. Matrosov and V. Rabinovich singled out one 70 million–ruble pilot project in Sverdlovsk for special attention but noted that several other major efforts to upgrade ventilation systems were underway elsewhere. Indeed, they observed that in 1970 scientific reports concerning the air quality in and around factories were bibliographic rarities, whereas in 1978 more than four hundred major studies were examining this single problem. Armed with scientific data and backed by criminal and civil sanctions, union safety inspectors have the right to enter any factory at will and inspect any area within that plant. If factory officials do not meet their demands, regional trade union and Party officials as well as officials of the regional office of the procuracy may intervene. Eventually the case can be taken to court.

In addition to the permanent safety inspectors hired by regional trade union organizations, individual factory trade union committees organize voluntary safety commissions. Each enterprise and shop has the right to organize their inspection system according to individual needs. The chairman of the safety commission must be a member of the factory trade union committee.

The commission theoretically inspects each shop at the start of a work shift. If a volunteer discovers a safety violation, he must report it to the shop foreman and the shop union steward. If the foreman does not correct that condition by the beginning of the next shift, the steward must report that failure to the factory union committee. Finally, if management persists in ignoring the violation, the factory trade union chairman can request that a professional inspector from the regional union council examine the plant. Once the regional inspector does so, the factory may become subject to legal action.

Nonetheless, serious safety violations continue to occur. During his tenure, former AUCCTU Chairman A. N. Shelepin frequently criticized local union officials for ignoring safety violations. He told the Fourteenth Trade Union Congress in 1968 that working conditions still wanted vast improvement[32] since neither the unions nor management enforced labor standards in all too many factories. Shelepin's successor, A. I. Shibaev, AUCCTU Deputy Chairman V. I. Prokhorov, and Party General Secretary L. I. Brezhnev have made similar pronouncements at other Party and union gatherings.[33]

In addition to a worker's right to appropriate employment and safe working conditions, the 1970 Fundamental Principles of Labor Legislation give the worker a legal right to an appropriate wage. Over the past twenty years, significant changes have occurred in the Soviet wage structure. Wage inequality (as opposed to total income inequality) has decreased as the result of major wage reforms in 1956 and 1968.[34] During the seven years between 1968 and 1975, the salary ratio between the top and bottom 10 percent of Soviet workers declined from $1:5$ to $1:4$.[35] Moreover, the Soviet minimum wage rose by nearly 150 percent from a pre-1956 level of 27 rubles per month to a 1978 level of 70 rubles per month. This increase in the base pay has occurred at the same time that upper-level salaries have become stabilized so that in coal mining a trust director's salary that was 450 rubles per month in 1960 and 1975 was eleven times the industry's minimum wage in 1960 but only 6.5 times the 1975 minimum.

The second of the two reforms established basic principles which determine Soviet wages to this day. Coming on the heels of the 1965 economic reforms, it sought greater flexibility in the calculation of individual wage levels. According to the new payment procedures, a Soviet industrial worker's job skills as well as various supplemental payments and union-sponsored social welfare benefits determine his take-home pay. The unions are able to exert influence over this process both nationally and locally.

Nationally, individual union central committees meet on a regular basis with representatives from the corresponding ministries in order to discuss changes in wage rates.[36] The law also requires the State Committee on Labor and Social Questions to examine all AUCCTU wage proposals. The AUCCTU itself maintains a staff of liaison officers who are in touch with both the State Committee on Labor and Social Questions and the State Planning Committee (Gosplan) in order to lobby for changes in the wage system. Indeed, one former AUCCTU liaison officer to Gosplan has boasted that some of his talks with that agency were so forceful that passers-by could hear them on the street. Locally, the wage commission of the factory or shop union committee acts to ensure the correct calculation of a worker's wage.

Marx's labor theory of value maintains that the value of a product is determined by the quantity of socially necessary labor required to produce it.[37] In an effort to translate that formula into a comprehensive wage system binding wages to the value of the labor performed, Soviet economists have identified half a dozen dimensions of work that should be considered in the formulation of an individual worker's wage: time, complexity, working conditions, skill, location, industry, and enterprise. Out of this theoretical formulation have arisen a base rate (*stavki*) establishing the amount payable to the least skilled worker in a given industry by industry, and three skill scales (*tarifnye setki*) establishing coefficients which, in the end, determine the pay rate of a given job at a specific enterprise. Additional coefficients relate the wage to working conditions and geographic region. Finally, various bonus systems are established by individual enterprises.

The first step in determining the wage of a specific worker is to ascertain the base rate of that worker's position from the *United Wage Qualifications Handbook for Mass Professions* (*Edinyi tarifno-kvalifikatsionnyi spravochnik skvoznykh professii*). This publication contains the industrywide base rates for persons filling jobs common to all or most branches of industry as they have been established by the USSR State Committee on Labor and Social Questions in accordance with an evaluation of the skills required by a given position and the desired maximum differential between minimum and maximum payment in a given industry. For example, if in 1975 the lowest-paid worker in the machine-building industry received a base rate of 1.0, a worker in the highest skill category would be assigned a multiplier of 1.71 times the base tariff.[38] As in the U.S. civil service, this rate is theoretically attached to a given position and not to the person who holds that position at any given time. The issue of coefficients arises only after the base rate has been established.

Three basic coefficients may increase the wage paid to a given employee: supplements granted for hazardous working conditions; supplements granted for less desirable geographic regions; and supplements accrued through work incentive programs.

The supplement for "hot, heavy, or hazardous conditions" is effected either through higher piece rates than those used under normal conditions (usually 5–15 percent higher) or, in those industries where abnormal working conditions are the rule, through increases in industrywide base rates contained in the *United Wage Qualifications Handbook*. In addition, supplements are paid for work in areas with less than desirable living or climatic conditions. These coefficients (which are established as a percentage increase in the base rate paid in the central, southern, and western regions of the European USSR) also compensate for regional variations in the cost of living (see Table 4.1). For example, workers in the far north receive time-and-a-half pay whereas workers on islands in the Arctic Ocean receive double time.[39] Finally, there are incentive supplements paid in accordance with the bonus funds established through socialist competition and the implementation of the 1965 economic reforms. These last supplements directly affect the salaries of nearly every industrial worker in the Soviet Union, although the 1978 average monthly monetary increase in the earnings of workers and employees in industry accrued from the Incentive Fund was only 14.30 rubles.[40] Such supplements also represent an area where factory-level union officials can and frequently do exert some influence.

The 1965 economic reforms established three funds derived

from enterprise profits: the Fund for the Development of Production supplies additional capital for construction and for technical innovation; the Incentive Fund encourages overachievers in socialist competition; and, finally, the Fund for Social and Cultural Needs raises more funds for the improvement of factory social, health, and recreational facilities. Some policy makers had hoped that enhanced incentives for individual workers and factories as a whole would stimulate production. Moreover, the creation of these surplus funds meant that a potentially larger proportion of a worker's total earnings may come from enterprise profits.

The use of new prerogatives by factory managers and factory union officials had led some Soviet labor law specialists to speculate that enterprise administrators now have the legal authority to establish local legal norms. The discussion of this controversial thesis intensified following the 1973 publication of a much-disputed work by Lvov University's R. I. Kondrat'ev, *Local Norms of Labor Law and Material Stimulation.*[41]

According to Kondrat'ev, the expansion of union and managerial prerogatives in numerous areas of joint decision making accompanied the post-1965 growth of enterprise autonomy. He argued that joint union–managerial decisions governing a broad sweep of enterprise activities amount to local control over legal and material labor norms. Factory authorities have begun to create legally binding norms that are largely independent of central decrees. Revealing further insight into the wage determination activities of factory officials, Kondrat'ev found that plant directors and factory union chairmen established the take-home pay an individual worker receives by exercising control over the distribution of profit-sharing premiums and benefits paid from union social funds.

Apart from the practical failures of the 1965 reforms, Kondrat'ev's critics challenge his definition of a legal norm. When the Labor Law Section of Leningrad State University's Juridical Faculty invited Kondrat'ev to discuss his work, A. S. Pashkov, chief of the section, took his guest to task for failing to appreciate the differences between locally constituted norms and local clarification of centrally established norms. In a 1978 textbook, the Ukrainian scholar retreated slightly from his earlier position,[42] suggesting that local norms actively involve union officials

Table 4.1. *Soviet wage coefficients based on branch rates and regional differentials, by branch and by region, ca. 1970*

Branch of Industry and Economy	Central	North-west	Volga-Vyatskiy	Central Black Earth	Volga	North Caucasus	Urals	West Siberian	East Siberian	Far East	Donetsk-Pridneprovskiy	South-west	Southern	Baltic	Trans-caucasian	Central Asian
Industry, total	1.00	1.22	0.97	0.92	0.99	0.98	1.10	1.15	1.33	1.66	1.13	0.91	1.00	1.07	1.00	1.00
Electric power	0.9	1.11	0.83	0.78	0.87	0.83	0.95	1.13	1.14	1.46	0.86	0.79	0.78	0.95	0.78	0.91
Fuel	1.21	2.37	0.95	0.81	1.11	1.57	1.50	1.69	1.40	2.00	1.79	1.35	0.99	1.30	1.37	1.33
Oil extraction	1.09	1.32	1.08	—	1.17	1.02	1.12	1.31	1.23	1.38	1.01	0.96	0.98	1.24	1.10	1.15
Coal	1.47	2.06	—	—	1.20	1.67	1.65	1.70	1.54	1.99	1.80	—	—	—	1.51	—
Coal mining	1.46	1.82	—	—	1.97	1.71	1.63	1.73	1.53	2.02	1.84	0.77	—	—	1.56	1.41
Peat	0.89	0.94	0.88	0.78	—	—	0.96	1.15	—	—	—	0.77	—	—	—	—
Peat mining	0.89	0.94	—	—	—	—	0.97	1.34	—	—	0.69	—	—	—	0.99	—
Ferrous metallurgy	1.18	1.39	1.08	1.16	1.17	1.17	1.27	1.34	1.59	—	1.19	1.01	1.15	1.26	1.23	1.33
Extraction and concentration of ores for ferrous metallurgy	0.97	2.25	—	1.19	2.00	—	1.31	—	1.84	—	1.32	—	1.11	—	1.26	—
Extraction and concentration of non-ore raw materials for ferrous metallurgy	1.07	1.04	—	1.09	—	1.03	1.12	—	1.38	—	1.04	0.97	1.08	—	1.10	—
Nonferrous metallurgy	1.14	1.71	1.13	—	1.23	1.29	1.25	1.38	2.71	2.68	1.15	0.99	1.04	1.17	1.37	1.33
Chemical and petrochemical industry (including chemical-pharmaceutical industry)	1.02	1.25	1.02	1.02	1.07	0.98	1.13	0.91	1.22	1.41	0.99	0.97	1.00	1.05	1.04	1.11
Chemical and petrochemical industry (excluding chemical-pharmaceutical industry)	1.03	1.29	1.03	1.04	1.08	0.99	1.14	1.15	1.24	1.54	1.01	0.98	1.03	1.06	1.01	1.14
Chemical	1.00	1.38	1.01	0.96	1.04	0.99	1.15	1.14	1.22	1.45	0.99	0.87	1.03	1.04	1.90	1.15
Wood chemistry	0.96	2.16	1.21	0.87	1.22	0.83	1.22	—	—	—	—	—	—	—	—	1.41
Petrochemical	1.11	1.12	1.14	—	1.14	1.02	1.13	1.03	1.32	—	1.09	0.96	—	—	1.18	1.09

Machine-building and metalworking (including medical instrument industry)	1.06	1.17	1.02	0.98	1.06	1.00	1.12	1.11	1.22	—	1.04	1.01	1.06	1.10	—	—
Machine-building and metalworking (excluding medical instrument industry)																
Machine-building	1.07	1.14	1.05	0.99	1.05	1.00	1.12	1.11	1.22	1.48	1.04	0.95	1.06	1.10	1.08	1.05
Energy	1.12	1.15	1.04	1.00	1.06	1.03	1.13	1.14	1.25	1.43	1.05	1.02	1.08	1.11	1.10	1.10
Repair of machinery and equipment	1.00	1.39	1.11	1.04	1.05	1.07	1.16	1.18	—	1.30	1.29	—	—	1.25	—	—
Timber, woodworking, pulp and paper	1.00	1.26	0.94	0.89	0.93	0.95	0.99	0.94	1.16	1.65	1.95	1.86	1.01	1.08	1.06	1.06
Woodworking	0.98	1.19	1.01	0.84	0.93	0.96	1.04	1.19	1.37	1.60	1.92	0.88	0.96	1.06	1.04	1.04
Construction materials	1.10	1.59	0.92	0.85	0.95	0.94	0.98	1.05	1.26	1.36	0.91	0.88	0.86	1.09	1.06	1.05
Nonmetallic ores	0.92	0.94	0.99	0.98	1.03	1.04	0.99	1.11	1.35	1.57	1.02	0.95	1.09	1.14	1.21	1.19
Light	0.88	0.88	0.70	0.75	0.79	0.68	0.78	0.81	1.40	1.13	0.78	0.78	0.86	0.94	0.84	0.85
Textile	0.90	1.34	0.83	0.78	0.85	0.84	0.83	0.91	0.99	1.70	0.85	0.83	0.88	0.96	0.88	0.92
Food	0.85	0.93	0.79	0.77	0.81	0.82	0.83	0.91	1.02	1.80	0.80	0.79	0.95	1.18	0.87	0.85
Transport[a]	1.05															
Communications[a]	0.75															
Construction[a]	1.12															

Note: Presumably dash indicates "not applicable."

[a] Only rates for the Central Region are shown in the original table, all others are blank, presumably indicating that the same rates apply, i.e., no differentials by region.

Source: V. P. Loginov, *Ekonomicheskaia effektivnost' mekhanizatsii na primere trudoemkikh proizvodstv.* Issued by the Academy of Sciences USSR, Institute of Economics, Moscow: Nauka, 1975, pp. 288–9, as published in M. Feshbach, "Regional and Branch Wage Differentials in the Soviet Union," *ACES Bulletin,* Vol. 17, No. 2–3, Winter 1975, pp. 58–9.

in managerial decision making. He argued that this process increased the effectiveness of regulations governing labor relations since workers felt directly involved in the creation of the rules that govern them. Kondrat'ev also conceded that such local regulations may only enhance but not supersede centrally established laws.

The theoretical aspects of Soviet wages should now be evaluated in terms of how all these base rates, coefficients, and supplements translate into individual paychecks, and whether or not those paychecks are sufficient to provide a Soviet worker with a comfortable existence. The first question is more easily addressed than the second. In 1978, the average monthly monetary earnings of a Soviet industrial wage worker was 176 rubles per month. (Table 4.2 provides a detailed accounting of the average monetary wage up to 1975 by industrial branch.) In addition, during any given year each Soviet worker and his or her family receive cash transfers (including old-age pensions, disability pensions, survivor pensions, long-service pensions, personal pensions, social insurance transfers, sickness benefits, maternity allowances, maternity grants, burial grants, holiday pay, educational stipends, child allowances, and family income supplements) as well as free or subsidized services (primarily in the areas of education, medical care, and housing).

As with any large-scale welfare program, wide discrepancies occur between theory and performance so that, in spite of equally legitimate claims to services, some workers benefit a great deal more from state-supported social programs than do others. On average, the net value accrued to a worker's cash income from such additional transfers and services as estimated by Soviet sources is approximately 67 rubles per month. Given the existence of an acknowledged discrepancy in services available to many workers (a topic discussed in greater detail in Chapter 6) and leaving aside the illegal payments required for many services that are nominally free, one is still left uncertain as to whether or not these averages allow the Soviet worker to live a "comfortable" existence.[43]

The cultural constraints attached to any definition of *comfortable* can be somewhat alleviated by comparing the average earnings in Table 4.2 with the officially recognized and calculated Soviet poverty (*maloobespechennost'*) level. That level has been established according to normative budgets containing

Table 4.2. *Average earnings of workers and salaried employees, by branch of industry, USSR, 1955–1975*

	Rubles per Month[a]		
	1955	1966	1975
All industry	78.3	106.8	162.2
Electric energy	85.0	113.2	167.3
Coal mining	126.8	195.3	274.9
Ferrous metallurgy	102.0	129.0	188.0
Chemicals	83.7	110.0	165.2
Machinery	84.0	106.5	164.1
Wood and paper	73.6	105.3	169.3
Timber	79.4	117.4	241.2
Wood working	64.7	93.8	155.3
Cellulose and paper	85.2	106.2	163.8
Construction materials	69.1	104.3	165.4
Light industries	57.6	81.3	124.6
Textiles	62.2	83.8	129.7
Garments	49.0	76.1	115.5
Shoes	56.7	85.1	131.9
Food industries	61.0	92.7	145.9
Milling	—	—	129.2
Bread	—	—	126.5
Beverages	—	—	122.9
Meat[b]	58.1	86.6	134.6
Sugar	52.0	81.1	—
Tobacco	—	—	136.3
Fish	109.2	181.2	—
Other food[c]	—	—	165.9

Note: Dash indicates not available.

[a] The figures for 1975 include all bonuses from the bonus fund and other sources. The figures for 1955 and 1966 include bonuses from the bonus fund only for those enterprises which had transferred to the reformed system. This may mean also that bonuses from the former "enterprise fund" are excluded.

[b] Both meat and milk for 1975.

[c] Refers to all of the food industry for which figures are not shown above.

Sources: For 1955–66: Tsentral'noe statisticheskoe upravlenie pri Sovete ministrov SSSR, *Trud v SSSR* (Moscow: Statistika, 1968), pp. 140–4; for 1975: *Vestnik statistiki*, No. 11, 1972, pp. 93–3, and, for 1976, No. 8, p. 90, as published in J. G. Chapman, "Recent Trends in the Soviet Industrial Wage Structure," in A. Kahan and B. Ruble (eds.), *Industrial Labor in the USSR* (Elmsford, N.Y.: Pergamon Press, 1979), p. 170.

expenditures for those goods and services deemed necessary for a minimum existence by various committees of experts. This method arrives at a poverty line of approximately fifty rubles per capita per month.[44] If this figure is taken as an absolute minimum, the average worker in light industry in the Soviet Union receives an income barely two and one-half times that of the subsistence level, whereas the average worker in coal mining lives on a salary averaging five times the official minimum. Although the average Soviet worker evidently does not starve, he must lead what even by Soviet standards can be considered only a modest existence.

In summary, over the past quarter-century the Soviet government has displayed relatively greater concern over the quality of life of its citizens than did various administrations under Stalin. Indeed, at least one Western observer, Vera Dunham, has spoken of the recent "embourgeoisement" of Soviet workers.[45] Furthermore, income differentials have narrowed significantly so that the living standards of the most poorly paid citizens (especially those living in rural areas) have improved the most. Leaving aside the issue of nonmonetary perquisites and privilege, Soviet policies affecting income disparities appear to be more effective than those of Western governments operating in a market economy. Income differentiation in strictly monetary terms tends to be lower in the Soviet Union than in the West. Still, it must be remembered that such calculations fail to take into account the rather shabby living standards experienced by all but the most privileged of Soviet citizens.

These changes in wage and income policies generally developed in accordance with national trade union policies and goals. Returning to the shop floor, questions remain as to how much and to what end factory union officials influence the size of workers' take-home paychecks. One must assess the two conflicting views of union activity raised by the *Trud* correspondent covering the Vecherenko affair: union officials can either exercise their authority to defend workers' legal rights, or they can choose not to do so.

Management has clearly decided to ignore workers' rights at the Sobkina Textile Factory.[46] In January 1978, that factory stopped making men's slacks and began producing blue jeans.

As a result of this switch, production norms and wage rates were adjusted, and in just three months average wages dropped by some forty to sixty rubles per worker per month. This reduction prompted K. Kashtanova, V. Zdrazhevskaia, and several other workers to question the factory director, A. Mavrin, who replied that this decline in income had been caused "by the jeans." Such an explanation appeared a bit contrived since employees at other textile factories manufacturing blue jeans had not experienced a similar decline in earnings. Eventually the workers prompted local union and republic ministerial officials to investigate. They found that administrative incompetence underlay much of the problem. Management quickly moved to correct the wage situation. Yet the factory union committee, having successfully defended the workers on that issue, began to dig deeper into managerial operations and found that a "bureaucratic carousel" of red tape undermined productivity. By this time, management had become defensive and refused to deal with union demands altogether. As a result, by July 1978 tensions had become so great that the plant could hardly function. By exercising available legal rights, at least one Soviet trade union organization evidently learned to place the rights of workers above those of management.

The formulation of a worker's wage is but one part of a factory trade union committee's total activity. Soviet trade unions administer a large number of social programs as well in that they supervise the budget for state social insurance and pension programs. Trade union officials refer to such programs as the social rights of each Soviet citizen, rights just as important as those of free speech, assembly, and religion.[47] Nevertheless, union performance in defense of these highly esteemed benefits remains uneven at best.

The factory trade union committee acts through its social insurance commission. Elected at the annual factory meeting, that commission oversees every aspect of social welfare administration.[48] Working through volunteer delegates, it reviews the distribution of monetary benefits and, more significantly, supervises medical treatment in many cases. According to Bernice Madison, there were over 2.3 million such delegates in 1977, or one for every forty-seven union members. When a worker becomes ill or disabled, a delegate is required to visit him at home and ensure that he follows recommended medical treatment. Should an employee fail to report to work, a delegate is required to investigate his absence.

These commissions supervise the distribution of welfare benefits drawn from social insurance funds. Their programs are financed by state revenues totaling some 32 billion rubles in 1979 alone collected through a 4.4–14 percent tax levied against each ministry's and enterprise's payroll.[49] Soviet union spokesmen have estimated that these programs (including temporary illness benefits for union members, maternity leave, child-care allowances for employees with a family income of less than sixty rubles per month, and reduction in fees charged for various health, recreational and child-care facilities operated by the unions in conjunction with the Ministry of Health and the Ministry of Education) increase the Soviet citizen's real income by nearly a third, from an average 1978 monthly take-home cash pay package for industrial wage workers of 176 rubles to a real value in cash, goods, and services of 243 rubles per month.[50]

Soviet plants distribute a variety of welfare benefits. There are numerous old-age, disability, and survivor pensions operated by the fifteen union republic ministries of social welfare. Union social insurance commissions perform an oversight function, monitor the distribution of pension funds, and publicize available benefits to factory employees. There are no less than three groups (loss of normal living capacity, loss of working capacity, and limited loss of working capacity) and eighteen different categories of payments based on the degree of disability, the cause of disability, the type of work, the work-related nature of the disability, the employee's tenure of service, the employee's work record, and the role played by alcohol in the disability (if there is such a role, there are no benefits). Such a plethora of factors governing the size of disability payments gives considerable discretionary authority to managerial officials. The unions provide the only recourse available to workers assuring that this authority is not abused.

In addition to their social insurance commissions, factory unions organize pension commissions. One such group at Moscow Watch Factory No. 2 in 1975 included fifteen members working out of the plant's personnel office. These volunteers went to that office after the completion of their work shifts and supervised the payment of wages and pensions to 300 pensioners once employed by the factory. Commission members periodically met with pensioners to discuss individual needs and worked closely with the Medico-Labor Expert Commission consisting of medical specialists and union officials charged with enforcing complex disability regulations.

Add these tasks to those already mentioned in the discussion of labor disputes, safety, and wages, and it becomes apparent that the one or two full-time union officials within a factory depend heavily on volunteer labor in order to meet their most basic legal obligations. Union supervision of volunteer social insurance pensions and medico-labor skills commissions requires a high level of employee participation in union and managerial affairs.

5

Do workers participate in Soviet management?

From the earliest days of their revolution Soviet labor leaders have portrayed their union organization as a legitimate framework for worker participation in management. This image has come to legitimize much of what Soviet trade unions say and do. Appearing before the Sixteenth Trade Union Congress in 1977, Communist Party General Secretary L. I. Brezhnev noted that the unions' primary duty must be to involve workers directly in economic, political, and social administration.[1] A little more than a year later, AUCCTU Chairman Shibaev praised the 121 million–member Soviet trade union organization as a powerful link between citizen and state, worker and management.[2]

A preeminent Soviet labor law specialist, the late N. G. Aleksandrov, once made the case for worker participation in Soviet management by describing a series of union endeavors: production conferences, joint union–management decision-making forums, socialist competition, union review of managerial innovation decisions, and union participation in national economic decision making.[3] Yet, these mechanisms – along with such already discussed union activities as dispute commissions, safety inspectors, and social insurance delegates – represent only indirect consultation at best.

Numerous structural constraints inhibit official familiarity with worker viewpoints. Union *nomenklatura* careers advance through selection from above. Quite naturally, many officials become less aware of rank-and-file demands than they are of their superiors' orders. The multifaceted nature of union obligations further aggravates this problem. The deputy union chairman of Moscow Watch Factory No. 2, I. Riabkova said during a 1975 interview that her duties include: organization

of socialist competition, consultation with management in economic planning sessions, distribution of social insurance and
welfare benefits, participation in educational and propaganda
programs, protection of workers from unsafe working conditions, administration of child care facilities, supervision of
union-operated housing and recreational operations, and resolution of labor disputes. Even though Riabkova can enlist the
help of scores of volunteer union workers (the *aktiv*), she alone
is ultimately responsible for all of these concerns. The factory
union chairman must be administrator and teacher, counselor
and housing superintendent, engineer and bookkeeper. No
matter how capable a chairman may be, he cannot possibly
maintain a close relationship with his members while scurrying
about trying to handle all of these bureaucratic duties.

The negative impact of the incredibly diverse demands facing
harried union officials can be seen regularly in the union
newspaper *Trud* and the union magazine *Sovetskie profsoiuzy*. N.
Belov of the Irkutsk Region writes of mismanagement of union
membership dues; N. Polovin at the Novokuznetsk Aluminum
Factory complains of irregularities in union election procedures;
I. Loboiko from the Khar'kov Region protests the disorderly
handling of socialist competition premiums by local union
officials; and V. Kotliarov and V. Nakonechnyi criticize union
and management incompetence in the operation of free factory
milk programs.[4] In all of these situations, factory union officials
have become estranged from their own union members – not
a new problem. In a 1925 speech before the Third Ivanov-
Voznesensk Provincial Trade Union Congress, then AUCCTU
Chairman Mikhail Tomsky expressed his exasperation over the
very same problem:

A worker knows what is happening in Bulgaria, what is happening
in Rumania; he knows what Poincaré thinks, he knows what Churchill
does at the League of Nations. But he does not know what his factory
union committee does. This can in no way be tolerated. Trade union
committees of the new type must understand that there is nothing
wrong, nothing to fear in placing the most serious questions of the day
on their agenda.[5]

Moreover, such isolation is not merely a Soviet phenomenon.
As Robert Michels's Iron Law of Oligarchy attests, Western
labor leaders may succumb to similar pitfalls.[6]

One device developed during the 1920s to resolve this problem was the production conference. Lenin endorsed the concept of joint managerial–worker production councils as an important method for involving blue collar and white collar workers in industrial decision making. Although the conferences have existed ever since, more authoritarian forms of industrial management brought them nearly to extinction during the 1930s. Official support for the conferences rebounded in the late 1950s, and they acquired their "permanent" legal status in 1958.

According to 1973 statutes governing the operation of the conferences,[7] all industrial establishments employing more than 300 persons are required to organize a conference of elected delegates representing 10 to 15 percent of the total work force. The law specifies that these bodies should represent the spectrum of professions (e.g. industrial laborers, engineers, economists, and administrators) and organizational alignments (e.g. management, union, Party, and Young Communist League) comprising the general plant population. Once formed, the production conference should convene at least twice each quarter under joint party and union supervision. The conference then elects a presidium having from five to twenty-five members to conduct its day-to-day business.

The actual size of the conference can be rather awesome. Difficult as it is to imagine, a conference in 1978 at the Minsk Motor Factory reportedly had some seventeen thousand members[8] who met to strengthen labor discipline and suggest improvements in production techniques. The first secretary of the Minsk Regional Party Committee claimed that its Party-supported work saved the motor factory over 1.14 million rubles in 1977 alone. The production conference at a Minsk Watch Factory, another model organization, generally reviewed labor and social discipline at the plant and sought to introduce new electronic clocks into production.[9] Its members were said to implement quality control procedures at the plant. In 1976, this group reviewed thirty-seven worker representations before passing thirty-two on to management, of which twenty were implemented, allegedly saving the factory more than 170,000 rubles in production costs.

These stories indicate that the conferences have obtained an enormous variety of theoretical rights and responsibilities. They can analyze the complete range of factory economic and social activities, including manpower utilization. The available evidence suggests that few conferences live up to many of these self-proclaimed goals.

Letters from conference chairmen published during 1977 in *Sovetskie profsoiuzy*[10] contained a litany of failures resulting from inexperience, insufficient time, and ill-defined roles. One letter from the Ukrainian port city of Simferopol' noted that the conferences do not convene very frequently. Another letter, by a conference chairman in Volgograd, laments that, even with major renovation work in progress at his plant, the factory's production conference has done little to leave its mark. Another critic complains that "a conference can recommend this, a conference can recommend that," but the administration does whatever it likes.[11] This being the case, union officers responsible for conference activities can obtain more substantial results through their efforts to obtain a beneficial collective agreement. At least that document has a modicum of legal authority.

In addition to the production conferences, Soviet trade union officers supervise a wide network of technical societies, the most visible of which are the Scientific-Technical Societies (NTO) and the All-Union Society of Innovators and Rationalizers (VOIR).[12] Both were established in the late 1950s and, according to recent Soviet reports, have expanded rapidly in recent years. Although local units of the Scientific-Technical Societies contain only 12 percent blue collar membership on average, nearly 50 percent of the members of the local societies of innovators and rationalizers come from the ranks of enterprise workers. Therefore this chapter focuses primarily on this second group.

The formal organization of the All-Union Society of Innovators and Rationalizers parallels that of trade union enterprise, regional, republic, and all-union committees, councils, conferences, and congresses.[13] At the factory level, the society advocates technological innovation and mobilizes support for innovation among workers, an activity which has been remarkably successful. Recent sociological surveys of Soviet workers show an overwhelmingly positive attitude toward automation.[14] According to American political scientist Rensselear Lee III, the societies propose new technologies to enterprise management, defend inventors' rights, and cut bureaucratic red tape inhibiting innovation.[15] In the Kamsk Cable Factory, volunteer rationalizers allocated over 5,000 rubles for the distribution of literature concerning technological innovation, an "exchange of experience" among society members, and lectures, seminars, and consultations.[16] Recently, the Red Boiler Maker Production Association in Taganrog initiated "worker dissertations," in which workers offer suggestions for improving plant production to a board of union, managerial, and technical examiners.[17] Should the worker demonstrate thorough knowledge of the relevant scientific literature, he receives a diploma. In 1977, fifty such dissertations saved the Taganrog association over 150,000 rubles.

Although Lee has observed that many of the society's activities involve its leaders directly in the managerial decision-making process, only one society leader in ten rises from the ranks of the workers. The recent expansion of the society may represent an expansion of the decision-making group within some Soviet industrial enterprises, but it has little or no significance for most rank-and-file union members.

The apparent paradox between the growth of the industrial decision-making circle and the exclusion of workers from the managerial process is echoed in several recent articles appearing in the Soviet press. The Twenty-Third Party Congress Tractor Factory in Lipetsk experienced considerable labor difficulties throughout the mid-1970s.[18] Labor turnover and discipline violations remained high, and, as might be expected, production fell sharply. By 1977, several workers at the plant, including Natal'ia Ionovna, had become concerned and concluded that the plant's problems had arisen largely because shop and factory union organizers ignored the opinions of workers.

Ionovna attempted to remove this obstacle singlehandedly. She spoke out at worker meetings and approached the factory trade union committee and the regional trade union council. No one listened. Finally, in desperation, she turned to the national union magazine, *Sovetskie profsoiuzy*.

The journal dispatched a special correspondent, L. Shcherbina, to Lipetsk. Shcherbina concluded that union and management officials had worked closely to establish artificially low wage rates in spite of complaints by the workers. The reporter concluded that union officials thought of themselves as managers and felt compelled to exclude the workers from informal and unofficial decision-making channels within the factory.

Meanwhile, the Riga Transistor Instrument Factory and the Riga Micro-Instrument Scientific Research Institute merged to form the Alpha Scientific Production Association.[19] Internal organizational structures from the two institutions similarly joined together to elect a single association union committee. Tensions arose as a result of psychological differences between scientific researchers and assembly-line workers. Opinions varied on almost every issue, from the menu at the association's cafeteria to housing assignments. Neither organizational changes nor the efforts of management could overcome the persisting difficulties; rather, the factory's new social dynamics undermined the union's legitimate role.

On the other hand, the local union organization functioned quite well across town at the Riga Experimental Factory of Technological Rigging.[20] Workers aired few complaints, and both union and management worked diligently to meet their mutual obligations. Still, shop foremen and shop stewards huddled when shipments arrived at the plant and approved illegal overtime work in order to meet production deadlines. Once again, workers found themselves being excluded from the decision-making process of the enterprise because union and management worked closely and because efforts to upgrade the status of Soviet trade unions had succeeded almost too well.

Some sociological surveys indicate that Soviet workers are aware of this situation. In response to a questionnaire, workers at the Tallin Earth Moving Factory in Estonia and at the May Uprising Textile Combine in Armenia indicated that they regularly attended factory and shop meetings.[21] Nevertheless, 60 percent of those attending meetings in Estonia and 40 percent in Armenia failed to join in discussions at those gatherings. Almost a majority of these workers stated that no one valued their suggestions and asked why they should even bother to let their union representatives know their opinions. To the extent that one can further refine the available indicators of worker participation, a more complex pattern emerges.

In assessing the general phenomenon of citizen participation in Soviet "sociopolitical activity," British political scientist Stephen White has concluded that such behavior represents an important aspect of contemporary political culture. Reviewing Soviet surveys from the 1920s and 1960s, White finds that the overall level of activism has increased dramatically throughout the Soviet period, and for all social groups – workers among them. In addition, White suggests that the content of this activity has become less "passive" in recent years. Nevertheless, turning to the beliefs and values underlying such activity, White echoes the views of the Estonian and Armenian workers who found no particular reason to speak up at their factory meetings: "It is a blend of conformity and dissent, of genuine commitment to the Soviet system and pride in its achievements combined with considerable cynicism with regard to those presently responsible for its management, then, that the contemporary Soviet political culture may perhaps most aptly be characterized."[22]

Even here, White's examination of the impact of social class, sex, and age on the emergence of political subcultures in the Soviet Union reaches the same conclusions as others have voiced concerning political systems elsewhere: better-educated persons tend to be more political than less-educated individuals; men more than women; and older persons more than younger. Extrapolating from White's findings, then, it would appear that in spite of quantitative growth in citizen participation most Soviet workers belong to a political subculture not at all encouraging to their active participation in management. Or, to quote White: "Technical and white collar staff, in particular, have been found in almost every study of this kind to be consistently more involved in sociopolitical activity than the mass of industrial workers. The amount of time devoted to such activity, for instance, tends to vary directly by social group."[23]

Thus far it would appear that the power structure of Soviet industrial life has changed in recent years to the extent that important decisions of managerial officials now take into account the viewpoint of union officials. Nevertheless, union officials themselves may be as distant from the reality of the assembly line as their managerial counterparts. Increased authority for the unions does not, in and of itself, guarantee worker participation. To understand why this is the case, one must review the history of participatory institutions over the past quarter-century or so.

Nikita Khrushchev praised the Soviet system for fostering widespread political participation. During his rise to power, Khrushchev and other Party spokesmen discussed in the Soviet press the withering away of the state and the eventual transferral of state functions to social organizations such as the trade unions. Concurrently, the statutory rights of factory trade union committees and of production conferences expanded, and the Scientific-Technical Societies and the All-Union Society of Innovators and Rationalizers came into being. During the mid-1960s, proposals were even aired for the election of factory managers.[24]

By the late 1960s, and particularly following the removal of Khrushchev, the adulation of socialist participatory democracy abated. Instead attention turned toward more technical issues of economic management. Although the legal gains of the unions not only remain intact but also grow in political significance, the ideological justification for worker participation becomes less strident. Despite an apparent rise in pro forma support for socialist competition, the broad outline of Communist Party policy over the past decade has been for a more meaningful involvement of the unions, not the workers, in the managerial process. The increasingly important role of union officials in disciplining workers may be seen in an examination of the decline of such a participatory institution as the comrades' courts.

Comrades' courts have existed in one form or another since the 1920s, although they virtually passed out of existence during the 1930s and 1940s.[25] These quasilegal tribunals embrace elected representatives of a given collective, at either a work site or a residential housing unit. To residential courts fall the unenviable task of resolving squabbles among families and neighbors; to the industrial courts, labor discipline problems.

One Leningrad residential court visited in 1974 met in the basement of a run-down building on the First Line of Vasil'evskii Island. Presiding over the court, a curmudgeonly mustached pensioner quickly called to mind the village elder of a not-too-distant Russian past. One among many cases that the court handled during an evening session involved "petty hooliganism." Called one summer night to break up a family dispute, a policeman found himself the object of a crude gesture. He carted off the offender and released him the next morning. Six weeks later, the policeman, the doorman, the defendant's wife, and her best friend all testified before the comrades' court. The tribunal deliberated for five minutes and fined the offender ten rubles. The case closed with a lecture on socialist norms of family life.

Although this scene occurred in a residential court, it illustrates the categories of problems heard by comrades' courts in both apartment blocks and factories. During the late 1950s and early 1960s, many factory courts dealt with labor discipline offenders, but by decade's end this had changed. According to one 1966 Soviet dissertation, comrades' courts handled no more than a handful of all disciplinary problems in Soviet factories.[26] When nearly a decade later a senior AUCCTU official responsible for the administration of the national system of union comrades' courts was asked about this finding, he concurred and added that other, more formal channels can best dispose of discipline problems.

Once again, the political leadership has abandoned a potential instrument for genuine worker participation in factory administration precisely at a moment when union officials have come to play a more significant role in plant management. One former union officer explained during a 1974 conversation that the factory union chairman sits in an office down the hall from that of the factory director and Party and Young Communist League chairmen. These officials frequently meet on the way to their offices, and, more often than not, get together each morning to resolve the day's most pressing concerns over a cup of tea. Meanwhile, the workers as well as most other union committee members are down on the assembly line or perhaps in a back alley drinking something stronger than tea. In any event, they do not participate in informal problem-solving sessions. Indeed, for the ordinary worker, there are few "informal" channels linking him to management.

During an off-the-record conversation, one Soviet labor relations specialist labeled this new breed of unionism the "white collar trade unions" of the Soviet present. It is not surprising that such unions exclude workers from their meetings with management. The growing complexity of demands placed upon union officers and factory managers alike requires increasingly sophisticated skills. The Moscow City Council of Trade Unions (encompassing some 19,500 primary trade union committees, 30,000 shop union organizations, 180,000 trade union groups, and 1.9 million union activists) supports several programs seeking an improvement of union skills in the Moscow region.[27] In 1978, it operated 575 schools and trained 240,000 persons each year through seminars, lectures, and courses. While much of this effort concentrated on political questions, the legal rights of union officers and union–management relations receive considerable treatment as well.

Similar training programs exist at the national level, but it is doubtful that they can substantially reduce the "white collar" syndrome. The 1978 entrance requirements of the Higher School of the Trade Union Movement in Moscow[28] grant preferential treatment to applicants with experience in Party, state, economic, and Young Communist League administration, medicine, and resort management and tourism. One must wonder how, in the face of predominantly white collar criteria, ordinary factory workers can enter responsible union positions. Even though improved skill requirements for union officials may result in more effective union performance, it will only widen the gap already existing between professional *nomenklatura* union officials and the rank-and-file membership.

This division often shows up in various unconscious gestures. Stephen White observes that changes in linguistic usage over the course of the past six decades generally reflects a broad democratization of social values.[29] In a book examining the use of the familiar and formal forms of the personal pronoun *you*, Vladimir Kantorovich described a meeting on a Moscow assembly line in which union members reprimanded a trade union committee member for greeting older workers with the familiar *ty* while the workers addressed him with the more respectful *vy*.[30] Such forms of address demonstrate a persistent social distance between union officials and workers which undermines union claims that worker participation in management can take place through union-controlled channels.

Many Soviet trade union officials are aware of these difficulties. Top-level union leaders appear to value competency more highly than participation. Some union spokesmen have proposed that shop-level officers improve their operations, thereby placing trained union personnel in closer proximity to frontline workers. In 1971, new regulations governing labor dispute resolution procedures adopted this approach giving broad authority to shop dispute commissions.[31] Yet one must remain skeptical about such measures reducing the considerable gap between Soviet theory and Soviet reality.

The discussion in this chapter of institutional channels for worker participation in Soviet factory management may have overemphasized the preeminence of full-time professional union officials. Less formal channels should be considered as well. In a study of spontaneous activity among Soviet industrial workers, British political scientist Alex Pravda examined the means by which workers express discontent.[32] Located on the fringes of, and in some cases even beyond, official institutional networks, such methods include labor turnover, labor discipline violations, letter writing, and collective protest, as in industrial actions, public demonstrations, and open dissent. Pravda was careful to point out that these manifestations of disenchantment in no way exhaust the options available to a disgruntled Soviet worker. Rather, he suggested, they represent forms of individual and collective activities that occur every day in Soviet factories.

Pravda uncovered a rich variety of worker activity. He concluded that, although accurate information is unavailable, the total number of individuals engaged in such activity during any one year could be as high as one in five workers. While the significance of these actions varies considerably (one cannot equate drunkenness on the job with holding a press conference for Western journalists), each action illustrates the difficulties of exercising control over the Soviet worker. Some Soviet industrial sociologists would agree with this assessment and turn to Western theories of informal group dynamics for explanations of industrial behavior patterns.[33] Even further beyond the edge of respectability, nonsanctioned demonstrations and disturbances occur in the Soviet Union, riots in Novocherkassk being the best known in the West.

Located on the banks of the Tuzlov and Aksai rivers approximately thirty miles from Rostov-on-Don, the city of Novocherkassk was founded in 1805 as a base for Russian military operations in the Northern Caucasus. An important industrial center, the city had a population of 130,000 during the early

1960s. On 1 June 1962, two independently revealed decisions brought about an open revolt in this normally peaceful community.[34] The first decision, announced in Moscow, raised the prices of meat and of butter; the second, announced in Novocherkassk itself, lowered the salary norms of workers at the Novocherkassk Electric Locomotive Factory by as much as 30 percent. On hearing of these decisions, workers stopped work at the forge and the foundry shops within the plant. After the plant director refused to talk to the workers, claiming that they could eat jam instead of meat, the strike spread throughout the plant, which is located two miles from the center of town on the opposite bank of the Tuzlov River. Soldiers sealed off the area, but discontent rose so quickly that by early afternoon workers began to tear up the nearby Rostov-Moscow rail line, and turmoil continued throughout the night.

The next morning, workers, picking up more marchers as they went, took their protest to Party headquarters in downtown Novocherkassk. At 11:00 A.M., thousands of city residents gathered and stormed the Party headquarters. At this point accounts vary. Red Army troops recaptured the Party building. Evidently the troops fired over the heads of the demonstrators to disperse them, but stray bullets hit children who had climbed into nearby trees for a better view. Pandemonium broke loose, with soldiers firing point-blank into the crowd. Within a few moments seventy to eighty bodies littered the town square.

By 1:00 P.M. the crowds had formed again. Worried Party officials called in tanks, and the protesters dispersed once more, only to gather later that evening. This cat-and-mouse game continued throughout the night until the morning of 3 June, when A. Mikoyan and F. Kozlov, both sent from Moscow to quiet the situation, warned the townspeople by local radio of "enemy provocateurs" in their midsts. The army then clamped down, and quiet returned to Novocherkassk by nightfall.

Although information is not sufficient to generalize from the Novocherkassk story to other disturbances, this and similar accounts indicate that Soviet workers can win immediate gains through strike actions, at least in the short run. In Novocherkassk, for example, the shops suddenly overflowed with a wide variety of foodstuffs, but the strike leaders there as well as in other smaller actions have suffered some harsh punishment.

According to another story, a wildcat strike took place in Leningrad during the 1960s over a wage dispute. Taxi drivers arrived at their garages one morning to find a reduction in their pay schedules. They refused to go onto the streets, and by midday the entire taxi system had ceased to operate. The protest soon threatened to spread throughout the city's transportation system. Senior Party officials arrived on the scene from Smolny (Leningrad Party headquarters) and began negotiating with the striking drivers. The Party leaders agreed to the workers' pay demands. The following day police arrested the strike leaders, who since then have not been in Leningrad garages again.

More widespread and perhaps more economically disruptive than rioting and striking are the thousands of personal decisions to leave a city or a region because of inadequate compensation.[35] This problem prevails in the far north and far east, where turnover is particularly high. During the five-year period 1966–70, more than 30,000 workers left the Bratsk Hydro-Electric Station Construction Site for other jobs, a figure slightly exceeding half the number of workers coming to the site during the same period.[36] Of this 30,000, one-third left as a result of inadequate housing and child care facilities, an indirect form of compensation in the Soviet context.

Several more stories concerning industrial unrest in the Soviet Union have recently surfaced in the West, with strikes and protest being reported in Moscow, Leningrad, Baku (Azerbaidzhan), Kaments-Podolskii (Ukraine), Temir-Tau (Kazakhstan), Chirchik (Uzbekistan), and Kaunas (Lithuania). During the spring of 1980, Western newspapers printed several unconfirmed reports of major work stoppages involving between 70,000 and 200,000 auto workers at Togliatti and Gorky.[37] Soviet trade union and Communist Party officials vehemently denied these reports.[38] But by far the most celebrated of these has been the actions of the so-called Klebanov Group.[39] During the winter of 1977–8, reports appeared in the Western press concerning the activities of a group of dissidents headed by Vladimir Klebanov, who it seems met other disgruntled citizens while waiting in reception roooms to complain to AUCCTU administrators, Supreme Soviet deputies, and national officials of the procuracy. They had come to Moscow to seek redress for complaints which, to their minds, local officials had mishandled.

Again and again they found the disputes resolution procedure inadequate. Shortly thereafter, seventy-two people from forty-two cities signed a letter of protest. A half-dozen of these petitioners, including Klebanov, turned to Western journalists for help. Several in the group were arrested for violations of Moscow residency laws, and Klebanov himself was detained at a psychiatric hopsital and later sent to corrective labor facilities.

An indirect relationship may exist between these unofficial and quasi-official activities and the previously discussed efforts to upgrade union performance. Klebanov and his co-protesters did not initially demand Western-style labor laws. They simply called for implementation of rights already guaranteed in Soviet law. They called for greater autonomy to determine their own destiny, a request not at odds with the strong official endorsements of worker participation in management. The Klebanov Group, the workers at Togliatti and Gorky, and the citizens of Novocherkassk outside the system, as well as the letter writers and job-leavers within officially sanctioned boundaries, all help to create an environment in which the informal working relationships between union and management become more complex. This complexity may not necessarily enhance the chances for worker participation. Nevertheless, when professional union officers gain increased access to managerial decision making (as they already have done), workers may have a greater chance of seeking similar powers. While the successes or failures of these demands depend in individual instances on the degree to which specific union officers and blue collar workers are able to communicate with each other, they help to determine more general patterns of union performance.

6

Patterns of union behavior

Soviet trade unions have neither entirely succeeded nor entirely failed in meeting their dual functions. Whether one discusses socialist competition or safety inspections, disputes commissions or health programs, an overall image of union performance is difficult to discern. Certainly there are glowing accounts by Soviet journalists of workers having managers fired; there are also harrowing accounts by Western journalists of managers having workers thrown in jail. If both images are correct – and many of the circumstances underlying such reports appear plausible – how can one make sense of them? What patterns, if any, are evident in union performance? Is it possible to predict when, where, and how a union official will meet his legal obligations? And what are the tensions within the present Soviet system of labor relations that might lead to future changes in union behavior?

The existence of tension within Soviet industrial life should not come as a surprise. Vera Dunham begins an examination of the worker in contemporary Soviet literature by observing:

Alarmingly, Soviet society has long since become not only pluralistic but torn. It is caught up in something resembling a class struggle, wedged between dynamism and stagnation; social mobility and social predestination; centralization and parochialism; metropolitanism and provincialism; overall embourgeoisement that pulls people up and internal colonialism that pushes people down; unifying chauvinism in the improbable all-Soviet recension and the imprudently convincing apartheid, deeply divisive, of the non-Russian nationalities. . . .

To grasp the lateral and vertical tensions in Soviet society, the overlapping conflicts at once, in one fell swoop as it were, is absolutely impossible. And yet nothing short of just that will do for the effort to understand any major problem, let alone the covert one of the regime's long standing ambivalence and indebtedness toward the growing ranks of the industrial workers.[1]

An examination of Soviet trade union behavior reveals two general sets of variables that have some predictive value. Union officials in heavy industry appear more likely to fulfill their duties than do those in light industry; union officials in traditionally industrialized regions appear more likely to fulfill their duties than do those in regions that have only recently undergone industrialization.

For the past half-century, Soviet investment priorities have favored heavy (Group A) over light (Group B) industry. As a result, discrepancies now exist in the quantity and quality of resources available to diverse forms of economic production. Not surprisingly, variations in the allocation of resources adversely influence the nature of benefits available to workers in light industry. For example, Leningrad's S. M. Kirov Metal Works maintains excellent (by Soviet standards) health-care facilities. Without disputing that fact, it is still noteworthy that many workers in Leningrad work in light industrial plants where the most basic social amenities are wanting. For this reason, important disparities in the Soviet distribution of wealth remain between heavy industry and light, as well as between light industry and nonindustrial sectors of the national economy. In other words, both managerial and blue collar personnel at Leningrad's Kirov Metal Works may receive higher wages and benefits than do the director and workers of a local bread factory.

Several national union policies only serve to exacerbate these inequalities so characteristic of the very structure of Soviet economic life. Recent efforts to improve union performance have concentrated primarily on factory union agencies. Yet local union officials remain isolated in several important ways. Factory union officers have limited horizontal contact with their peers. This segregation of factory union officials from each other, in addition to the basic investment priorities described above, creates a situation in which heavy industrial enterprises maintain the best health and recreational facilities without ever opening them up to outsiders. Meanwhile, union organizations in light industry offer but the limited conveniences that are guaranteed as constitutional rights.

Table 6.1. *Monthly average salaries of all
employees, salary range of factory trade union
chairmen, by branch of the national economy, 1975
(rubles)*

Branch	Employee average salary	Union salary range
Industry	162.2 ⎫	
Transport	173.5 ⎬ up to 240	
Communications	123.6 ⎪	
Construction	176.8 ⎭	
Scientific research	155.4	180–220
Agriculture	126.8 ⎫	
Trade	108.7 ⎬ 90–120	
Remaining nonindustrial	—	

Source: L. Chavpilo; I. Shimko; and B. Ivashkin,
Finansovaia rabota profsoiuzov (Moscow: Profizdat, 1975),
pp. 127–9; TsSU SSSR, *Narodnoe khoziaistro v 1975
g.* (Moscow: Statistika, 1975). pp. 546–7.
Note: Dash indicates not available.

Inequalities within the wage structure of union officials are
most pronounced at the enterprise level. Significantly, the salary
of a Soviet factory trade union chairman is linked to that of the
enterprise director (usually 70% of the director's salary). In
1975, a factory chairman's monthly wage could reach a maximum of 240 rubles per month with special AUCCTU approval.[2]
(As was already mentioned, in 1977 the average monthly
monetary earnings of a Soviet industrial worker was 176 rubles).[3] Salaries are generally higher in heavy industry, particularly when such enterprises make an effort to keep highly
qualified managers, so that the 240 ruble ceiling may mask
considerable variation among industrial, transport, communication, and construction concerns. Even so, the variation between industrial and nonindustrial wages is significant, the 240
ruble figure being exactly twice that for the highest paid union
chairmen in agriculture, trade, and remaining nonindustrial
sectors of the economy (see Table 6.1). Striking wage differentials are also evident among regional safety and technical

Table 6.2. *Monthly salary range of regional technical
and safety inspectors, by branch of the national
economy, 1975 (rubles)*

Branch	Salary range[a]
Mining	
Metallurgy	} 100 210
Petrochemical	
Aviation	
Defense	
Machine construction	
Shipbuilding	
Forestry, paper and pulp	} 180–200
Construction	
Electric power and electro-technical	
Transportation	
Geological surveying	
All remaining branches	160–80

[a] Chief safety inspectors receive the same salary as other
department chiefs.
Source: L. Chavpilo; I. Shimko; and B. Ivashkin, *Finansovaia rabota profsoiuzov* (Moscow: Profizdat, 1975), p.
135.

inspectors: as much as a thirty-ruble monthly variation may
exist between a metallurgical inspector and a construction
inspector (see Table 6.2).

The variation in salaries of union officials working in differing
branches of the economy becomes less significant as they move
up the *nomenklatura* career ladder to serve district city union
and regional union committees (see Table 6.3). Even if other
incentives have not already driven the most talented union
officers out of light industry, however, the impact of these
reduced differentials on union performance at the local level
must be minimal at best.

By the winter of 1974–5 Leningrad union officials were
beginning to discuss various measures to reduce differences
between industrial sectors.[4] The Leningrad Regional Trade
Union Council sought to alleviate the most noticeable inequalities by pressuring individual enterprise trade union organizations to exchange jealously guarded vacation passes (*putevki*) so

Table 6.3. *Monthly salaries of republic, regional, city, and district trade union committee officials, by branch of the national economy, 1975 (rubles)*

Position	Non-Group	Group I	Group II
Republican committees			
Chairman	220–270		200–240
Secretary	190–240		170–210
Department chief	160–190		140–180
Head bookkeeper	130–160		130–155
Instructor	140–150		130–145
Deputy head bookkeeper	120–150		120–145
Regional, city, and district committees			
Chairman	190–250	170–190	160–180
Secretary	160–210	140–170	140–160
Departmental chief and head bookkeeper	130–150	130–140	120–130
Inspector	110–130	110–120	110

Source: L. Chavpilo; I. Shimko; and B. Ivashkin, *Finansovaia rabota profsoiuzov* (Moscow: Profizdat, 1975), pp. 129, 130, 133.
Note: Non-Group includes metallurgy and railway transport; Group I, industry, construction, communication, non-railway transport, and agriculture; Group II, trade, service, educational, and cultural.

that husbands and wives could spend their holidays together; by urging the larger, wealthier factories such as the Kirov Works to donate unused space in their vacation facilities and at health spas so that workers from smaller and poorer enterprises could use them; and, finally, by opening a special rest home on the Gulf of Finland so that mothers and their children could vacation together. Workers of the entire Leningrad region may share accommodations at this home, but workers from smaller factories enjoy distinct advantages in the distribution process.

Even though Leningrad union officials have taken steps to equalize services among area enterprises, union officials at factories maintaining the best social facilities have been reluctant to relinquish control over them. Ultimately, if the inequitable distribution of social benefits is to end, regional trade union councils must obtain increased authority to act as brokers among area factories. In his 1978 speech before the USSR Supreme Soviet, AUCCTU Secretary A. Viktorov indicated that pressure exists to do just this.[5] The Viktorov speech contained the most overt references to date to the wide disparities in services available to workers. Significantly, Viktorov strongly supported the role of intraunion councils in distributing social benefits more widely among various sectors of the economy and to the more than 700,000 primary trade union organizations at work throughout the Soviet Union.

Party policies, state laws, and union decrees charge each primary union cell with an almost infinite number of duties ranging from labor protection to organizing folk dance competitions.[6] If factory trade union committees are ever to fulfill even the most pressing of these obligations, they must draw upon a vast array of talent. This talent may be found mainly in traditional industrial centers such as Leningrad, where enterprises attract and keep the most gifted workers in the country, factories employ the most efficient full-time trade union professionals, and plants draw administrators already conversant in the latest managerial techniques. This does not appear to be the case in many recently industrialized regions of the Soviet Union.

Moscow, Leningrad, and a handful of other European cities offer a quality of life seldom found in the rest of the Soviet Union. The competition for employment in these areas remains intense even today. Their factories attract the best workers and channel many talented employees into union work. The *nomenklatura* system and union salary structures reward successful union officials in other regions by relocating them in one of the major European industrial centers. Taken together these factors underlie the superior performance of union organizations located in traditional industrial centers over those in recently industrialized regions.

Few factories in the Soviet Union are more important or have a more prestigious past than the Kirov (formerly Putilov) Metal Works in Leningrad.[7] "*Putilovtsy*" played an instrumental role in the revolutions of 1905 and 1917. Worker brigades from the famous plant literally stopped German tanks at the factory's gates during World War II. Lenin, Stalin, Khrushchev, Brezhnev, and a host of other important Party officials have given major addresses before meetings of *putilovtsy*. To be a worker at the Kirov, to be a *putilovets*, is deemed a great honor.

Work on the assembly line at the Kirov works offers substantial material rewards by Soviet standards. The success of the plant in socialist competition ensures a worker regular bonus payments. The union committee and factory administration operate some of the best housing, medical, and recreational facilities in the Soviet Union. The vacation center operated by the Kirov on the Black Sea coast is among the largest and very best in the country. Kirov metalworker Konstantin Vasil'evich Govorushin described some of the extensive cultural programs in his autobiography:

Tens of thousands of theater tickets are distributed in a year by our trade union activists. Factory houses of culture and clubs annually host about 3,000 film presentations, hundreds of amateur concerts, and dozens of symphony and chamber music concerts. Since 1956, already nearly twenty years ago, the Leningrad Philharmonic has performed a special series of concerts for Kirov audiences. Long before the season begins, programs for the concerts are posted in shops (the programs having been discussed previously by representatives of the factory and of the Philharmonic), and workers may subscribe to a concert series. Here one must not slip up: even the great white-columned hall of the Symphony with its loges and balconies cannot hold all the Kirov music lovers. This is especially the case if the great friend of our collective, E. A. Mravinskii, is scheduled to conduct.

I myself prefer ballet. You can forget about the fatigue accumulated from a week of labor, and about the big and little troubles of social affairs [obshchestvennye-dela] when, for an evening, one moves to the magical world of music and dance.

We Leningraders can make great use of our leisure. Sometimes, on the morning of our days off, my grandson and I go to the Hermitage together, or to the Russian Museum.[8]

Union officials at the Kirov are said to be among the most effective in the Soviet Union. From 1963 to 1973 the AUCCTU praised few enterprises more often than the Kirov,[9] and the Leningrad Regional Trade Union Council often cites union work at the plant as a model for other enterprises to follow.[10] Nikolai Ivanovich Zinov'ev, then chairman of the Leningrad Regional Committee of the Trade Union of Machine Construction Workers and now chairman of that union's central committee, concluded a 1975 interview by observing:

Finally, in answer to your question, no, we do not need any new legislation extending the rights of trade union organizations. Enough legislation already exists for union officials to do their job. Look at the Kirov! Unfortunately, various trade union officials do not always use those rights. They do not choose to act as if they were at the Kirov. But, that is a problem of education and not a problem of legislation.[11]

In short, Zinov'ev, the Leningrad Regional Trade Union Council, and other national union officials believe that "Putilov" union leaders have created a trade union organization that fits the optimal Leninist model as closely as any operating in the Soviet Union today.

Another model factory, the Moscow Furniture Assembly Combine, offers yet another glimpse into Soviet trade union operations During the early months of 1977, this factory held its annual election meeting for union officers. The meeting quickly degenerated into harsh criticisms of both managerial and union representatives by the plant's workers. A year later a reporter from the AUCCTU's bimonthly magazine *Sovetskie profsoiuzy* returned to the factory to see exactly what impact the meeting had had on the operation of the plant.[12]

During the course of the year, shop union officials had consulted regularly with administration officers and held frequent meetings with workers as well. Many improvements in the production process resulted from these sessions, including a beginning on the reconstruction of an obsolete ventilation system. The *Sovetskie profsoiuzy* reporter observed that the development of a system for ranking workers' proposals made such improvements possible. The factory or shop union committee selected easily achieved proposals but rejected more difficult ones while focusing their efforts on more important questions. They then presented each of these decisions to open factory meetings.

Union officials had also received a large number of complaints concerning the operation of the plant cafeteria. Most of the criticisms came from workers on the night shift, when the menu was more limited than during the day. Twice during the year union officials had addressed the director of the enterprise food service, A. Ledbeva, to request improvement of the cafeteria service. As a result, *Sovetskie profsoiuzy* reported proudly, the food had improved, and the number of complaints had declined sharply.

As the story concluded, factory production performance was improving dramatically. The authors credit the success of the assembly line to a spirit of cooperation emerging from the union–management and union–worker meetings. The physically and psychologically healthier work environment encouraged employees to work more diligently. The reporter mentioned little about the enterprise's lighting system, sanitation, child care, or transportation facilities. Can one assume that they were in excellent condition? Given the other conditions described in the article, that is unlikely to be the case.

Whatever else one can say about the union officials praised in this story, they, like their counterparts at Leningrad's Kirov Metal Works, showed considerable concern for the welfare of the workers who elected them. But, unlike the Kirov, these officials must rank worker's suggestions in order of feasibility. Perhaps this factor can explain why renovation had only just begun on the ventilation system, which "remained on the level of the first years." As a light industrial plant, the Moscow Furniture Assembly Combine did not have adequate resources to do all that it should. The inability of union agencies to deliver adequate social and health services reflected their limited resources.

The Soviet petroleum industry undertook massive efforts during the early 1930s to exploit oil found near the Bashkir capital of Ufa. In the late 1940s production increased further, and by the early 1960s Bashkiriia was producing more oil than any other area in the Soviet Union except for the neighboring Tatar Autonomous Republic to the west.[13] During this great expansion teams of oil workers created new towns, including Salafat, Sterlitamak, and Ishimbai. These communities joined Ufa as major centers for the Urals petrochemical industry. One might expect such enormous highly technical and capital-intensive industries naturally to maintain a high degree of commitment to labor safety standards. One might further anticipate a highly trained managerial staff like that of the Kirov Metal Works as well as plentiful human and financial resources, unlike those of the Moscow Furniture Assembly Combine. This is not the case.

In December 1972, the secretariat of the AUCCTU berated the management and union officials of the Bashkir Oil Association for inadequate working conditions.[14] Specifically, the central union council charged that workers did not wear legally required protective clothing. Moreover, no facilities existed for the distribution, cleaning, repair, and storage of such attire.

The secretariat then instructed the Central Committee of the Union of Oil Workers to consult with the relevant ministries to ensure that the association's director, E. V. Stoliarov, fulfilled his obligation to clothe and protect his production workers properly.

Unlike the Moscow Furniture Assembly Combine, Bashkir's problems did not stem from a shortage of funds. Rather it appears that Comrade Stoliarov did not meet his legal obligations. The responsible factory, association, and regional union organizations could not, or simply would not, force him to do so.

Stories such as these are not unusual in newly developed regions of the Soviet Union. The notion that the enterprise maintains an obligation to ensure minimum safety norms apparently has not penetrated the consciousness of provincial union personnel, let alone managerial personnel. This is true even in heavy industries where resources should not create abnormal constraints on the fulfillment of safety regulations. Efforts to improve the work of factory trade union committees remain inadequate. This situation is even worse in light industry, as the Bukhara weaving industry demonstrates.

The name *Bukhara* has been synonymous with high-quality weaving for centuries. Uzbek artisans create beautiful rugs, gorgeous fabrics, and exquisite embroidery. Unlike the skilled craftsmen of centuries past, present-day workers turn out many of these stunning items by machine. A trip to a factory manufacturing such goods can highlight a visit to ancient Bukhara.[15] The guide more often than not will be friendly, the workers happy to see a new face or two; and the production process itself is fascinating. Skilled seamstresses using antiquated electric looms and sewing machines produce most of the goods. The need to move one's hands quickly has increased exponentially with the introduction of machinery into the weaving and sewing process.

Unfortunately, one finds little opportunity to converse with workers in factories such as the Ten Years of October Silk Factory in Bukhara. Sewing machines create an ear-shattering noise. Less than five minutes in such a din engenders a sense of impending insanity; yet women spend their entire work careers in this unhealthy environment. Dangerously high levels of noise present work hazards in a number of industrial settings. No society has dealt successfully with this problem. Distressingly, the Bukhara plant appears to have done absolutely nothing to control the intense sound.

One may blame outdated machinery for some of the difficulty. Even so, officials could do much more. They could reduce the number of machines per room or install acoustical devices to muffle the metallic shrill. Inadequate resources may be helping to create the noise problem. Even more important, union officials and the workers themselves are all seemingly unaware that the problem exists. When asked why the noise level was so high, the guide shrugged her shoulders, smiled, and replied, "Machines make noise!"

Not long ago, a Soviet citizen directly concerned with union affairs remarked, "Trade unions are like traffic laws; you never think of them until there has been an accident." Unfortunately, the further one moves away from primary sectors of the Soviet economy, the worse the highways and the trade unions become. Union efforts to guarantee the social rights of workers appear to be most successful in those few enterprises such as the Kirov where administrators face only minimal human and financial shortages. Once compromise becomes necessary, as at the Moscow Furniture Assembly Combine, union performance begins to fall short of legally established norms. Finally, when both adequate financial and human resources are wanting, the ability of enterprise union agencies to protect even the most basic social rights suffers considerably.

One may still sound a positive note on the social activities of Soviet trade unions. Today's Soviet worker is undoubtedly better off than his predecessors. The base level of union performance continues to rise and, perhaps even more important, the number of institutions in which local union officials follow behavior norms of Party, state, and union continues to increase. Considerably more improvement is necessary, however, before actual union performance can even approximate the demands of Party, state, and union decrees – and before Soviet trade unions will perform as well as they claim to in their publications. Whether or not union behavior will continue to improve depends on the resolution of several tensions within the unions themselves.

First, the unequal distribution of trade union health and recreational facilities among enterprises in various branches of the national economy is a major source of long-term conflict both within the trade union organizations and between union officers on the one hand and Party and state administrators on the other. Concern over the disparate conditions of social services in heavy industrial and light industrial enterprises has already generated considerable discord among Leningrad trade union officials. There is little reason to believe that the situation in just this one city constitutes a special case.

Second, the 1965 economic reforms led to the creation of local legal norms. As the scholarly debate concerning the legal significance of such norms continues, the practical implications of locally established rules and regulations will grow. Those who argue that standards established by municipal and factory officials constitute law help to create an atmosphere in which greater autonomy for enterprise management and union officials becomes possible. If their debate moves out of the juridical faculties into the offices of managers and union chairmen, it is quite possible that the union relationship with management will undergo a profound change, one which could ultimately improve union defense of workers' rights as defined by Soviet law.

Third, labor legislation has expanded the rights of the shop trade union committee in a number of areas, particularly those relating to the resolution of labor disputes. These new laws recognize difficulties in union administration arising from the separation of trade union chairmen from factory workers. In an effort to make the local union organization more responsive to the worker, Soviet legislators have moved the central locus of union activities from the factory committee to the shop-level union organization. Such a change may eventually reduce worker alienation from shop-level union officers. On the other hand, it also could increase the tension between shop officials who are sympathetic to workers' problems and superior union officers and factory administrators who are less so.

Fourth, the AUCCTU, several branch trade union central committees, and numerous regional interunion councils have expanded educational programs designed to train union officers.[16] These efforts already have helped thousands of union representatives to understand their obligations to defend the rights of workers. If programs such as these continue to expand, it is probable that union organizations would alleviate some of the previously mentioned imperfections in the program to transform theoretical union functions into daily practice. This increased knowledge could also lead to increased tension between union officials and factory administrators.

The resolution of these tensions could lead to dramatic changes in the behavior of Soviet trade union officials. They are an integral part of the total environment in which a union officer must function. Union officials after all are neither saints nor sinners. Rather, they are bureaucrats who work in a vast ministry of labor–type organization in which they attempt to deal with numerous contradictions and serve multiple constituencies. The fact that the Soviet unions are staffed neither by saints nor by sinners should not come as a surprise; nor should the fact that tensions are evident within union ranks. And although Soviet officials might offer Marxist-Leninist catechism concerning the "absence of antagonistic relationships under socialism," ambiguities apparent in many of the policies discussed thus far suggest that they are aware of such difficulties. Accepting the existence of difficulties, one must wonder how long the pressures within the Soviet labor relationship might be expected to last.

Some Western social scientists are coming to believe that tensions and contradictions are inevitable in industrial relations not because of property or authority relations but as a result of the separation of family and work life within industrial society. American sociologist Rosabeth Moss Kanter has summarized this position by arguing:

If early corporations tried to swallow up the family in paternalistic company towns and welfare programs, modern ones tend to disclaim any responsibility for family lives of members. And social scientists as well as organization officials have often treated people in one world as though they have no connection with another. Consideration of linkages between work and family systems has generally been confined to analysis of how the quantity or type of "output" from one system (such as money or prestige from the work world or labor power from the family) enter into the operation of the other. So, historical-ideological reasons for the myth of separate worlds are compounded by the neglect of social science to close the gap.[17]

Soviet managers, for their part, appear to have a distinct

advantage in dealing with the interrelationship between work and personal life. Never having accepted what Kanter has labeled the "myth of separate worlds," Soviet union and managerial officials should be relatively comfortable in dealing with the "whole worker" rather than merely with the "worker at work." Indeed, it could be argued that the social programs described above "swallow up the family in paternalistic company towns and welfare programs," just as Kanter's early corporations tried to do.

On the practical side, however, Soviet political and economic institutions are singularly unprepared for such an approach to the work relationship. Union social welfare programs already fall short of their targets as a result of bureaucratic compartmentalization. This tendency isolates two plants located next to each other because they answer to differing ministries and, hence, to differing unions. Moreover, the complete bureaucratization of Soviet industrial life does not bode well for the high degree of flexibility in managerial decision making urged by Kanter. One cannot for example imagine as widespread use of flexitime in Soviet industry as Kanter does in the United States.

Returning, then, to the question of the persistence of ambiguities and tensions within Soviet industrial life over time, one must conclude that such pressures will continue well into the future. Even if Soviet union officials come reasonably close to meeting their present goals as they themselves define them (a feat yet to be accomplished), it is likely that those self-defined goals will undergo considerable evolution. The concern over a labor relationship that treats the whole man and not just the man at work is, to a considerable degree, a product of affluence. Put in a slightly different cast, flexitime results from the postindustrial, not the preindustrial, revolution. As Soviet aggregate and personal wealth increases, similar subtle changes may occur in the thinking of Soviet union officials and managers. This study has suggested that just such a change has already begun; even though Soviet labor relations in the future may lack the so-called antagonistic relationships of the capitalist West, they will not lack conflict.

By examining the Soviet worker, factory trade union chairmen, their milieu, and their place within the factory, the national trade union organization, and the national political arena, this study has arrived at some basic observations about Soviet union behavior. Yet, as the union daily *Trud* proclaims, Soviet workers and unions are not alone in this world. The time has come to shift focus and to examine the relationship between Soviet workers and the world beyond the Soviet Union.

7

The international activities of Soviet trade unions

International efforts to create workingmen's solidarity anticipate Russian unionism by several decades. As a result, when the Bolsheviks attempted to participate in these efforts, they found themselves moving into a world they had done little to create. Moreover, the newly legitimized Russian labor politicians suddenly had opponents whose working-class credentials were *at least* as solid as those of Moscow.

The concept of labor solidarity dates from the founding of the First International by Karl Marx in 1864. Doctrinal squabbles led to the demise of that body, and a quarter of a century later, the Second (or Socialist) International came into being. In the meantime, several independent efforts to foster union cooperation were underway. The 1890s witnessed the birth of the International Trade Secretariats (ITS), organizations which represent individual unions in similar industries from around the world. Then in 1903 the International Secretariat of National Trade Union Centers developed as the economic arm of the Second International.[1] In spite of Samuel Gompers's opposition to the International's socialist convictions, the American Federation of Labor (AFL) joined its union arm, which was then known as the International Federation of Trade Unions (IFTU), in 1909. As Europe headed to war, the IFTU appeared to be moving toward universal trade union unity.

IFTU members supported the tradition that only one union center could be admitted from any one country.[2] Therefore, powerful Czech unions were preempted from joining by their Austrian counterparts, as were many important non-AFL labor groups from North America. The selective nature of the IFTU membership combined with mounting strains between the Ger-

119

mans and English within the Second International to tax European labor unity severely. The Second International did not survive World War I; the IFTU and the independent ITS did.

The AFL pulled out of the IFTU shortly after the treaty ceremonies at Versailles.[3] A year later, European Christian unions formed their own international – the International Federation of Christian Trade Unions (IFCTU) – and by that time, the International Labour Organisation (ILO) had begun operations as well.

The ILO was established as the answer of Versailles to Bolshevism.[4] Based on British proposals, the organization and its complex tripartite system of union, employer, and government representation were logical extensions of late nineteenth-century paternalistic idealism. Together with the IFTU and the IFCTU, the ILO encouraged pluralist (i.e., noncommunist) unionism with an antirevolutionary and an anti-Soviet bias, a fact not lost on Western or Soviet observers.[5]

By 1920, M. Tomsky, A. Lozovsky, and their colleagues faced an arsenal of hostile union groups intent on further isolating them. They turned to the leaders of the Third (or Communist) International, who moved to create a union affiliate. Events in the West did little to dissuade them from this pursuit. During the summer of 1920, unionists excluded from the IFCTU, ICFTU, and ILO gathered in Moscow. A rather diverse group, the meeting attracted such motley characters as so-called anarchosyndicalists and secret reformers. Sharing in the rejection of the IFTU, the conference participants formed a Temporary International Council of Trade Unions. One year later that organization became, with the direct assistance of the Communist International, the Red International of Labor Unions, or the Profintern. Headquartered in Moscow, it set out to splinter the Amsterdam-based IFTU.[6]

The opening rounds of the interwar conflict between Moscow and Amsterdam were sounded by Lenin, whose article "Left-Wing Communism – An Infantile Disorder" bitterly attacked social democratic union traditions.[7] Both the Profintern and the IFTU quickly made their memberships mutually exclusive, and by 1923 the Russian organization had established international propaganda committees to counter the successful ITS. This polarization of European (and, hence, world) labor was clearly understood by Profintern chief A. Lozovsky when he addressed that organization's first congress in 1921: "Each bourgeois organization which supports the bourgeois order with its own methods and capabilities is a godsend to the bourgeois system, and no sort of metaphysical responsibilities or spiritless theories of the bourgeoisie in their struggle with the proletariat can be accepted because it is impossible to separate politics from economics."[8]

Given the relatively limited resources available to each side, both Moscow and Amsterdam found their salvos counterproductive. Once both sides began to realize that the world Bolshevik revolution must wait for another day, the need for a modus vivendi became compelling.[9] In 1923, Russian food workers quietly joined the International Food and Drink Workers Federation, and shortly thereafter the first tentative steps toward Anglo-Soviet trade union cooperation were taken. The rather boisterous history of the short-lived Anglo-Russian Trade Union Committee has been carefully chronicled by Daniel F. Calhoun.[10]

According to Calhoun, the Soviet members failed to agree on objectives. Tomsky saw personal and political gain from enhanced prestige abroad, whereas Lozovsky stood to lose his Profintern post should that organization disband. It was Tomsky who pursued reconciliation with the British most stridently.

The British for their part were similarly divided among "soft" and "hard" lines. Their goals, however, were more clearly defined. From the very beginning, the British sought the integration of the Soviet trade unions into the mainstream of the international labor movement. They moved to open channels of communication with the Soviets while bringing considerable pressure to bear on the IFTU to accept a Soviet application. In the end both efforts failed.

In June 1924, debate over the efficacy of united front policies dominated the Fifth Congress of the Communist International and the subsequent Third Profintern Congress. In spite of considerable acrimony, the meetings confirmed the theoretical validity of cooperation with European social democrats, while warning against the temptations of opportunism. During the debate over united front tactics, Lozovsky mentioned an Anglo-Russian trade union committee as an example of the kind of cooperation that was now possible.

It took some time for the Anglo-Russian Trade Union Committee to come into being. The defeat of the MacDonald Labor government and the role of the so-called Zinoviev letter in that loss did little to encourage the British Trade Union Congress. When the committee was formally established in September 1925, it appeared to be already doomed to failure and collapsed within half a year.

The circumstances surrounding the committee's demise scarred both British and Soviet unionists for a generation. The British believed themselves compromised by Soviet financial support of the 1926 general strike, aid which provided opponents of the strike with much lethal ammunition. Furthermore, when the strike failed the British did not appreciate being labeled weak and opportunistic by their Soviet brethren. The Soviets, for their part, raised a considerable amount of money and resented seeing it squandered on a strike action that could not be won. This experience and the failure of Soviet aid to bolster labor actions in Germany, China, and elsewhere only strengthened the position of those within the Soviet leadership opposed to united front tactics.[11] In 1928 the Sixth Congress of the Communist International and the Fourth Profintern Congress denounced the united front.

By the early 1930s, Soviet trade union leaders had lost much of their authority for independent action in international affairs just as they had in domestic. The removal of Tomsky and his colleagues from senior union posts marks the end of efforts by Soviet labor officials to build constituencies abroad. For many years to come, Soviet trade unions would only have one constituency in questions of foreign affairs – the Communist Party of the Soviet Union. At a time when the goal of that Party was to build "socialism in one country," the opportunities for building bridges to social democratic unions in Europe were virtually nonexistent. For their part, those social democrats saw no reason to make peace with an enemy calling them social fascists, an attitude that would persist until the rise of Hitler forced the Soviet Union to seek friends and foreign support. For the unions, that search involved the ILO and the IFTU.

Although the Soviets had been hostile to the ILO from the time of its formation by the Treaty of Versailles, in 1934 the Soviet Union joined the League of Nations and thus became a member of the ILO. Although the Soviet Union never applied officially for membership in the League's labor branch, it did send unofficial delegations, including employer representatives and delegates from labor and government. The credentials of these officials were never accepted by the ILO, and the USSR did not ratify any of that agency's conventions. Still, the tone on both sides remained cordial and constructive. Soviet participation in the ILO came to an abrupt end in 1939 as a result of the expulsion of the Soviet Union from the League of Nations following the commencement of hostilities against Finland.

Dr. Christopher Osakwe, an international law specialist who has written on Soviet conduct in international organizations, evaluated this episode in Soviet-ILO relations by noting:

> In the name of peaceful coexistence the Soviet Union thought it a betrayal of the International Labour Movement to have anything to do with the ILO between 1919 and 1934. In the name of peaceful coexistence, the Soviet Union found it tolerable to enter into some form of constructive dialogue with the ILO between 1934 and 1939. In the name of peaceful coexistence, the Soviet Union opened yet a new wave of battle of words against the ILO between 1939 and 1953. Finally, in the wake of peaceful coexistence, the Soviet Union considered full membership in the ILO in 1954 not bad after all.[12]

While attempting to improve relations with the ILO, Soviet union officials were also seeking improved relations with the IFTU. Accounts of this episode have been colored by events following World War II, with Soviet commentators claiming that the IFTU turned its back on the Soviet Union at the time of the Hitler threat and many Western observers indicating that the Soviets negotiated in bad faith. Whichever position is most accurate, serious moves were taken by neither side until 1937, when the British Trade Union Congress (TUC) made a concerted effort to upgrade the IFTU. That organization had been severely weakened by the loss of the strong German unions in 1933. In 1937, the AFL joined the IFTU, and the British perceived a unique opportunity for transforming the IFTU once and for all into a universal labor organization.

In accordance with the 1934 endorsement of the united front by the Communist International and stimulated by discreet overtures by the British, the Profintern began to curtail its operations throughout 1937, disbanding altogether in December of that year.[13] Serious negotiations began between both sides with this last institutional obstacle to Soviet membership in the IFTU removed. The talks that followed soon collapsed when the Soviets demanded that the IFTU select two presidents and two secretaries, one of each being a Soviet citizen. Moreover, the Soviet Union requested that it be exempt from IFTU membership dues. Soon thereafter the outbreak of war destroyed the IFTU altogether.[14]

It can be argued that the 1930s were marked by a growing importance of the union component to Soviet foreign policy. Yet whatever gains the unions may have made came at a very high price. The erosion of union authority in domestic affairs gave their leaders absolutely no room to maneuver, and the unions became a direct arm of the Soviet government at home and abroad. The loss of revolutionary union leadership plus the expansive fluctuation in general foreign policy objectives allowed the unions to reach out to the West, but only as a pragmatic step in the larger struggle against fascism. Just as the unions had come to act as the equivalent of the defunct People's Commissariat of Labor in domestic policy, they began to function as the labor equivalent of the government's foreign policy apparatus abroad. Just as the liquidation of the people's commissariat marked an important gain in union domestic responsibilities, the total integration of union international programs with those of the government ironically proved to be beneficial. This integration meant that the unions had become too important to be allowed to pass out of existence. In the end, this fact may do more to explain Stalin's decision to upgrade the unions systematically during the postwar period than any discussion of reconstruction manpower needs or consumer demands.

A spirit of cooperation developed between British and Soviet unionists during the war. AUCCTU Chairman Shvernik traveled to England in 1942 and again in 1943, and subsequently an Anglo-Soviet Trade Union Committee was formed.[15] British labor leaders hoped to extend this growing partnership among all the allies and proposed the formation of an Anglo-Soviet-American Trade Union Committee to the AFL. The Americans refused and, as if their own refusal was not sufficient, warned the British TUC not to approach the Congress of Industrial Organizations (CIO). CIO President Philip Murray was rather dismayed by the AFL's presumptuousness and quickly informed both the British and the Soviets that the AFL did not speak for the entire American labor movement. In November 1942, the CIO's national convention granted its leadership the authority to establish communications with the Soviet unions, and in 1944 a CIO delegation traveled to the USSR.[16] By war's end the CIO had joined the British TUC and the Soviet AUCCTU in proposing the formation of a new international labor federation.

Preliminary organizational meetings for that body were held in London in 1945, with the World Federation of Trade Unions (WFTU) being established at meetings held in Paris later that year. The new association's policies and objectives had a political cast from the very beginning.[17] The favorable wartime experience of the immediate past, however, convinced many Western unionists that accommodation with the Soviets was now possible. The negotiations concerning the WFTU charter and its first elections reflected a delicate balance of interests acceptable to all participants. This quickly changed, however, as East–West relations began to chill. Soviet demands concerning Spain, Greece, Germany, and the United Nations placed the fledgling WFTU under considerable strain. Finally, the rejection of the CIO's proposal to endorse the Marshall Plan led to the departure of the powerful U.S., British, and Dutch unions in 1949. Joined by the AFL, these groups founded the International Confederation of Free Trade Unions (ICFTU) to rival the WFTU.[18] The WFTU was forced to move its headquarters out of Paris to the Soviet-occupied sector of Vienna and later to Prague. The ICFTU shared its opposition to the WFTU with the Christian IFCTU, and the international labor movement became hopelessly polarized once more.[19]

The debacle of the late 1940s has become a subject of considerable controversy in the West. The ever anticommunist AFL has gone to great lengths to point to the WFTU's early years as a vivid example of why Western unionists should never cooperate with Soviet unions.[20] Nonetheless, more dispassionate observers such as Morton Schwartz have suggested that the WFTU was both a product and a victim of the Soviet Union's spasmodic relationship with her wartime allies.[21]

The confrontation politics of the WFTU forced the Soviet unions and government to increase their commitment to international union activities. Any failure to meet the challenge of either the ICFTU or the IFCTU would be interpreted correctly by unionists around the world as a Soviet defeat. The expansion of international operations may be seen in the increasing number of foreign trade union delegations visiting the Soviet Union, from an average of ninety delegations per year during the early 1950s, to 750 during the mid-1960s, and 900 during the mid-1970s. (Soviet trade union delegations traveling abroad similarly increased on average from fifty during the early 1950s to 800 during the mid-1970s.)[22] Still, the 1940s and early 1950s witnessed fewer union officials actually engaged in the foreign policy-making process. American political scientist Edwin Morrell has concluded that by the late 1950s only a small group within the AUCCTU Presidium and Secretariat had any role in establishing policy, and, at that, these men probably took their cue directly from the Central Committee of the Communist Party.

The growing Soviet union foreign policy enterprise began to expand following the death of Stalin. In 1954, the Soviet Union and the other socialist states moved to join the ILO. The Soviet application created a profound crisis within that body, and the ideological polemics of the 1940s became the rule of the day at ILO meetings well into the 1970s.[23]

The central focus of East–West confrontation centered on the issue of tripartism. When the ILO passed from the League of Nations to the United Nations, it retained its distinctive system of representation. Each member state continued to send three separate delegations representing employers, trade union officials, and government officials. During the early dialogue between the Soviet Union and the ILO in the 1950s, the Soviets chose not to send all three delegations, refusing to admit that there were employers in the Soviet Union. Meanwhile, many Western delegations refused to admit that there were unions in the Soviet Union.

In contrast to the principle of tripartism, some ILO members proposed a new operating principle, that of universalism,[24] arguing that as a worldwide agency the ILO could not limit its membership to representatives of any single ideological, economic, or social system. The goal of universal membership must take precedence over that of tripartism. In addition, several blue-ribbon commissions examined Soviet labor relations and government–union cooperation worldwide,[25] reporting that, although the degree of government involvement in Soviet internal trade union affairs was perhaps greater than in the West, a strict reading of the ILO charter would disqualify many if not most ILO members. Therefore union autonomy and independence could not be viewed as a prerequisite for admission to the ILO.[26] As a result of this judgment, single-party African states joined the ILO during the 1960s without the issue of tripartism ever being raised.

Throughout the 1950s and well into the 1960s and 1970s, a series of conflicts arose over Soviet ILO activities. These disputes threatened to destroy the organization on several occasions, and the survival of the agency depended on Director General D. A. Morse's ability to build and maintain a broad consensus among various factions. One must recognize, however, that many of the less overtly ideological clashes may have been inevitable. During the 1950s and 1960s the entrance of new member states from the developing world was transforming the ILO from a forum for establishing international labor standards into a service-oriented agency offering training and support services to member states.[27]

Shortly after joining the ILO, the Soviets demanded that one of the assistant directorships be filled by a Soviet citizen.[28] In 1960, Morse judged that this request could not be denied and moved to make such an appointment. The strong protests of the AFL-CIO and the U.S. government forced Morse to deny the request. Morse, an American, resigned. A year later he was reelected, and the issue of Soviet representation in senior ILO management remained unresolved. Morse retired in 1970, and his successor appointed a Soviet delegate as ILO assistant director general. As a protest, the U.S. Congress suspended the payment of U.S. contributions to the agency. This began a gradual U.S. withdrawal from the ILO, which ended when the United States left the organization altogether in 1977 as a protest over the extension of observer status to the Palestine Liberation Organization.[29] The Americans returned in 1980 once organizational reforms had been completed.

Writing in 1972, Osakwe characterized Soviet participation in the ILO as "somewhat weak" but not as that of an "outsider."[30] From 1954 to 1972, the Soviet Union ratified 40 of 130 ILO conventions (as opposed to 80 by the French, 65 by the British, and 7 by the Americans). Moreover, along with the United States, Britain, Italy, and Japan, the Soviet Union served on 9 of 10 industrial committees (a record surpassed only by India). In conclusion, Osakwe noted, aside from overtly ideological issues and the discomfort that the Soviet presence created for the AFL-CIO, the Soviet Union had compiled a respectable record on day-to-day nuts-and-bolts issues.

While the Soviet role in the ILO was slowly emerging, Soviet trade unions continued their battles with Western labor organizations through the WFTU. One prime area of conflict focused on the International Trade Secretariats (ITS).[31] Even before the break-up of the WFTU in 1949, Soviet representatives attempted to co-opt the ITS into the new organization. The Western unions and the ITS successfully resisted, pointing to the fierce independence of the ITS during the interwar period. The WFTU has little hope of gaining ascendancy within the international labor community without solid control over these workhorses of the labor movement. It eventually established the parallel Trade Internationals (TIs), which have not enjoyed the success of the much older ITS.

The nations of the developing world became yet another arena for sustained conflict between East and West.[32] Here, the ICFTU has been joined by the Christian IFCTU and its successor, the World Confederation of Labor (WCL), in efforts to create regional trade union organizations free from Soviet influence. When the ICFTU/IFCTU created the African Trade Union Conference (ATUC) during the early 1960s, the WFTU established the All-African Trade Union Federation (AATUF). When the ICFTU/IFCTU gained the upper hand in Latin America, the WFTU established the Permanent Committee for Labor Unity in Latin America (CPUSTAL). In the Middle East, the WFTU's initial successes with the International Confederation of Arab Trade Unions (ICATU) have been cast in doubt by the withdrawal of Egyptian support for Soviet-backed causes.[33] And although the ICFTU has been forced to cut back operations following the 1968 departure of the AFL-CIO over a dispute over the maverick United Auto Workers (UAW), the WFTU may not be able to fill the remaining void.[34]

In many ways, the WFTU is a troubled organization. The refusal of Chinese unions to repay past debts cost the WFTU substantial currency reserves. Moreover, Western participants do not always accept a pro-Soviet line. The Soviet invasion of Czechoslovakia in 1968 split the WFTU, and just as it appeared that the Soviet Union would be able to reassert control over the organization the Italian General Confederation of Labor (CGIL) withdrew, and French members threatened to withdraw in protest over the treatment of dissidents in the Soviet Union and East Europe.[35]

One might suggest, then, that both the weakened ICFTU and the divided WFTU have entered into periods of decline, which may have been generated by forces stronger than ideological conflict. As noted above, the ILO has increasingly become a service organization in recent years, and the pressures on the U.N.-sponsored agency are shared by the ICFTU, WFTU, and WCL. Under such conditions ideological strife may become an unwanted vestige of the past.[36] Nevertheless, it is doubtful that the more general division of the international labor movement into two wings will come to a precipitate end. Such fissures have continued for more than a century despite two world wars and numerous revolutions.

Writing in 1946, British historian E. H. Carr had considerable difficulty defining the two currents of international labor.[37] He noted that the basic schism included but was not limited to five deep divisions within world labor, namely those between the Second International and the Third; between reformist unions and revolutionary; between political unions and neutral; between industrial unions and craft; and between unions from the developed and the developing world. Many of these discontinuities are evident today.

Because Soviet trade unions have been forced to respond to an increasingly complex world arena during the 1960s and 1970s, organizational and educational efforts have had to expand, thus widening the issues confronting union foreign service officers. Whereas Morrell could note a decline in the attention paid to international affairs at trade union gatherings of the 1950s, an observer in the 1970s must be struck by their increase. As in domestic affairs, Soviet union leaders have developed more sophisticated responses to policy issues, a sophistication readily apparent in an examination of the contemporary Soviet foreign affairs union bureaucracy.

In the 1920s, international affairs remained an important issue within Soviet trade union circles. Policy alternatives were hotly debated both at union congresses and within the AUCCTU itself. During the 1930s, union foreign policy making became considerably more restricted with the unions performing as a co-opted agent of the Communist International. By the early 1950s, only a handful within the AUCCTU Secretariat and AUCCTU Chairman Kuznetsov had any impact on the determination of foreign labor policies. At the end of the 1950s, this situation began to change as the AUCCTU staff charged with implementing international policies began to grow. The number of union delegations traveling to and from the Soviet Union increased greatly, as did the attention paid to international affairs at union gatherings. Finally, once Shelepin became AUCCTU chairman, the international profile of the unions became more pronounced. The powerful new chief attempted to use the unions' foreign connection much as Tomsky had to enhance his own stature with the Party's leadership by improving his image abroad. These developments are reflected in the changes within the AUCCTU foreign affairs bureaucracy over the past two decades.

According to Edwin Morrell,[38] in 1960 the International Department, one of ten AUCCTU departments, had some forty staff members subdivided into at least six sectors: capitalist and colonial countries; socialist countries; international union federations; the ILO and Unesco; information services; and interpreting services. Reporting directly to newly elected AUCCTU Secretary Petr Piminov, the International Department was among the largest within the union structure and was responsible for every contact with foreigners.

One and one-half decades later, yet another American observer of Soviet international trade union operations, Roy Godson, described a department that had rapidly expanded.[39] According to Godson, the International Department, now under the direction of V. Mozhaev and still reporting directly to Piminov (as it would until his death in May 1980), remained one of the largest divisions of the AUCCTU. The department's staff had grown to approximately one hundred professionals, including many area specialists trained by the Soviet Union's leading foreign affairs institutions. These experts were divided into at least five sectors: capitalist states; the Middle East and Africa; Asia; Latin America and the Caribbean; and international organizations. In addition, several branch unions and AUCCTU departments employed their own international affairs advisors, as did the AUCCTU Secretariat; and the Higher School of the Trade Union Movement, which employed 300 instructors, including 48 doctors and 200 candidates of science, established a separate international program in 1961.[40]

During the first fifteen years of operation, the international program of the Higher School of the Trade Union Movement trained some 3,300 unionists from Africa, Asia, and Latin America as labor economists.[41] Students participate in a special ten-month degree program and are frequently joined at the school by unionists from socialist countries participating in two-month programs. Groups of labor representatives from around the world also visit the school for month-long union training programs. Aside from the Higher School of the Trade Union Movement, the AUCCTU provides direct support to the Patrice Lumumba Friendship University in Moscow, where foreign unionists may choose to enter formal university degree programs. The Academy of Sciences' Institute of the International Worker Movement has even greater influence on formulating union positions on international problems.

Established as a department within the Academy's Institute of World Economics and International Relations in 1966, the center became an autonomous establishment within the research network of the USSR Academy of Sciences two years later.[42] The institute, which has been under the direction of Academician T. T. Timofeev since its creation as a research department, examines the problems of the "international worker, antimonopolistic, and communist movements" and criticizes "anticommunist, opportunistic, and reformist" social and economic theories. More specifically, the institute studies the economic position of the working class, the social consequences of technological innovation and change in that class, and social composition of the proletariat both in the West and to a far lesser degree at home in the Soviet Union. Its research mandate includes the study of Eurocommunism as well as leftist and union movements in industrialized and developing countries. As a research center within the Academy of Sciences, the institute offers graduate training in international relations, international economics, and labor economics. Many alumni of these programs now work for the AUCCTU's International Department.

In the early 1960s, Morrell suspected that foreign policy decisions affecting the unions came directly from the Communist Party's Secretariat.[43] In the mid-1970s, even as skeptical an observer as Godson allows for some deviation, be it ever so slight, in union positions on international issues from those of the Party.[44] This view is supported by I. Dimant's examination of variations in attitudes of the Soviet press toward the Middle East.[45] Dimant observes significant differences in the coverage of the Middle East by the Communist Party's daily *Pravda* and by the unions' own *Trud*. While no observer denies the considerable influence the Central Committee's International Department must exert over the AUCCTU, the expansion of the unions' own staff of foreign affairs specialists makes conflict and deviation increasingly plausible. With its own set of experts and its own bridges to the outside world, the AUCCTU of today need not be as vulnerable or as isolated as it had been under Stalin.

The desire for increased collaboration among various segments of the world labor movement is probably the most basic operating principle of current Soviet trade union international activities. Present-day Soviet authors and union officials ascribe a wide variety of possible benefits to such joint action, ranging from justice for the Palestinians and democracy for Portugal to an end to the nuclear arms race and world peace. These same spokesmen directly blame "reactionary, reformist, and opportunistic" elements of world labor for the lack of such unity.[46] Soviet leaders themselves claim to favor improved bilateral and international relations with unionists from all ideological backgrounds and, in particular, encourage joint action by the ICFTU, the WCL, and the WFTU. Speaking before the Sixteenth Trade Union Congress in 1977, Leonid Brezhnev addressed this last point:

We welcome any step furthering the quest of . . . cooperation between the major trade-union centers . . . the World Federation of Trade

Unions, the International Confederation of Free Trade Unions, and the World Confederation of Labor.

And although the attainment of unity is a long and complex process, we are convinced that it will proceed in a positive direction. In any case, Soviet trade unions work and will work precisely in this direction.[47]

In spite of the dramatic increase in trade union activities around the globe since the end of World War II, Europe has remained at the center of the international labor movement since the mid-nineteenth century. Understandably, Soviet unionists have come to attach considerable importance to their European connection. It is, of course, natural for the Soviet trade unions to maintain their long-standing ties with communist unions in West Europe and to cement economic and strategic interests in East Europe by expanded union integration. More interesting, perhaps, are the recent Soviet efforts to establish working relationships with noncommunist unions on the continent.

With the American AFL-CIO retreating from the European labor scene throughout the past decade, the Soviet union representatives have made several overtures to the ICFTU and to several major European groups.[48] Early Soviet proposals for a European Conference on Security and Cooperation (which finally convened in Helsinki in 1975) were first made through union channels. In addition, the 1970s have been marked by improving relations with socialist unions in West Germany and with Christian unions in France, Italy, and Belgium.

In connection with these approaches, the Soviets proposed annual European trade union conferences to be held in Geneva to discuss the Humanization of the Work Environment. The first such meeting in 1974 proved a success insofar as there were no confrontations between ideologically diverse groups. Several subsequent conferences were postponed owing to vacancies in key AUCCTU leadership positions, but in 1977 a second conference convened. This time the story was different. Coming shortly after the Charter '77 protest letter in Czechoslovakia,[49] the conference was dominated by criticisms from Italian and French communist delegates concerning the treatment of Soviet and East European dissidents. The sessions drew to a close in confusion, and a third all-European trade union conference was postponed indefinitely.

Soviet policies toward North American unions are even more

trenchantly defined.[50] Open hostility exists between the AFL-CIO and the AUCCTU, and the Soviet policy of international union cooperation has been ineffective. Once U.S. visa restrictions were lifted in 1977, a few delegations of Soviet union officials came to the United States, but in the post-Afghanistan era the large AFL-CIO shows no sign of altering its official position and the U.S. Department of State is no longer granting visas to Soviet unionists. Meanwhile the Canadian Labor Congress has made more contacts with the Soviet Union than has its U.S. neighbors.

Just as Soviet relations with Western labor have been based on their evaluations of the possibilities for revolution and a collapse of capitalism (or a lack thereof), so, too, are union relations with the Third World. Some Soviet observers believe that union-led revolt has been severely inhibited in many developing nations.[51] They consider labor movements in these countries to be polarized according to nationality, race, religion, tribe, and myriad other factors, while unions lacking the revolutionary tradition of Europe fall prey to what are seen as bourgeois ideologies. The Soviet unions generally link their basic ties with Africa, Asia, Latin America, and the Middle East to general Soviet foreign policy objectives in a given region. Whenever Soviet prospects improve, representatives of the WFTU and AUCCTU frequently appear with quick dispatch.

Soviet performance in Africa has been mixed.[52] During the early 1960s, the AUCCTU established direct relations with several newly independent states, including Algeria, Morocco, Senegal, Ghana, and Gabon. Yet many of these initial ties deteriorated throughout the decade. In 1961, the Soviets and the WFTU welcomed the formation of the All-African Trade Union Federation (AATUF) in Nkrumah's Ghana. Following that leader's demise, the AATUF became officially nonaligned, although friendly relations have been maintained with Moscow and Prague. In 1973, the Organization of African Unity sponsored the creation of the Organization of African Trade Union Unity (OATUU). Some Soviet spokesmen initially denounced that organization's leadership as consisting of "bourgeois vassals." By the late 1970s, proper but restrained communications were initiated between the OATUU and the AUCCTU.

In Asia and Latin America, the record of Soviet–local trade union relations is less spectacular, although arguably more sound. The Soviet unions have been able to develop solid long-term working relationships with labor movements in India, Sri Lanka, Vietnam, and Bangladesh. Moreover, a dialogue exists with most other Asian union groups, with the notable exception of the People's Republic of China.[53] In Latin America, pro-Soviet labor groups and the WFTU have attempted to counterbalance the strong AFL-CIO presence in the region as well as the activities of the Latin American Federation of Christian Trade Unions (LAFCTU) through the establishment of CPUSTAL.[54] Initially headquartered in Brazil, that organization was forced to move by a military coup and resettled in Chile, where it fared even worse.[55] While some training activities have been relocated in Havana, Soviet unionists have had difficulty finding a new home for CPUSTAL on the Latin American mainland.

Soviet-sponsored union groups have had their greatest success in the Middle East.[56] Assisted by Arab reaction against U.S. support of the Israeli Histadrut, the WFTU and AUCCTU strongly supported the formation of the International Confederation of Arab Trade Unions (ICATU). Initially dominated by Egyptian trade unions (which remain the region's most developed outside of Israel), the ICATU has fallen on hard times in more recent years, with the vocal support of Soviet trade unions for their government's intervention in Afghanistan only exacerbating an already deteriorating situation.[57] This decline has not affected bilateral Arab-USSR labor relationships and the AUCCTU maintains strong ties with Syrian unions in particular.

In many regions of the developing world, Soviet unions have been able to exploit anti-Western sentiment to develop strong ties with indigenous labor groups.[58] In so doing, the Soviets appear willing to take high risks for large short-term political gain. In the developed world, Soviet policies are far less ambitious and frequently more successful. Yet, as American labor observer Benjamin Martin has noted, success is never total, and whatever political advantages accrue from a particular action may prove to be the result and not the cause of more general Soviet achievements in any given part of the world.[59]

The Soviet trade unions share in the trend over recent years for international labor groups to develop the service component of their programs more than their political operations.[60] Education remains one such service which more established union centers in Europe and North America have to offer. As already mentioned above, the AUCCTU's Higher School of the Trade Union Movement has steadily expanded its international program throughout its nearly two-decade existence. More than 15,000 non-Western unionists have attended the courses sponsored by the AUCCTU and WFTU over the past two decades, and another 10–15,000 labor leaders have participated in Soviet and East European–sponsored regional seminars.[61]

Although these programs are not devoid of ideological content, it would be a mistake to assume that political considerations are the sole or even the paramount reason for their apparent success. Union leaders around the world need to know how to finance housing projects, establish health clinics, create consumer cooperatives, manage their union's budget, and so forth, and precisely these concerns frequently dominate U.S.-sponsored and even Soviet-sponsored training programs.

Evaluating such instruction during the early 1960s, H. K. Jacobson wrote:

Whether a young trade unionist attends the ILO's International Institute for Labour Studies in Geneva, the ICFTU's Labour College in Kampala, the AFL-CIO sponsored Institute of Free Labor Development in Washington, or Histadrut's Afro-Asian Institute, the labour college at Conakry which is supported by various communist donors, or the WFTU training centre in Budapest, elements of the curriculum will be very similar. Regardless of one's ideological preferences, only limited variations are possible in efforts to impart knowledge about such practical matters as trade union administration.[62]

This similarity, of course, does not mean that communist-sponsored programs (Soviet or otherwise) do not contain Marxist elements or that the AUCCTU does not attempt to win lifelong friends. What it does suggest is that someone from a developing nation who attends a Soviet training program need not become a Marxist or join a pro-Soviet "fifth column." In education as in the rest of the international labor movement, reality is simply too complex to make such large assumptions.

The complexity of the international labor arena has created a situation in which each actor must operate with growing sophistication. Soviet labor representatives can no longer credibly talk of "social fascists" or "secret reformists." If they are to have any impact on the world around them, Soviet unions must continue to refine their understanding of how that world operates. The relationship between domestic and foreign trade union policies derives its special significance precisely because of this process of realization.

During the early 1970s, a group of union bureaucrats in charge of recreational facilities throughout the Leningrad region traveled to Czechoslovakia in order to examine its union reports. The leader of that delegation returned home to Leningrad and demanded that similar facilities be created there. This request was not favorably received. First there was the problem of limited space. Then there was the problem of coordinating vacation schedules. Finally there was the problem of conflicting union memberships. How could Ivan and Masha be expected to vacation together if they did not even work in the same plant? The delegation leader responded to such claims with some success because he was able to point out that similar problems have been resolved by socialist Czechoslovakia and asked why they couldn't be handled in the socialist Soviet Union. Shortly thereafter, construction of a special vacation camp for mothers and children of the Leningrad region got under way on the shores of the Gulf of Finland.

This story illustrates the impact that the outside world might have, indeed, already has had, on Soviet union administrators. This influence is both explicit and indeterminate. It is explicit in that the relationship between a tour of Czechoslovakia and the construction of a new form of recreational facility may be easily discerned. It is indeterminate in that the significance of that camp for the entire system of Soviet labor relations is impossible to evaluate. There are other manifestations of foreign influence on domestic union policies which, although less overt, may prove more significant.

The growth of the AUCCTU's foreign policy role has created a need for even more specialists to be employed by that organization and has brought about significant change in the functions of many union institutions such as the Higher School of the Trade Union Movement. Numerous other areas of union activity can benefit from staff and organizational changes. An increase in the number of labor law specialists could improve union protection of workers' rights; similarly, more labor management specialists could help union production efforts, and a greater number of hotel management trainees could advance union vacation programs. Given the growing complexity of union operations, any improvements in the quality of the union staff comparable to those which have already occurred in international affairs can only enhance general union performance. Although it remains uncertain whether the process of refinement of union international programs is antecedent or simultaneous to a similar development at home, both processes undoubtedly can be mutually reinforcing.

Conclusion

The performance of Soviet trade unions has already been evaluated by several scholars and observers from the West. Obviously such a body of academic literature will contain conflicting viewpoints, and Western opinion seems to fall into three groups: Some argue that Soviet trade unions are worthy of study only insofar as they can be shown to be weak. Others believe significant trade union activity is evident in the Soviet Union but disagree about its importance and the role played by local union organizations. This group minimizes the role of factory trade union agencies, either because of widespread Soviet democratic centralism or because of more universal institutional dynamics that make local bureaucrats more accountable to central bureaucracies than to local constituencies. The third group acknowledges centralizing tendencies but considers their overall effect on local union organization to be less than crippling.

Writers who share the first opinion focus on features of Soviet trade unions such as their inability to conduct meaningful collective bargaining, strike, and express concern over short-term economic conditions. They believe that these characteristics define Soviet trade union activity in the past and the present. If the unions have no basic rights, Jay Sorenson and others argue, whatever they do benefits only the state.[1] They conclude that Soviet trade unions are inherently ineffectual as labor organizations.

The second group believes that Soviet trade unions perform several essential managerial, educational, and advocacy functions. These writers emphasize centralizing forces within Soviet society that force the overall unions to be subservient to Party

139

interests and to make local union officials overly dependent on their superiors. Edwin Morrell finds parallels between Soviet trade union operation and that of the weak public service unions in the United States.[2] Others, like Thomas Lowit[3] and George Vedel,[4] stress centralizing tendencies that are universal to all modern industrial societies and note that the position of Soviet unions is distinctive because a single locus of power is centered in the Communist Party. Nonetheless, the dominance within the Soviet trade union hierarchy of central officials finds parallels elsewhere. Isaac Deutscher,[5] for his part, identifies Russian underdevelopment as a root cause of the highly centralized union and political structures identified by the others. Had Russia been more industrialized in 1917, he argues, and had the trade unions been able to play a more important role in the revolutionary process, perhaps their position in Soviet society would have been significantly different. None of these authors – Morrell, Lowit, Vedel, or Deutscher – denies the authority of the Communist Party over the unions. They argue that such authority need not prohibit the unions from having a limited impact on the formation of and major control over the implementation of Soviet labor policies. In short, Soviet trade unions, at least at the national level, are significant institutions.

The third group accepts as given the fact that Soviet trade unions are significant institutions. Like the others, these investigators deny neither the authority of the Communist Party nor the supremacy of central trade union officials. Nevertheless, they contend that if these relationships are accepted as premises and attention is then directed to the actual work of trade union committees at the factory level, considerable activity having a favorable influence on the lives of Soviet workers can be discerned. Emily Clark Brown[6] expresses this viewpoint in her examination of Soviet labor relations and trade union activity, and Louis Greyfie de Bellcombe[7] shows that Soviet collective agreements at the factory level became increasingly significant throughout the 1950s. Mary McAuley[8] focuses on dispute resolution in Leningrad from 1957 to 1965, and finds that many factory union leaders try to secure decisions beneficial to workers. The conclusions of this study support the position of the last group of scholars.

This book has described union activities both in the international and the domestic arenas. Moreover, it has identified several areas of continuity and change – continuity in the sense that the principles underlying union operations are as Leninist today as they were sixty years ago. Inside the country, union officials attempt to mobilize workers behind production goals and to defend those same workers from managerial "bureaucratism." Abroad, the unions still seek to lead a global anticapitalist trade union movement. Yet the manner in which the unions attempt to obtain these desired ends has changed dramatically throughout six decades of Soviet rule and a quarter-century of post-Stalinist government.

Most changes are results of pressures placed by current events (large and small) on Marxist-Leninist theory. Union performance at the factory level might indicate that individual personality is more important than the 1970 Fundamental Principles of Labor Legislation. Forums for worker participation in management might suggest that the demand for high productivity favors expertise and not representative membership as a key to union success. In having to face multiple constituencies all trying to achieve multiple ends, union officials from the shop floor to the AUCCTU find that they must compromise and negotiate. This process of adjusting theory to reality has led to fundamental changes within union policies and performance even though Leninist theories of union–management relations under socialism have remained relatively unaltered.

In real life, then, union administrators seek practical solutions to intractable problems. The often divergent demands of the Communist Party, management, union supervisors, and rank-and-file workers have forced the Soviet trade union officer to choose from among several undesirable options. If, for example, a factory does not receive supply shipments on a regular basis, a union official must decide whether to protest illegal overtime work when necessary materials finally do arrive or to look the other way in the hope of gaining cooperation from management on larger social programs. This dilemma becomes more compelling when we recognize that neither union nor management controls the supplier. Any real solution to illegal overtime work must deal with inadequacies in Soviet supply networks, an issue far larger than the unions themselves. In failing to take on such a problem, are the union leaders dupes of the Communist Party? Practical men choosing to deal only with the realm of the possible? Or, simply incompetent? There can be no easy answer.

Changes that have taken place in union performance and the dilemmas from which they evolved demonstrate that all desired ends cannot be obtained in an economy of scarcity. No matter how sympathetic a factory director may be, he cannot accede to union demands for improved health services or recreational facilities if he does not have the resources to provide them. In spite of rapid economic advances, the Soviet Union simply cannot afford the kind of society it has defined for itself, and social programs such as those of the unions are more often than not within the category of the unaffordable. The unions and the Soviet government may be dishonest in proclaiming un-realizable goals as reality, but should they be faulted for seeking what they cannot obtain? The answer is hardly clear-cut.

Soviet union officials are not unaware of these difficulties and have sought to alleviate them through a growing dependency on specialization in both domestic and international affairs. Factory-level union officials face an almost infinite array of assigned duties, each requiring considerable expertise. Over the past twenty years, senior union officials have worked to improve local union performance by upgrading the training of factory union representatives. Union organizations at various levels have instituted formal degree programs, special seminars, lectures, and conferences in an effort to improve the quality of local union personnel. These programs have been moderately successful in many priority industries and geographic regions. With this investment in expertise, career union bureaucrats quite naturally have usurped the position of rank-and-file members in many localities.

In the international arena, training programs have similarly improved, and the AUCCTU has established a direct working relationship with the Academy of Sciences through the Institute of the International Workers' Movement. Moreover, the AUCCTU's own staff of area specialists has expanded throughout most of the 1960s and 1970s. Present-day union international policy is established by people who frequently know more about labor conditions abroad than they do about the industrial environment at home.

The growing reliance on expertise has led to an increased sophistication in many policy areas. Internationally, the Soviet unions take local traditions and conditions into account in their dealings with the developing world. Domestically, the official approach to labor discipline violations has moved nearly 180 degrees away from what it was under Stalin. Four decades ago, a truant would have been sent to jail or to a forced labor colony. Today he can hardly even be fired, a turnabout resulting from an increasing awareness of the social causes of labor discipline violations.

Thus far, considerable emphasis has been placed on changes in union behavior brought about by the pressures of daily administration. It would be a mistake to conclude on this note, though, since the continuity so evident in union behavior often runs dangerously close to becoming stagnation.

Even though the Leningrad Regional Trade Union Council has created some vacation programs for entire families, the reader should not forget that such advances have been limited in scope and have come only after considerable effort. The bureaucratic compartmentalization of Soviet life frequently prevents factory administrators located right next door to each other from acting together on issues of mutual benefit. If husband and a wife do not work in the same industry, chances are that they will not vacation together. The inflexibility of union administrators demonstrated in this one minor policy dispute could be magnified a hundred, a thousand, perhaps even a million times when one considers more sensitive and less obviously beneficial proposals.

The tension between growing sophistication and continued obstinance creates a national agenda for union reform for the 1980s much as it did for the 1950s. As manpower reserves shrink and the center of the Soviet population shifts to the east, the central role of the traditional European industrial base can be maintained only through advances in productivity. Such an increase can occur through innovation – technological and administrative – as modern production techniques make the draconian responses of the 1930s less attractive. However, the vary inventiveness that will be required to resolve many of the more serious economic problems of the 1980s was in short supply during the 1970s.

Pressure exists to narrow the gap between theory and practice in Soviet labor relations. To do so depends on forces beyond the jurisdiction of the unions alone. Further change in Soviet economic and social relationships are in order. This probably means that the issue of union reform will be only one of several awaiting any post-Brezhnev leadership group.

Notes

Introduction

1 "Konstitutsiia razvitogo sotsializma," *Sovetskie profsoiuzy*, 1977, No. 19, pp. 2–3; "Profsoiuzy SSSR v tsifrakh i faktakh," *Sovetskie profsoiuzy*, 1977, No. 6, pp. 4–5; "Boevaia programma deistvii," *Sovetskie profsoiuzy*, 1977, No. 9, pp. 2–4; M. Binyon, "How Docile Are Russia's Unions?" *London Times*, 20 December 1979, p. 19; and "The Workers' Interests and the Trade Unions," *Soviet Union*, 1980, No. 10, pp. 8–9.

2 This book will examine primarily the work of trade unions within Soviet industrial enterprises. Coverage of union activities within offices and scientific establishments as well as in stores and on state and collective farms will be minimal. Concerning agricultural unions, readers may consult P. J. Potichnyj, *Soviet Agricultural Trade Unions, 1917–1970* (University of Toronto Press, 1972).

3 For example, D. C. Heldman, *Trade Unions and Labor Relations in the USSR* (Washington, D.C.: Council of American Affairs, 1977); and P. Barton, "'Trade Unions' in the USSR," *AFL-CIO Free Trade Union News*, Vol. 34, No. 9S, 26 September 1979, pp. 1–16.

4 *Washington Post*, 16 January 1980, p. A–22.

5 V. Haynes and O. Semyonova (eds.), *Workers Against the GULAG* (London: Pluto Press, 1979).

6 S. Schwarz, *Labor in the Soviet Union* (New York: Praeger, 1952), pp. 100–15.

7 A. Kahan and B. A. Ruble (eds.), *Industrial Labor in the USSR* (Elmsford, N.Y.: Pergamon Press, 1979).

8 P. H. Solomon, Jr., *Soviet Criminologists and Criminal Policy* (New York: Columbia University Press, 1978), pp. 15–64.

9 N. M. Shvernik, *Otchetnyi doklad XI s"ezdu profsoiuzov o rabote Vsesoiuznogo tsentral'nogo soveta professional'nykh soiuzov* (Moscow: Gospolitizdat, 1954), p. 17.

10 E. Morrell, "Communist Unionism: Organized Labor and the Soviet State" (Ph.D. dissertation, Harvard University, Cambridge, Mass., 1965), pp. 103–8.

11 I. A. Arabian, "Ustranenie prichin narusheniia trudovoi distsipliny," *Sovetskoe gosudarstvo i pravo*, 1978, No. 1, pp. 124–7.

12 *Bol'shaia sovetskaia entsiklopediia*, 3rd Ed. (Moscow: Sovetskaia entsiklopediia, 1978), Vol. 30, pp. 615–16.

Chapter 1. Soviet trade union development: 1917–1956

1 I. O. Snigireva, L. S. Iavich, *Gosudarstvo i profsoiuzy* (Moscow:
   Profizdat, 1967).
2 E. H. Carr, *The Bolshevik Revolution* (Middlesex: Penguin, 1966),
   Vol. 2, pp. 105–20, 220–29. This discussion will not deal with
   union development before 1917. Among the numerous excellent
   studies of prerevolutionary Russian workers' movements are: O.
   Anweiler, *The Soviets: The Russian Workers', Peasants' and Soldiers'
   Councils: 1905–1921*, trans. R. Hein (New York: Random
   House–Pantheon, 1973); V. Grinevich, *Professional'noe dvizhenie
   rabochikh v Rossii* (Moscow: Krasnaia nov', 1923); S. P. Turin, *From
   Peter the Great to Lenin* (London: Frank Cass, 1935); M. Gordon,
   Workers Before and After Lenin (New York: Dutton, 1941); and J. L.
   H. Keep, *The Russian Revolution* (New York: Norton, 1976), to name
   but a very few.
3 Various accounts of this debate are to be found in such works as
   O. Anweiler, *The Soviets*, pp. 244–53; S. Cohen, *Bukharin and the
   Bolshevik Revolution* (New York: Knopf, 1972), pp. 102–6; R. Day,
   Leon Trotsky and the Politics of Economic Isolation (Cambridge Uni-
   versity Press, 1973), pp. 42–44; I. Deutscher, *Soviet Trade Unions*
   (New York: Oxford University Press, 1950), p. 17; I. Deutscher,
   Stalin (New York: Oxford University Press, 1966), pp. 222–4; M.
   Dewar, *Labour Policy in the USSR* (New York: Royal Institute of
   International Affairs, 1956), pp. 82–6; F. Kaplan, *Bolshevik Ideology
   and the Ethics of Labor* (New York: Philosophical Library, 1968); A.
   Kollontai, *The Workers' Opposition in Russia* (Chicago: Industrial
   Workers of the World, 1921); and A. Ulam, *The Bolsheviks* (New
   York: Collier, 1965), pp. 468–70. The propositions of the three
   positions as well as transcripts of the debate at the Congress may
   be found in *Kommunisticheskoia partiia Sovetslcogo soiuza, X s"ezd
   RKP(b): Stenograficheskii otchet.* (Moscow: KPSS–Partizdat, 1963),
   pp. 337–401. The following account is based primarily on materials
   and interpretations offered by M. Dewar.
4 J. B. Sorenson, *The Life and Death of Soviet Trade Unionism: 1917–1928*
   (New York: Atherton, 1969).
5 International Labour Office, *Labour Conditions in Soviet Russia* (London: Harrison, 1920).
6 V. I. Lenin, *On the Trade Unions* (Moscow: Progress, 1970), pp.
   469–70.
7 D. Langsam, "Pressure Group Politics in NEP Russia: The Case of
   the Trade Unions" (Ph.D. dissertation, Princeton University, Princeton, N.J., 1974); International Labour Office, *The Trade Union
   Movement in Soviet Russia: Studies and Reports*, Series A, No. 26

(Geneva: I.L.O., 1927); and M. P. Tomskii, *Izbrannye stat'i i rechi* (Moscow: VTsSPS, 1928).

8 E. Morrell, "Communist Unionism: Organized Labor and the Soviet State" (Ph.D. dissertation, Harvard University, Cambridge, Mass., 1965), p. 402; I. Deutscher, *Soviet Trade Unions*, p. 17; E. H. Carr, *The Interregnum* (Middlesex: Penguin, 1969), pp. 67–8.

9 M. P. Tomskii, *Izbrannye*, p. 449.

10 I.L.O., *Studies and Reports*, Series A, No. 26.

11 Citing data found in an unpublished Soviet candidate's dissertation (I. E. Efimov, "Bor'ba Kommunisticheskoi partii za mobilizatsiiu profsoiuzov na vosstanovlenie narodnogo khoziaistva (1921–1922gg.)," Candidate's dissertation, Leningrad State University, 1956), E. Morrell states that during the period beginning April 1922 and ending March 1923, 219 Communists were assigned to district and local trade union bodies. During the following year, 360 more Communists were assigned to the staffs of central union bodies as well as to leadership positions in regional union councils (E. Morrell, "Communist Unionism," pp. 40–43).

12 Ibid., p. 60. Similar data appear in Vaskov, "Voprosy profkadrov," *Udarnik*, 1932, No. 2, pp. 56–60. According to that study, the percentage of union officials in 1929 in eight regions who had been affiliated previously with political parties other than VKP(b) was 22.2 percent; in 1931–2, 2.7 percent.

13 S. Shvarts, "Pod znakom piatiletki," *Sotsialisticheskii vestnik*, 1930, No. 234, pp. 6–8; and S. Shvarts, "Nuzhny li profsoiuzy?" *Sotsialisticheskii vestnik*, 1930, No. 236, pp. 5–6.

14 N. M. Shvernik, "Itogi VI plenuma VTsSPS," *Voprosy profdvizheniia*, 1937, No. 9/10, pp. 6–30.

15 Unless otherwise indicated, this discussion of labor protection and safety is based on M. Dewar, *Labour Policy*; and S. Schwarz, *Labor in the Soviet Union* (New York: Praeger, 1952).

16 E. H. Carr and R. W. Davies, *Foundations of a Planned Economy* (Hammondsworth: Penguin, 1969), Vol. 1, pp. 648–51.

17 Vsesoiuznyi tsentral'nyi sovet professional'nykh soiuzov, *Profsoiuzy SSSR; Dokumenty i materialy* (Moskow: Profizdat, 1963), Vol. 2, pp. 689–91, 700–3.

18 Z. M., "Zabolevaemost' i travmatism sredi stakhanovtsev i nestakhanovtsev," *Voprosy profdvizheniia*, 1936, No. 10, pp. 59–63.

19 S. Schwarz, *Labor*, pp. 258–307.

20 Unless otherwise indicated, this discussion is based on M. McAuley, *Labour Disputes in Soviet Russia, 1957–1965* (Oxford: Clarendon, 1969), pp. 9–39.

21 A more detailed account of the history of the Soviet collective agreement may be found in L. G. de Bellcombe, *Les Conventions collectives de travail en Union soviétique* (Paris: Mouton, 1958); and M. McAuley, *Labour Disputes*, pp. 11–17.

22 A point frequently commented on by Solomon Schwarz, see: S. Schwarz, *Labor*, pp. 182–3; S. Shvarts, "Profsoiuznyi tupik," *Sotsi-*

alisticheskii vestnik, 1931, No. 258, pp. 9–10; S. Shvarts, "Pered novoi koldogovornoi kampanii," *Sotsialisticheskii vestnik*, 1933, No. 288, pp. 10–11.

23 S. Trubnikov, "Nuzhny li koldogovory," *Voprosy profdvizheniia*, 1937, No. 7/8, pp. 68–70; and L. Kudriatsev, "Koldogovory nuzhnyi," *Voprosy profdvizheniia*, 1937, No. 7/8, pp. 68–70.

24 P. Moskatov, "O vyborakh profsoiuznykh organov," *Voprosy profdvizheniia*, 1937, No. 16, pp. 1–8.

25 L. Pogrebnoi, "Kollektivnyi dogovor sotsialisticheskogo predpriiatii," *Profsoiuzy SSSR*, 1938, No. 13, pp. 104–12.

26 "Uchenyi plan dlia kursov profaktiva, 9 maia, 1939g.," *Profsoiuzy SSSR*, 1939, No. 6, pp. 65–72.

27 A. Bergson, *The Structure of Soviet Wages* (Cambridge, Mass.: Harvard University Press, 1944), pp. 207–9.

28 M. McAuley, *Labour Disputes*, pp. 11–19.

29 S. Schwarz, *Labor*, pp. 147–51, 162–3.

30 L. Berezanskii, *Proizvodstvennoe soveshchanie: Chto takoe proizvodstvennoe soveshchanie i kak v nem rabotat'* (Moscow: Doloi negramotnost', 1927).

31 "Socialist emulation" are various methods used to stimulate production through cooperative action. For a discussion of "emulation" that would be contemporary to the period under discussion, see A. S. Aluf, *The Development of Socialist Methods and Forms of Labour* (Moscow: Co-Operative Publishing Society of Foreign Workers in the USSR, 1932).

32 A. Vvedenskii, "Sotssorevnovanie nakanune XVII s″ezda," *Voprosy profdvizheniia*, 1934, No. 1, pp. 47–54.

33 N. M. Shvernik, *Stakhanovskoe dvizhenie i zadachi profsoiuzov* (Moscow: Profizdat, 1935).

34 S. Schwarz, *Labor*, pp. 94–100.

35 S. Shvarts, "'Zhestkaia' politika," *Sotsialisticheskii vestnik*, 1930, No. 223, pp. 10–11; A. Deviakovich, "Rabota proizvodstvenno-tovarishcheskikh sudov," *Voprosy profdvizheniia*, 1933, No. 10, pp. 78–81; and "Puti istochniki rosta proizvoditel'nosti truda sel'khozmashinostroenii," *Voprosy profdvizheniia*, 1934, No. 8/9, pp. 63–79.

36 S. Schwarz, *Labor*, pp. 100–15.

37 E. Genkin, "NKVD-Vigilant Guard of Soviet Fatherland," *Moscow Daily News*, December 27, 1937, p. 2.

38 M. Dewar, *Labour Policy*, pp. 111–17.

39 E. H. Carr and R. W. Davies, *Foundations*, Vol. 1, pp. 490–503.

40 B. Madison, *Social Welfare in the Soviet Union* (Stanford University Press, 1968), pp. 34–62.

41 *Profsoiuzy SSSR*, Vol. 2, pp. 697, 703–4; S. Schwarz, *Labor*, pp. 100–10.

42 E. H. Carr, "Marriage of Inconvenience," *New York Review of Books*, May 18, 1978, pp. 42–43.

43 E. Morrell, "Communist Unionism," pp. 88–98.

44 In terms of circulation, *V pomoshch' FZMK*, which began publication in 1940, was the leading union journal during the late 1940s. When this journal was taken off wartime footing in January 1947 and became a bimonthly, its circulation was established at 50,000, 20,000 higher than previously. In April 1950, the title was changed to *V pomoshch' profsoiunznomu aktivu*, and its circulation was established at 70,000. The retitled journal offered little that was new in terms of content, form, or editorial board. Its circulation fluctuated between 70,000 and 75,000 until publication ceased in August 1953.

By contrast, the broader orientation of topics in the monthly *Professional'nye soiuzy* was limited to a much smaller circulation. Between 1948 and 1950, 15,000 copies were issued monthly. This figure rose in May 1950 to approximately 30,000, where it remained until June 1952, when it was cut to approximately 24,000 copies per monthly edition. This journal's format and circulation remained stable until the end of 1953.

During the fall of 1953, a major reorganization of trade union publications occurred. *Professional'nye soiuzy* and *V pomoshch'* both ceased publication. In January 1954 a new journal, *Sovetskie profsoiuzy*, began publication on a monthly basis. The reorganization went much further. The editorial boards of *V pomoshch'* and *Professional'nye soiuzy* merged under a new chief editor, M. A. Sivolobov, who had no apparent ties to either publication. The new journal served the combined audience of *V pomoshch'* and *Professional'nye soiuzy*. The number of pages per issue increased, and sections of the journal were set aside for discussions of local concerns (discussions which previously had appeared in *V pomoshch'*). The circulation of *Sovetskie profsoiuzy* remained designated at between 90,000 and 105,000 until January 1960, when it jumped to over 130,000. During this period, the editorial board underwent major reorganization on three occasions (November 1955, November 1958, and July 1959). The journal became a bimonthly in August 1958. The circulation of *Sovetskie profsoiuzy* has risen steadily throughout the 1960s and 1970s, reaching over 730,000 in 1974 before falling back to a 1 January 1980, circulation of 525,090. With that growth, the content has become increasingly popularized, with more serious discussions of union affairs being carried out in smaller, more specialized journals such as *Okhrana truda i sotsial'noe strakhovanie*, which began publication in July 1958; *Okhrana truda na predpriatii*, which began to appear in 1967; and *Sotsialisticheskoe sorevnovanie*, which first came out in April 1976. *Sotsialisticheskii trud*, the journal of the USSR State Committee for Labor and Social Questions (formed in 1955), has frequently treated labor concerns since it began publication in 1956.

Trud, which began publication in 1921, remained the unions' daily spokesman throughout the period, as well as continuing to serve as a major Soviet daily newspaper.

45 For a discussion of the events leading up to reimplementation of the collective agreements, see: L. G. de Bellcombe, *Les Conventions*, and M. McAuley, *Labour Disputes*, pp. 43–45. It is interesting to note that Soviet trade union officials believed it necessary to have model collective agreements drawn up for foreign delegations before they were actually reintroduced on a mass scale. For example, in 1944, a U.S. trade union delegation visiting Moscow was told that wages and working conditions were determined by collective agreements between union and management. Congress of Industrial Organizations, *Report of the C.I.O. Delegation to the Soviet Union* (Washington, D.C.: C.I.O., 1945), p. 8.

46 N. V. Popova, "O rabote s profsoiuznymi kadrami," *Professional'nye soiuzy*, 1948, No. 1, 20–30.

47 The resolutions of the Tenth Trade Union Congress are found in *Profsoiuzy SSSR*, Vol. 3, pp. 632–51. Accompanying commentary may be found in *Professional'nye soiuzy*: S. Egurazdov, "Navstrechu X s"ezdu professional'nykh soiuzov," *Professional'nye soiuzy*, 1948, No. 11, pp. 19–22; "Navstrechu X s"ezdu profsoiuzov," *Professional'nye soiuzy*, 1948, No. 3, pp. 3–6; "X s"ezd professional'nykh soiuzov SSSR," *Professional'nye soiuzy*, 1949, No. 4, pp. 3–6; "Boevaia programma raboty profsoiuzov," *Professional'nye soiuzy*, 1949, No. 6, pp. 3–6; and S. Egurazdov, "Povysit' rol' sobranii profsoiuznogo aktiva," *Professional'nye soiuzy*, 1950, No. 2, pp. 27–30.

48 After examining unpublished material at the AUCCTU Library, E. Morrell concluded that measures were taken in July 1951 to reduce sanctions against absenteeism and truancy that had been in effect since the late 1930s (E. Morrell, "Communist Unionism," pp. 103–7). These changes altered judicial and administrative penalties for absenteeism and truancy. Both remained criminal offenses until 1956.

49 "Uluchshat' i sovershenstvovat' rabotu profsoiuzov," *Professional'nye soiuzy*, No. 12, pp. 1–9; and "Povysit' uroven' rukovodstva profsoiuznymi organizatsiiami," *Professional'nye soiuzy*, 1953, No. 6, pp. 1–6.

50 These articles began to appear in the first edition of *Sovetskie profsoiuzy* in January 1954 and continued to the congress. See, for example, "Profsoiuznaia zhizn': otchety i vybory profsoiuznykh organov," *Sovetskie profsoiuzy*, 1954, No. 1, pp. 32–35; Z. Sokolov, "Demokratizm sovetskikh profsoiuzov," *Sovetskie profsoiuzy*, 1954, No. 5, pp. 28–39; and "XI s"ezd professional'nykh soiuzov SSSR," *Sovetskie profsoiuzy*, 1954, No. 5, pp. 1–8.

51 *Sovetskie profsoiuzy*, 1954, No. 2, pp. 1–7; 1954, No. 3, pp. 9–14.

52 *Trud*, 12 March 1956, p. 2; 31 March 1956, pp. 1–2; 29 June 1956, p. 2; and V. Prokhorov, "Profsoiuzy v bor'be za vysokuiu proizvoditel'nost' truda," *Sotsialisticheskii trud*, 1956, No. 5, pp. 8–17.

Chapter 2. Soviet trade union development: 1957–1980

1 V. V. Grishin was elected AUCCTU chairman in March 1956, probably at the strong urging of N. Khrushchev. The forty-two-year-old Grishin had previously served as second secretary of the Moscow City Party Committee and remained with the AUCCTU until 1967, when he became first secretary of the Moscow City Party Committee. Although Grishin had no previous union experience, he had worked as a locomotive engineer and had held several positions in the Young Communist League. E. Morrell, "Communist Unionism: Organized Labor and the Soviet State" (Ph.D. dissertation, Harvard University, Cambridge, Mass., 1965), pp. 113–14.

2 For a general discussion of these events, see W. Leonhard, *The Kremlin Since Stalin* (New York: Oxford University Press, 1962), pp. 193–241.

3 Many of these letters dealt with the proposed boundaries of specific regional districts, the impact of the proposed changes on "socialist competition," and the importance of economic reorganization for technological innovation. Letters of this latter type often focused on the need for a national association of innovators under union leadership. Such an association came into being in January 1958.

4 In particular, see "Leninskie printsipy upravleniia khoziaistvom," *Trud* 9 April 1957, p. 1; I. Gureev, "Uluchshit' organizatsionnoe postroenie profsoiuzov," *Trud*, 18 April 1957, p. 1; and N. Kovalev, "Proizvodstvennye printsipy: Osnova postroeniia sovetskikh profsoiuzov," *Trud*, 21 April 1957, p. 2.

5 "V interesakh gosudarstva i naroda," *Sovetskie profsoiuzy*, 1957, No. 3, pp. 1–4.

6 "Za dal'neishee sovershenstvovanie upravleniia promyshlennost'iu i stroitel'stvom," *Sovetskie profsoiuzy*, 1957, No. 4, pp. 7–10; "Obsuzhdaem tezisy doklada tov. N. S. Khrushcheva," *Sovetskie profsoiuzy*, 1957, No. 4, pp. 7–29.

7 "Vazhnyi etap v zhizni sovetskikh profsoiuzov," *Sovetskie profosiuzy*, 1957, No. 5, pp. 1–5; "Za novye uspekhi v kommunisticheskom stroitel'stve," *Sovetskie profsoiuzy*, 1957, No. 6, pp. 1–4.

8 V. V. Grishin, "Povysit' rol' profsoiuzov v khoziaistvennom stroitel'stve," *Pravda*, 2 April 1957, p. 4.

9 Letters were published from enterprise union officials on 4 April and 28 April; summaries of discussions in *Leninskoe znamia* and in *Sovetskie profsoiuzy* were published on 8 April and 4 May, respectively, and nine letters from ten union officials of various ranks were summarized in the article "Osushchestvit' perestroiku raboty profsoiuzov," *Pravda*, 29 April 1957.

10 F. Siumakov, "Nuzhnaia novaia struktura profsoiusov," *Pravda*, 15 April 1957, p. 4.

11 Verkhovnyi sovet SSSR, *Zasedaniia Verkhovnogo soveta SSSR, chet-*

vertogo sozyva (7–10 maia, 1957); Stenograficheskii otchet (Moscow; Izdatel'stvo Verkhovnogo soveta SSSR, 1957), pp. 12–64.

12 This account is based on W. Leonhard, *The Kremlin*, pp. 242–51. Readers are also directed to C. A. Linden, *Khrushchev and the Soviet Leadership, 1957–1964* (Baltimore: Johns Hopkins University Press, 1966), pp. 40–57; and to R. Conquest, *Power and Policy in the USSR* (New York: St. Martin's Press, 1962), pp. 292–328.

13 *Trud*, 12 June 1957, pp. 1–3.

14 "Osushchestvit' perestroiku raboty profsoiuzov," *Pravda*, 17 June 1957, p. 1.

15 Kommunisticheskaia partiia Sovetskogo soiuza, *KPSS o profsoiuzakh* (Moscow: Profizdat, 1963), pp. 71–84.

16 For example, N. S. Khrushchev, "O kontrol'nykh tsifrakh razvitiia narodnogo khoziaistva SSSR na 1959–1965 gody," *Pravda*, 28 January 1969, p. 10; and L. I. Brezhnev, "Resheniia XXIV s"ezda KPSS: Boevaia programma deiatel'nosti sovetskikh profsoiuzov," *Sovetskie profsoiuzy*, 1972, No. 8, pp. 4–11.

17 Kommunisticheskaia partiia Sovetskogo soiuza, *KPSS o profsoiuzakh* (Moscow: Profizdat, 1974), pp. 301–4.

18 V. V. Grishin, "O zadachakh professional'nykh soiuzov v sviazi s resheniiami XXIII s"ezda KPSS," *Trud*, 27 April 1966, p. 2.

19 A. N. Shelepin, "XIV s"ezda professional'nykh soiuzov SSSR," *Trud*, 28 February 1968, pp. 2–6.

20 This discussion is based on J. Hough, "Policy-Making and the Worker," in A. Kahan and B. Ruble (eds.), *Industrial Labor in the USSR* (Elmsford, N.Y.: Pergamon Press, 1979), pp. 367–96.

21 E. Morrell, "Communist Unionism," pp. 110–11.

22 *Trud*, 26 March 1977, p. 1.

23 N. N. Romanov, "O merakh po dal'neishemu uluchsheniiu raboty s profsoiuznymi kadrami i aktivom," *Trud*, 3 October 1968, p. 2.

24 N. N. Romanov, "O dal'neishem uluchshenii raboty pervichnykh profsoiuznykh organizatsii," *Trud*, 17 April 1969, p. 2.

25 Such as the May 1979 resolution of the CPSU Central Committee, "On the Work of the Karaganda Regional Party Committee Concerning the Fulfillment of the 25th CPSU Congress on Party Leadership of Trade Union Organizations and the Improvement of Their Role in Economic and Cultural Construction," as described in the *Trud* editorial, "Vazhnye zadachi profsoiuzov," *Trud*, 26 May 1979, p. 1.

26 J. Hough, "Policy-Making."

27 "Vazhnye zadachi profsoiuzov," *Trud*, 24 November 1979, p. 1.

28 Soviet social welfare and health programs are too complex to be dealt with here. Readers are advised to consult: B. Madison, *Social Welfare in the Soviet Union* (Stanford University Press, 1968); and V. Navarro, *Social Security and Medicine in the USSR* (Lexington, Mass.: Lexington Books, 1977).

29 Shelepin left the AUCCTU in May 1975 and was appointed one

of five deputy chairmen of the State Committee on Vocational and Technical Education on 26 May 1975.

30 For example, it was Prokhorov who presented the AUCCTU report at the Twenty-Fifth Party Congress in February 1976 (Kommunisticheskaia partiia Sovetskogo soiuza, *XXV s"ezd, Stenograficheskii otchet* (Moscow: Politliteratura, 1976), Vol. 2, pp. 128–33.

31 "Informatsionnoe soobshchenie o plenume Vsesoiuznogo tsentral'nogo soveta professional'nykh soiuzov," *Trud*, 24 November 1976, p. 1.

32 A. Viktorov, "V interesakh liudei truda," *Trud*, 1 December 1978, p. 2.

Chapter 3. Union–management–Party relations at the plant

1 A fact never overtly stated by Soviet journalists but frequently alluded to (see, for example, V. Zenkov, "Osoboe mnenie," *Trud*, 6 June 1978, p. 2) and by legal scholars (see, for example, R. I. Kondrat'ev, *Sochetanie tsentralizovannogo i lokal'nogo pravovogo regulirovaniia trudovykh otnoshenii* [Lvov: Vishcha shkola, 1977]).

2 V. Smoliarchuk, *Prava profsoiuzov v regulirovanii trudovykh otnoshenii rabochikh i sluzhashchikh* (Moscow: Profizdat, 1973), pp. 5–11.

3 D. P. Hammer, *USSR: The Politics of Oligarchy* (Hinsdale, Ill.: Dryden Press, 1974), p. 174.

4 See discussion Ts. A. Iampol'skaia, "O sisteme profsoiuzov SSSR," in Ts. A. Iampol'skaia and A. I. Tsepin (eds.), *Pravovye aspekty deiatel'nosti profsoiuzov SSSR* (Moscow: Nauka, 1973), pp. 41–93.

5 The regulations governing trade union elections are found in Vsesoiuznyi tsentral'nyi sovet professional'nykh soiuzov, *Spravochnik profsoiuznogo rabotnika* (Moscow: Profizdat, 1974), pp. 21–29. This account of trade union elections is based on discussions with several Soviet trade union officials and is substantiated by the regulations.

6 For a general discussion of Soviet personnel procedures, including the *nomenklatura* system, see J. Hough, *The Soviet Prefects* (Cambridge, Mass.: Harvard University Press, 1969), pp. 149–77. For a discussion of the trade union *nomenklatura* system, see E. Morrell, "Communist Unionism: Organized Labor and the Soviet State" (Ph.D. dissertation, Harvard University, 1965), pp. 174–90.

7 For example, in January 1977 approximately 80 percent of the factory trade union chairmen in Voronezh were Communist Party members (V. Adashchik, "Printsipal'no po delovomu," *Trud*, 5 January 1977, p. 2). In January 1980, 62.9 percent of all factory trade union chairmen in the Uzbek SSR were Community Party members (N. Makhmudova, "Sovershenstvovanie form i metodov profsoiuznoi raboty," *Kommunist Uzbekistana*, 1980, No. 1, pp. 44–52).

8 This account is based on discussions with Soviet trade union officials.

9 This account is based on discussions with Soviet trade union officials.
10 This account is based on discussions with Soviet trade union officials.
11 I. Slovinskii, "Doverie obviatyvaet," *Sovetskie profsoiuzy*, 1979, No. 11, pp. 22–23.
12 This account is based on discussions with Soviet trade union officials.
13 I. O. Snigireva and L. S. Iavich, *Gosudarstvo i profsoiuzy* (Moscow: Profizdat, 1967), pp. 165–216.
14 For a discussion of Soviet collective agreements, see N. G. Aleksandrov, *Sovetskoe trudovoe pravo* (Moscow: Iuridicheskaia literatura, 1972), pp. 209–23.
15 R. Hutchings, *Soviet Economic Development* (New York: Barnes & Noble, 1971), pp. 135–7.
16 B. M. Richman, *Management Development and Education in the Soviet Union* (East Lansing: Michigan State University Press, 1967), pp. 80–94.
17 R. Hutchings, *Soviet Economic Development*, pp. 148–66; and M. Z. Bor, *Aims and Methods of Soviet Planning* (New York: International Publishers, 1967), pp. 37–50.
18 M. Z. Bor, *Aims and Methods*, pp. 50–4.
19 A. Katsenelinboigen, *Studies in Soviet Economic Planning* (White Plains, N.Y.: M. E. Sharpe, 1978), pp. 159–60.
20 D. Granick, *Managerial Comparisons of Four Developed Countries: France, Britain, United States and Russia* (Cambridge, Mass.: MIT Press, 1972), pp. 50–4.
21 J. Hough, *Prefects*, pp. 80–100.
22 A fact which prompted the celebrated Shchekino experiment designed to reduce overemployment. See K. W. Ryavec, *Implementation of Soviet Economic Reforms* (New York: Praeger, 1975), pp. 209–11.
23 D. Granick, *The Red Executive* (Garden City, N.Y.: Doubleday, 1961), pp. 230–4.
24 See, for example, I. A. Arabian, "Ustranenie prichin narusheniia trudovoi distsipliny," *Sovetskoe gosudarstvo i pravo*, 1978, No. 1, pp. 124–7.
25 D. Granick, *Red Executive*, pp. 148–50.
26 This account is based on discussions with Soviet trade union officials.
27 See, for example, Kommunisticheskaia partiia Sovetskogo soiuza, *KPSS o profsoiuzkh* (Moscow: Profizdat, 1974), pp. 331–8.
28 L. I. Brezhnev, *Sovetskie profsoiuzy – vliiatel'naia sila nashego obshchestva* (Moscow: Politizdat, 1977), pp. 13–14.
29 J. Berliner, *The Innovation Decision in Soviet Industry* (Cambridge, Mass.: MIT Press, 1976).
30 This account is based on discussions with Soviet trade union officials.

31 This account is based on discussions with Soviet trade union officials.

32 Kamskii kabel'nyi zavod imeni 50-letiia SSSR, *Kollektivnyi dogovor na 1974 god* (Kudymkar: Kudymkarshaia tipografiia, 1974).

33 A. S. Paskhov (ed.), *Sovetskoe trudovoe pravo* (Moscow: Iuridicheskaia literatura, 1976), p. 171.

34 As testified to in part by the numerous training programs established in recent years for union officials. Discussion of collective agreement procedures are found in manuals used in Perm and Vologda regional trade union seminars. V. P. Burov, *Rabota profsoiuzov po zakliucheniiu i proverke vypolneniia kollektivnykh dogovorov* (Perm: Profkursy Permskogo soveta profsoiuzov, 1970); Vologodskii oblastnoi sovet professional'nykh soiuzov, uchebnometodicheskii kabinet profsoiuznykh kursov, *Metodicheskoe pis'mo po organizatsii shkol i postoianno-deistvuiushchikh seminarov po obucheniiu profsoiuznogo aktiva* (Vologda: Oblastnaia tipografiia, 1972).

35 M. Haraszti, *A Worker in a Worker's State* (New York: Universe Books, 1977), p. 96.

36 D. C. Heldman, *Trade Unions and Labor Relations in the USSR* (Washington, D.C.: Council on American Affairs, 1977).

37 By 1935, collective agreements ceased to exist in the USSR. Except for a twelve-month period in 1937–8, this situation remained unchanged until 1947. M. McAuley, *Labour Disputes in Soviet Russia, 1957–1965* (Oxford: Clarendon, 1969), pp. 36–38.

38 V. K. Fedinin, *Sotsialisticheskoe sorevnovanie na sovremennom etape* (Moscow: Ekonomika, 1974).

39 Kamskii kabil'nyi zavod, *Dogovor*, pp. 4–15, 31–7.

40 This account is based on discussions with Soviet trade union officials.

41 A comment made during an interview with a Soviet trade union official.

42 V. Mikulich, "Kommunist v profsoiuznoi organizatsii," *Trud*, August 1, 1978, p. 2.

43 M. I. Kornikova, *Vospitatel'naia rabota v trudovom kollektive* (Moscow, Profizdat, 1975). For a more general examination of political socialization in the USSR see S. White, *Political Culture and Soviet Politics* (London: Macmillan, 1979), pp. 75–83, 113–42.

44 A. I. Tsepin, "Obshchaia kharakteristika professional'nykh soiuzov," in Ts. A. Iampol'skaia and A. I. Tsepin (eds.), *Pravovye aspekty*, pp. 12–40, 25.

45 Vsesoiuznyi tsentral'nyi sovet professional'nykh soiuzov, *Profsoiuzy SSSR: Dokumenty i materialy* (Moscow: Profizdat, 1974), Vol. 5, pp. 505–16.

46 "Vliiatel'naia sila sovetskogo obshchestva," *Trud*, 10 June 1978, p. 2.

47 "V tsentral'nom komitete KPSS," *Trud*, 2 April 1978, p. 1.

48 Dom politicheskogo prosveshcheniia LK i LKG KPSS, "Tekushchii moment (material v pomoshch' dokladchikam lektoram i politinformatoram)," Unpublished report, Leningrad, May 1974.

49 N. A. Petrovichev, *Partiinoe stroitel'stvo* (Moscow: Politliteratura, 1976), pp. 346–7.

Chapter 4. The legal and social rights of Soviet workers

1 V. Zenkov, "Osoboe mnenie," *Trud*, 6 June 1978, p. 2.
2 Vsesoiuznyi tsentral'nyi sovet professional'nykh soiuzov, *Spravochnik profsoiuznogo rabotnika* (Moscow: Profizdat, 1971), pp. 7–47; and B. F. Khrustalev, "Istochniki trudovogo prava," in A. S. Pashkov (ed.), *Sovetskoe trudovoe pravo* (Moscow: Iuridicheskaia literatura, 1976), pp. 91–108.
3 *Sbornik zakonodatel'nykh aktov o trude* (Moscow: Iuridicheskaia literatura, 1974), pp. 942–55.
4 This discussion of Soviet disputes resolution practice is based on interviews with union officials in Leningrad as well as on B. I. Ushkov, "Poriadok rassmotreniia trudovykh sporov," in A. S. Paskhov (ed.), *Pravo*, pp. 471–89.
5 *Biulleten' Verkhovnogo suda SSSR*, 1968, No. 6, pp. 37–9.
6 Ibid.
7 Ibid., 1970, No. 5, pp. 7–10; 1971, No. 6, pp. 3–11; 1972, No. 1, pp. 37–44; 1974, No. 2, 45–7; 1974, No. 3, 19–27.
8 Ibid., 1977, No. 3, pp. 29–37.
9 Ibid., 1978, No. 6, pp. 1–6.
10 Ibid., pp. 2–3.
11 Ibid., 1978, No. 11, pp. 12–16; 1979, No. 9, pp. 1–5, 9–12.
12 Ibid., 1973, No. 1, p. 4.
13 Ibid., 1971, No. 7, pp. 1–2.
14 Ibid., 1979, No. 8, p. 2.
15 "Vliiatel'naia sila sovetskogo obshchestva," *Trud*, 20 June 1978, p. 2.
16 Such studies began to appear during the mid-1960s. It was not until after the appearance of A. A. Abramova's *Distsiplina truda v SSSR* (Moscow: Iuridicheskaia literatura, 1969), and V. I. Nikitinskii's *Effektivnost' norm trudovogo prava* (Moscow: Iuridicheskaia literatura, 1971), that such investigations became more commonplace. Although neither Abramova's nor Nikitinskii's work has appeared in English, translations of similar studies are to be found in M. Yanowitch (ed.), *Soviet Work Attitudes* (White Plains, N.Y.: M. E. Sharpe, 1979).
17 V. Ponomarev, "Reshenie prinimaet zavkom," *Vechernii Leningrad*, 22 October 1974, p. 2.
18 For a synopsis of this work, see V. Dunham, "The Worker and the Soviet System – A Literary Study," Unpublished manuscript, 1980, pp. 13–18.
19 "Vysokaia rol' trudovogo kollektiva," *Trud*, 12 April 1978, p. 3.
20 "Krepit' trudovuiu distsiplinu," *Pravda*, 28 October 1974, p. 1; "V Tsentral'nom komitete KPSS," *Pravda*, 7 January 1975, p. 1.

21 I. A. Arabian, "Ustranenie prichin narusheniia trudovoi distsipliny," *Sovetskoe gosudarstvo i pravo*, 1978, No. 1, pp. 124–7.

22 "V TsK KPSS, Prezidiume Verkhovnogo soveta SSSR, Sovete ministrov SSSR, i VTsSPS o dal'neishem ukreplenii trudovoi distsipliny i sokrashenii tekuchesti kadrov v narodnom khoziaistve," *Trud*, 12 January 1980, pp. 1–2. For examples of accompanying commentary, see "Krepit' distsipliny truda," *Trud*, 13 January 1980, p. 1; and "Smotr okhrany truda," *Trud*, 20 January 1980, p. 1.

23 A. M. Kuznetsov, "Okhrana truda," in A. S. Pashkov (ed.), *Pravo*, pp. 405–35.

24 Kamskii kabel'nyi zavod imeni 50-letiia SSSR, *Kollektivnyi dogovor na 1974 god* (Kudymkar: Kudymkarskaia tipografia, 1974).

25 A. Sharov, "Nam otvechaet," *Trud*, 18 June 1978, p. 2.

26 "Vliiatel'naia sila," *Trud*, 20 June 1978.

27 "The Workers' Interests and the Trade Unions," *Soviet Union*, 1980, No. 10, 8–9.

28 "Vilnius Trade Union Official Removed from Post," *Foreign Broadcast Information Service Daily Report: Soviet Union (FBIS-SOV-80-227)*, 21 November 1980, R-8.

29 Sakharov; Akimov; et al., "Vmesto ventiliastii skvozniaki," *Trud*, 24 March 1978, p. 2; A. Rostovtsev, "Vot tak my i zhivem," *Trud*, 24 March 1978, p. 2; Novak; Rak; Kolosov; Biuko; et al., "V ozhidanii konveiera," *Trud*, 18 June 1978, p. 2.

30 "Sozniatel'naia rol' sovetskikh profsoiuzov," *Rabochii klass i sovremennyi mir*, 1977, No. 2, pp. 3–9, 7–8.

31 A. Matrosov and V. Rabinovich, "Industriia chistogo vozdukha," *Trud*, 24 August 1978, p. 7.

32 *Trud*, 28 February 1968, pp. 2–6.

33 Kommunisticheskaia partiia Sovetskogo soiuza, *XXV s"ezd KPSS; Stenograficheskii otchet* (Moscow: Politliteratura, 1976), Vol. 1, pp. 109–10; Vol. 2, pp. 128–33; *Sovetskie profsoiuzy*, 1972, No. 8, pp. 4–33; 1977, No. 8, pp. 5–29.

34 For further discussion of these reforms, see J. G. Chapman, *Wage Variation in Soviet Industry: The Impact of the 1956–1960 Wage Reform* (Santa Monica, Calif.: RAND, 1970); L. J. Kirsch, *Soviet Wages: Changes in Structure and Administration Since 1956* (Cambridge, Mass., MIT Press, 1972); A. McAuley, *Economic Welfare in the Soviet Union* (Madison: University of Wisconsin Press, 1979); and J. G. Chapman, "Recent Trends in the Soviet Industrial Wage Structure," in A. Kahan and B. A. Ruble (eds.), *Industrial Labor in the USSR* (Elmsford, N.Y.: Pergamon Press, 1979), pp. 151–83.

35 K. I. Mikul'skii (ed.), *Effektivnost' sotsialisticheskogo proizvodstva i khoziaistvennyi mekhanizm* (Moscow: Nauka, 1979), p. 219.

36 This discussion of the union role in wage policy formation is based on interviews with Soviet trade union officials, and G. I. Guliaev, "Pravovoe regulirovanie zarabotnoi platy," in A. S. Pashkov (ed.), *Pravo*, pp. 349–404.

158   *Notes to pp. 79–91*

37 This discussion is based on A. McAuley, *Economic Welfare*, pp. 174–97.
38 J. Chapman, "Recent Trends," p. 153.
39 Ibid., p. 160.
40 A figure calculated by dividing by 12 the quotient of dividing the total earnings of the Material Incentive Fund for 1978 (6,166 million rubles) by the total number of workers and employees in industry for that year (36,014,000). Tsentral'noe statisticheskoe upravlenie SSSR, *Narodnoe khoziaistvo SSSR v 1978 g.* (Moscow: Statistika, 1979), pp. 366, 530.
41 R. I. Kondrat'ev, *Lokal'nye normy trudovogo prava i material'noe stimulirovanie* (Lvov: Vishcha shkola, 1973).
42 R. I. Kondrat'ev, *Sochetanie tsentralizovannogo i lokal'nogo pravovogo regulirovaniia trudovykh otnoshenii* (Lvov: Vishcha shkola, 1977).
43 This discussion is based on A. McAuley, *Economic Welfare*, pp. 260–301, and TsSU SSSR, *Narodnoe khoziaistvo, 1978*, p. 371.
44 A. McAuley, *Economic Welfare*, pp. 16–20.
45 V. Dunham, "The Worker and the Soviet System," pp. 22–25.
46 F. Podnii, "Norma," *Trud*, 26 July 1978, p. 2.
47 E. L. Kuz'min, "Kritika burzhuaznykh i revisionistskikh vozzrenii na gosudarstvo i demokratikiiu," *Sovetskoe gosudarstvo i pravo*, 1977, No. 3, 125–33; "Prava cheloveka: sut' spora, sut' problemy," *Novyi mir*, 1978, No. 10, pp. 185–216.
48 B. Q. Madison, "Trade Unions and Social Welfare," in A. Kahan and B. A. Ruble (eds.), *Industrial Labor*, pp. 85–115.
49 Ibid. Also see A. D. Zaikin, "Pravovye voprosy gosudarstvennogo sotsial'nogo strakhovaniia," in N. G. Aleksandrov, *Sovetskoe trudovoe pravo* (Moscow: Iuridicheskaia literatura, 1972), pp. 530–70; M. Binyon, "How Docile Are Russia's Unions?" *London Times*, 20 December 1979, p. 19; and I. Smirnov, *Profsoiuzy SSSR: 100 voprosov – 100 otvetov* (Moscow: Profizdat, 1972), p. 111.
50 TsSU SSSR, *Narodnoe khoziaistvo, 1978*, p. 371.

Chapter 5. Do workers participate in Soviet management?

1 L. I. Brezhnev, *Sovetskie profsoiuzy – vliiatel'naia sila nashego obshchestva* (Moscow: Politizdat, 1977), pp. 14–15.
2 "Vliiatel'naia sila sovetskogo obshchestva," *Trud*, 10 June 1978, p. 2.
3 N. G. Aleksandrov, "Prava profsoiuzov v oblasti uchastiia v upravlenii proizvodstvom," in N. G. Aleksandrov, *Sovetskoe trudovoe pravo* (Moscow: Iuridicheskaia literatura, 1972), pp. 196–201.
4 "Poriadok naveden," *Sovetskie profsoiuzy*, 1978, No. 7, p. 35; "Spravedlivost' vosstanovlena," *Sovetskie profsoiuzy*, 1978, No. 7, p. 35; I. Loboiko, "U nas kritika ne v pochete," *Trud*, 28 March 1979, p. 2; and V. Kotliarov and V. Nakonechnyi, "Vpustuiu teriaem vremia," *Trud*, 18 January 1979, p. 1.

5 M. P. Tomskii, *Izbrannye stat'i i rechi, 1917–1927* (Moscow: VTsSPS, 1928), p. 381.

6 R. Michels, *Political Parties*, trans. E. Paul and C. Paul (New York: Dover, 1959).

7 Vsesoiuznyi Tsertral'nyi sovet professional'nykh soiuzov, *Spravochnik profsoiuznogo rabotnika* (Moscow: Profizdat, 1974), pp. 66–71.

8 V. Mikulich, "Kommunist v profsoiuznoi organizatsii," *Trud*, 1 August 1978, p. 3. In January 1980, nearly one-third of all laborers were said to participate in production conferences in the Uzbek SSR. N. Makhmudova, "Sovershenstvovanie form i metodov profsoiuznoi raboty," *Kommunist Uzbekistana*, 1980, No. 1, p. 49.

9 L. Ianovskii, "Vyigryvaet proizvodstvo," *Sovetskie profsoiuzy*, 1977, No. 23, pp. 14–15.

10 Ia. Dumchev, "Kak povysit' rol' PDPS?" *Sovetskie profsoiuzy*, 1977, No. 6, pp. 16–17; "Proizvodstvennoe soveshchanie ili rabochee sobranie," *Sovetskie profsoiuzy* 1977, No. 12, pp. 16–17; "PDPS: Koordinaty effektivnosti," *Sovetskie profsoiuzy*, 1977, No. 23, pp. 14–15; and B. Khaitovich, "S uchetom spetsifiki," *Sovetskie profsoiuzy*, 1977, No. 23, p. 14.

11 L. Ianovskii, "Vyigryvaet."

12 S. M. Alekseev, "Dvizhenie izobretatelei i ratsionalizatorov v SSSR (1966–1975)," *Istoriia SSSR*, 1975, No. 4, pp. 3–22.

13 F. M. Leviant and A. V. Mavrin, "Professional'nye soiuzy: Uchastie rabochikh i sluzhashchikh v upravlenii proizvodstvom," in A. S. Pashkov (ed.), *Sovetskoe trudovoe pravo* (Moscow: Iuridicheskaia literatura, 1976), pp. 139–63.

14 M. N. Nochevnik and V. I. Usenin, "Rabochii klass, avtomatizatsiia i profsoiuzy," *Rabochii klass i sovremennyi mir*, 1977, No. 2, pp. 10–13.

15 R. Lee III, "The Factory Trade Union Committee and Technological Innovation," in A. Kahan and B. A. Ruble (eds.), *Industrial Labor in the USSR* (Elmsford, N.Y.: Pergamon Press, 1979), pp. 116–34.

16 Kamskii kabel'nyi zavod imeni 50-letiia SSSR, *Kollektivnyi dogovor na 1974 god* (Kudymkar: Kudymkarskaia tipografiia, 1974), pp. 4–11.

17 N. Misiuchenko, "Moia dissertatsiia," *Sovetskie profsoiuzy*, 1978, No. 20, p. 14.

18 L. Shcherbina, "Chto za obidoi?" *Sovetskie profsoiuzy*, 1978, No. 17, pp. 10–11.

19 V. Kharchenko, "Preimushchestva ob"edineniia," *Trud*, 6 June 1978, p. 2.

20 E. Suvvi, "Prava, kotorye nam dany," *Sovetskie profsoiuzy*, 1977, No. 17, pp. 36–37.

21 V. A. Maslennikov, "Trudovye proizvodstvennye kollektivy v sotsial'no-pravovykh issledovaniiakh," in Akademiia nauk SSSR, Institut gosudarstva i prava, *Pravo i sotsiologiia* (Moscow: Nauka, 1973), pp. 291–3.

22 S. White, *Political Culture and Soviet Politics* (London: Macmillan, 1979), pp. 89–112, 154–65.
23 Ibid., p. 162.
24 Ia. S. Kapeliush, "Public Opinion on Electing Managers," in M. Yanowitch (ed.), *Soviet Work Attitudes* (White Plains, N.Y.: M. E. Sharpe, 1979), pp. 60–80.
25 H. J. Berman, *Justice in the USSR* (Cambridge, Mass.: Harvard University Press, 1963), pp. 289–98.
26 N. N. Borodina, "Gosudarstvenno-pravovye i obshchestvennye mery ukrepleniia distsipliny truda rabochikh i sluzhashchikh v SSSR" (Candidate dissertation, Institute of State and Law of the USSR Academy of Sciences, Moscow, 1966).
27 K. Smirnov, "Aktiva – prochee znanie," *Sovetskie profsoiuzy*, 1978, No. 3, pp. 28–29.
28 "Pravila priema v vysshie profsoiuznye shkoly VTsSPS na 1978 god," *Trud*, 7 December 1977, p. 4.
29 S. White, *Political Culture*, p. 86.
30 V. Kantorovich, *Ty i vy* (Moscow: Sovetskaia Rossiia, 1974), p. 11.
31 V. D. Arkhipov; N. I. Koniaev; and P. S. Khoren, *Kommentarii k polozheniiu o poriadke rassmotreniia trudovykh sporov* (Moscow: Iuridicheskaia literatura, 1976).
32 A. Pravda, "Spontaneous Workers' Activity in the Soviet Union," in A. Kahan and B. A. Ruble (eds.), *Industrial Labor*, pp. 333–66.
33 V. G. Vasil'ev, *Problemy povysheniia proizvoditel'nosti truda na prepriiatiiakh promyshlennosti i transporta* (Moscow: Nauka, 1974), pp. 330–52; M. Yanowitch (ed.), *Soviet Work Attitudes*.
34 Several accounts of the events in Novocherkassk have appeared in the West, the most extensive being found in A. Solzhenitsyn, *The Gulag Archipelago*, Vol. 3 (New York: Harper & Row, 1978), pp. 506–14.
35 W. Teckenberg, "Labour Turnover and Job Satisfaction: Indicators of Industrial Conflict in the USSR?" *Soviet Studies*, 1978, Vol. 30, No. 2, pp. 193–211.
36 G. L. Mel'nikov, "Formirovanie proizvodstvennogo kollektiva stroiki," in Ministerstvo vysshego i srednego spetsial'nogo obrazovaniia RSFSR, Irkutskii gosudarstvennyi universitet im. A. A. Zhdanova, *Kollektiv i lichnost'* (Irkutsk: Irkutskii gosudarstvennyi universitet, 1972), pp. 3–20; Zh. Medvedev, "Dissent in the Soviet Union," Lecture, U.S. Department of State, Washington, D.C., 28 October 1976.
37 *New York Times*, 14 June 1980, p. 3; 18 June 1980, p. A31.
38 *Izvestiia*, 21 June 1980, p. 5.
39 B. Barton, "'Trade Unions' in the USSR," *AFL-CIO Free Trade Union News*, 26 September 1979, pp. 1–16, 13; D. K. Shipler, "Soviet Workers Tell of Hazards of Complaining," *New York Times*, 2 December 1977, pp. A1, A12; D. Satter, "Soviet Workers Sign Public Protest Letter," *Washington Post*, 8 February 1977, p. A10; K. Klose, "Angry Soviet Workers Form Unauthorized Trade

Union," *Washington Post*, 8 February 1978, p. A20; C. R. Whitney, "Dissident Unionists in Moscow Pledge Continuing Struggle," *New York Times*, 28 February 1978, p. A7; E. C. Scheetz, "Disaffected Workers Publicly Defend Their Rights," Radio Liberty Research, 28 February 1978, RL 4 7/78; H. Jamieson, "Arrested Workers Protest Corruption," *Labour Focus on Eastern Europe*, Vol. 1, No. 6, p. 17; and L. Sergeeva, "Golos i sovest' rabochikh," *Posev*, 1978, No. 3, pp. 2–3; and V. Haynes and O. Semyonova (eds.), *Workers Against the GULAG* (London: Pluto Press, 1979).

Chapter 6. Patterns of union behavior

1 V. Dunham, "The Worker and the Soviet System: A Literary Study (the Nineteen Sixties and Seventies)," Unpublished manuscript, 1980, pp. 3–4.

2 L. Chavpilo; I. Shimko; and B. Ivashkin, *Finansovaia rabota profsoiuzov* (Moscow: Profizdat, 1975), pp. 127–61. I would like to thank Professor Alastair McAuley of the University of Essex for calling my attention to this work.

3 Tsentral'noe statisticheskoe upravlenie, *Narodnoe khoziaistvo SSSR v 1978 g* (Moscow: Statistika, 1979), p. 371.

4 This discussion is based on interviews with Leningrad trade union officials and is touched upon in N. Aitov, "Zhelannaia gorizontal'," *Literaturnaia gazeta*, 20 August 1975, p. 10.

5 A. Viktorov, "V interesakh liudei," *Trud*, 1 December 1978, p. 2.

6 For a brief review of these duties, see A. I. Tsepin, *Kontrol' FZMK za sobliudeniem zakonodatel'stva o trude* (Moscow: Profizdat, 1975), and V. I. Smoliarchuk, *Prava profsoiuzov v regulirovanii trudovykh otnoshenii rabochikh i sluzhashchikh* (Moscow: Profizdat, 1973).

7 Leningrad, Institut istorii partii, *Istoriia Kirovskogo (byv. Putilovskogo) metallurgicheskogo i mashinostroitel'nogo zavoda v Leningrade* (Moscow: Izd. Sotsial'no-ekonomicheskaia literatura, 1961–6).

8 K. V. Govorushin, *Za narvskoi zastavoi* (Moscow: Politizdat, 1975), p. 330.

9 In Volume 5 of the collection Vsesoiuznyi tsertral'nyi sovet profsoiuzov, *Profsoiuzy SSSR; Dokumenty i materialy* (Moscow: Profizdat, 1974), ten decrees praising the Kirov appear, the same number of times as the Lenin Metallurgical Enterprise Group in Magnitogorsk and the "Uralkhimmash" chemical machinery factory in Sverdlovsk. The Fifty Years of the USSR Metallurgical Factory in Cherepovets is praised in twelve decrees, whereas the "Svetlana" industrial association in Leningrad appears in eleven.

10 *Profsoiuzy SSSR*, Vol. 5, No. 204, pp. 624–34.

11 Interview, 11 April 1975.

12 L. Zhelnina, "Posle sobraniia," *Sovetskie profsoiuzy*, 1978, No. 5, pp. 34–35.

13 This discussion of the petroleum industry in the Bashkir Autonomous Republic is based on R. Khakimova and A. Bushkina,

Sovetskaia Bashkiriia (Moscow: Sovetskaia Rossiia, 1969), and A. P. Rozhdestvenskii, *Bashkiriia: Putevoditel'* (Ufa: Bashkirskoe knizhnoe izdatel'stvo, 1970).
14 *Sbornik postanovlenii VTsSPS*, 1972, No. 4, pp. 69–71.
15 This account is based on a May 1975 visit to the factory by the author. A discussion of the Bukhara textile factory may be found in U. Kh. Kamalov, A. A. Muzafarov, V. G. Saakov, *Bukhara: Putevoditel'* (Tashkent: Tsk KP Uzbekistana, 1973), pp. 11–56.
16 *Sbornik postanovlenii VTsSPS*, 1971, No. 4, pp. 16–20.
17 R. M. Kanter, *Social Science Frontiers No. 9: Work and Family in the United States: A Critical Review and Agenda for Research and Policy* (New York: Russell Sage Foundation, 1977), p. 17.

Chapter 7. The international activities of Soviet trade unions

1 J. P. Windmuller, *Labor Internationals* (Ithaca, N.Y.: Cornell University Press, 1969), pp. 3–7.
2 E. H. Carr, "Two Currents in World Labor," *Foreign Affairs*, Vol. 25, No. 1, pp. 72–81.
3 J. P. Windmuller, *Internationals*, pp. 8–9.
4 C. Osakwe, *The Participation of the Soviet Union in Universal International Organizations* (Leiden: Sijthoff, 1972), pp. 63–9.
5 D. Dubinsky, "World Labor's New Weapon," *Foreign Affairs*, Vol. 28, No. 3, pp. 451–62; H. K. Jacobson, "The USSR and the ILO," *International Organization*, 1960, No. 3, pp. 402–28; and G. Kanayev, *Soviet Trade Unions and the International Trade Union Movement* (Moscow: Novosti Press, 1971), pp. 14–15.
6 M. Mukhtasipov, *Sovetskie profsoiuzy v bor'be za mezhdunarodnoe edinstvo rabochego klassa, 1918–1939g.* (Moscow: Mysl', 1966), pp. 18–28; G. M. Adibekov, "Profintern v bor'be za edinstvo mezhdunarodnogo rabochego i profsoiuznogo dvizheniia," *Novaia i noveishaia istoriia*, 1971, No. 4, pp. 16–32; and Vsesoiuznyi tsertral'nyi sovet professional'nykh soiuzov, *Profsoiuzy SSSR; Dokumenty i materialy* (Moscow: Profizdat, 1963), Vol. 2, No. 156, pp. 255–57.
7 V. I. Lenin, *On Trade Unions* (Moscow: Progress, 1970), pp. 354–63.
8 A. Lozovskii, "Komintern i profintern: Rech' na I Kongresse profinterna 10 iiulia, 1921g.," in A. Lozovskii, *Desiat' let bor'by za profintern* (Moscow: VTsSPS, 1930), Vol. 1, pp. 298–304, in particular p. 301.
9 E. H. Carr, "Marriage of Inconvenience," *New York Review of Books*, 18 May 1978, pp. 42–43.
10 D. F. Calhoun, *The United Front: The TUC and the Russians, 1923–1928* (Cambridge University Press, 1976).
11 *Profsoiuzy SSSR*, Vol. 2, Nos. 253, 258–79, 328–31, pp. 421–23, 429–31, 560–4; V. A. Kuz'ko and Iu. A. Livunin, "Pomoshch' trudiashchikhsia SSSR rabochim Germanii v 1923–1924 gg.," *Voprosy istorii*, 1973, No. 12, pp. 200–4; M. Mukhtasipov, *Sovetskie*

profsoiuzy, pp. 72–76; and P. I. Iakovlev, *Ocherki po istorii mezhdunarodnoi solidarnosti trudiashchikhsia* (Moscow: Nauka, 1974).

12 C. Osakwe, *Universal International Organizations*, pp. 67–71.

13 M. Schwartz, "Soviet Policy and the World Federation of Trade Unions, 1945–1949" (Ph.D. dissertation, Columbia University, New York, 1963), pp. 32–39.

14 D. Dubinsky, "World Labor's New Weapon"; J. P. Windmuller, *Internationals*.

15 L. Pogrebnoi, "Vydaiushchiesia deiateli sovetskogo profdvizheniia," *Sovetskie profsoiuzy*, 1978, No. 9, pp. 28–29; *Profsoiuzy SSSR*, Vol. 3, Nos. 286–294, pp. 452–57; J. P. Windmuller, *Internationals*, pp. 10–11; G. Kanayev, *Soviet Trade Unions*, pp. 22–28; and E. Nash, "Wartime Activities of the Soviet Trade Unions," Unpublished report, Editorial and Research Department, Bureau of Labor Standards, U.S. Department of Labor, Washington, D.C., 1944.

16 Congress of Industrial Organizations, *Report of the C.I.O. Delegation to the Soviet Union* (Washington, D.C.: CIO, 1945).

17 M. Schwartz, "Soviet Policy," pp. 126–37.

18 V. Reuther, "The International Activities of American Trade Unions," in W. Haber (ed.), *Labor in a Changing America* (New York: Basic Books, 1966), pp. 298–310; D. Dubinsky, "World Labor's New Weapon"; D. Dubinsky, "Rift and Realignment in World Labor," *Foreign Affairs*, Vol. 27, No. 2, pp. 232–45; and J. P. Windmuller, *Internationals*, pp. 11–13.

19 J. P. Windmuller, "ICFTU After 10 Years: Problems and Prospects," *Industrial and Labor Relations Review*, Vol. 14, No. 2, pp. 257–72.

20 R. Godson, "American Labor's Continuous Involvement in World Affairs," *Orbis*, Vol. 19, No. 1, pp. 93–116.

21 M. Schwartz, "Soviet Policy," p. 340.

22 E. Morrell, "Communist Unionism: Organized Labor and the Soviet State" (Ph.D. dissertation, Harvard University, Cambridge, Mass., 1965), pp. 526–27; B. Martin, "The International Activities of Soviet Trade Unions," in A. Kahan and B. A. Ruble (eds.), *Industrial Labor in the USSR* (Elmsford, N.Y.: Pergamon Press, 1979), pp. 135–48; and K. A. Guseinov, *Trade Union Associations: USSR, Asia and Africa* (Moscow: Nauka, 1967), p. 49.

23 R. W. Cox, "ILO: Limited Monarchy," in R. W. Cox and H. K. Jacobson (eds.), *The Anatomy of Influence: Decision Making in International Organizations* (New Haven: Yale University Press, 1973), pp. 102–38, 105–7.

24 Ibid., pp. 107–8.

25 C. Osakwe, *Universal International Organizations*, pp. 72–75.

26 International Labour Office, *Trade Union Rights in the USSR; Studies and Reports*, New Series, No. 49 (Geneva: ILO, 1959).

27 H. K. Jacobson, "The USSR and the ILO," pp. 414–417.

28 R. W. Cox, "ILO."

29 S. M. Schwebel, "The United States Assaults the ILO," *American*

Journal of International Law, 1971, No. 1, pp. 136–42; K. DeAnzheli, "Za MOT, kotoraia sluzhila by trudiashchimsia," *Vsemirnoe profsoiuznoe dvizhenie*, 1978, No. 8, pp. 6–9; B. Martin, "International Activities"; and "America's Contribution to the I.L.O.," *New York Times*, 18 February 1980, p. A16.

30 C. Osakwe, *Universal International Organizations*, pp. 76–88.
31 J. P. Windmuller, *Internationals*.
32 Ibid.
33 B. Martin, "International Activities."
34. A. O. Hero, Jr. and E. Starr, *The Reuther–Meany Foreign Policy Dispute* (Dobbs Ferry, N.Y.: Oceana, 1970), pp. 66–76.
35 B. Martin, "International Activities."
36 J. P. Windmuller, *Internationals*, pp. 62–67.
37 E. H. Carr, "Two Currents."
38 E. Morrell, "Communist Unionism," pp. 522–35.
39 R. Godson, *The Kremlin and Labor: A Study in National Security* (New York: Crane, Russak, 1977), pp. 28–29.
40 V. Putiatina, "VShPD," *Sovetskie profsoiuzy*, 1979, No. 23, pp. 16–17.
41 J. Svetlicnij, "At Moscow, a University for Trade Unions from All over the World," *World Trade Union Movement*, 1976, No. 10, pp. 30–31.
42 O. N. Melikian, "Institut mezhdunarodnogo rabochego dvizheniia AN SSSR na rubezhe piatiletke," *Rabochii klass i sovremennyi mir*, 1976, No. 2, pp. 172–9.
43 E. Morrell, "Communist Unionism," pp. 522–35.
44 R. Godson, *The Kremlin and Labor*, p. 2.
45 I. Dimant, "*Pravda* and *Trud*; Divergent Attitudes Towards the Middle East," Research Paper No. 3, Soviet and East European Research Center, Hebrew University, Jerusalem, 1971.
46 V. V. Zagliadin (ed.), *The World Communist Movement* (Moscow: Progress, 1973), pp. 188–235; M. Baglaia, "Osnova dlia edinykh deistvii," *Sovetskie profsoiuzy*, 1979, No. 9, pp. 40–41; "Kommunisty i profsoiuznoe dvizhenie," *Rabochii klass i sovremennyi mir*, 1975, No. 5, pp. 3–20.
47 L. I. Brezhnev, *Sovetskie profsoiuzy – vliiatel'naia sila nashego obshchestva* (Moscow: Politizdat, 1977), p. 17. Also see, "My gotovy vmeste s VKT. . . ," *Vsemirnoe profsoiuznoe dvizhenie*, 1978, No. 2, p. 12; and L. Petrov, "Delo srodnivshee nas," *Sovetskie profsoiuzy*. 1979, No. 10, pp. 29–30.
48 B. Martin, "International Activities."
49 Ibid.; Associated Press Dispatch, "Soviets Challenged on Rights of Workers," 23 April 1978.
50 R. Godson, *The Kremlin and Labor*, pp. 54–58; S. Haseler, "Visas for Soviet Trade Unionists?" *Policy Review*, 1977, No. 1, pp. 81–8; F. Bonoski, "Profsoiuzy SShA: Esli prigliadet'sia vnimatel'nei. . . ," *Sovetskie profsoiuzy*, 1978, No. 14, pp. 40–42.
51 V. V. Zagliadin, "Izmeneniia v mire i kommunisticheskoe dvi-

zhenie," *Rabochii klass i sovremennyi mir*, 1975, No. 5, pp. 3–20; V. V. Zagliadin (ed.), *The World Communist Movement*.

52 B. Martin, "International Activities."

53 R. Godson, *The Kremlin and Labor*, pp. 39–42; A. Davydov, "'Novye Veleniia' i starye dogmy," *Sovetskie profsoiuzy*, 1979, No. 5, pp. 43–44.

54 Kh. Kroes, "Trudiashchiesia Latinskoi Ameriki i VFP," *Vsemirnoe profsoiuznoe dvizhenia*, 1978, No. 3, pp. 3–4; A. V. Kondrat'ev, "Latino-amerikanskii proftsentr trudiashchikhsiia (KLAT)," *Rabochii klass i sovremennyi mir*, 1975, No. 3, pp. 174–6; G. Kanayev, *Soviet Trade Unions*, pp. 64–8.

55 R. Godson, *The Kremlin and Labor*, p. 39.

56 B. Martin, "International Activities."

57 Ia. Skliarevskii, "Afganistan: Novyi etap revoliutsii," *Sovetskie profsoiuzy*, 1980, No. 7, p. 30.

58 R. Godson, *The Kremlin and Labor*, pp. 58–70.

59 B. Martin, "International Activities."

60 A. Zack, *Labor Training in Developing Countries* (New York: Praeger, 1964), pp. 97–112; and H. K. Jacobson, "Ventures in Polity Shaping: External Assistance to Labor Movements in Developing Countries," in R. W. Cox (ed.), *The Politics of International Organizations* (Washington, D.C.: Praeger, 1970), pp. 195–205.

61 R. Godson, *The Kremlin and Labor*, pp. 40–41.

62 H. K. Jacobson, "Ventures," p. 202.

Conclusion

1 J. B. Sorenson, *The Life and Death of Soviet Trade Unionism, 1917–1928* (New York: Atherton, 1969); R. Godson, *The Kremlin and Labor: A Study in National Security* (New York: Crane, Russak, 1977); D. C. Heldman, *Trade Unions and Labor Relations in the USSR* (Washington, D.C.: Council on American Affairs, 1977); A. Broadersen, *The Soviet Worker* (New York: Random House, 1966); R. Conquest, *Industrial Workers in the USSR* (London: Bodley Head, 1967); F. S. Haylenko, *Trade Unions and Labor in the Soviet Union* (Munich: Institute for the Study of the USSR, 1965); P. Barton, "'Trade Unions' in the USSR," *AFL-CIO Free Trade Union News*, 26 September 1979, pp. 1–16.

2 E. Morrell, "Communist Unionism: Organized Labor and the Soviet State" (Ph.D. dissertation, Harvard University, Cambridge, Mass., 1965).

3 T. Lowit, *Le Syndicalism du type soviétique* (Paris: Colin, 1971).

4 G. Vedel, *Les Organizations de masse en Union soviétique* (Paris: Cujas, 1965).

5 I. Deutscher, *Soviet Trade Unions* (New York: Oxford University Press, 1950).

6 E. C. Brown, *Soviet Trade Unions and Labor Relations* (Cambridge, Mass.: Harvard University Press, 1966).
7 L. G. de Bellcombe, *Les Conventions collectives de travail en Union soviétique* (Paris: Mouton, 1958).
8 M. McAuley, *Labour Disputes in Soviet Russia, 1957–1965* (Oxford: Clarendon, 1969).

Classified bibliography

I. Soviet works

A. Communist Party and union officials

Brezhnev, L. I. *Following Lenin's Course*. Moscow: Progress, 1972.
Leninskim kursom. Moscow: Politeratura, 1973.
Otchetnyi doklad Tsentral'nogo komiteta KPSS XXIII s"ezdu Kommunisticheskoi partii Sovetskogo soiuza. Moscow: Politeratura, 1966.
Sovetskie profsoiuzy − vliiatel'naia sila nashego obshchestva. Moscow: Politizdat, 1977.
K. Marks i F. Engel's o profsoiuzakh. Moscow: Profizdat, 1959.
Kalinin, M. *Na putiakh k sotsializmu*. Leningrad: Priboi, 1926.
Khrushchev, N. S. *Otchetnyi doklad Tsentral'nogo komiteta Kommunisticheskoi partii Sovetskogo soiuza XX s"ezdu*. Moscow: Gosizdat, 1959.
Kollontai, A. *The Workers' Opposition in Russia*. Chicago: Industrial Workers of the World, 1921.
Kuznetsov, V. V. *Sotsialisticheskoe sorevnovanie i zadachi profsoiuzov*. Moscow: Profizdat, 1947.
Lenin, V. I. *Collected Works*. Moscow: Foreign Language Publishing House, 1960−4.
On Trade Unions. Moscow: Progress, 1970.
Lenin i Stalin o trude. Moscow: Profizdat, 1941.
Lenin o trude i prave. Leningrad: Leningradskii gosudarstvennyi universitet, 1970.
Lozovskii, A. *Desiat' let bor'by za profintern*. Moscow: VTsSPS, 1930.
Za edinstvo mirovogo profdvizheniia. Moscow: Partizdat, 1935.
Molotov, V. *Organizatsionnyi otchet Tsentral'nogo komiteta XIV s"ezdu Rossiiskoi kommunisticheskoi partii (bol'shevikov)*. Moscow: Gosizdat, 1926.
Shelepin, A. *Report of the All-Union Central Council of Trade Unions to the 15th Congress of the Trade Unions of the USSR*. Moscow: Profizdat, 1972.
Shvernik, N. M. *Doklad na XII plenume VTsSPS*. Moscow: Profizdat, 1954.
O zadachakh VTsSPS i professional'nykh soiuzov v sviazi s peredachei im funktsii Narkomtruda. Moscow: Profizdat, 1933.

167

Otchetnyi doklad XI s"ezdu profsoiuzov SSSR o rabote Vsesoiuznogo tsen-tral'nogo soveta professional'nykh soiuzov. Moscow: Gospolitizdat, 1954.
Perezakliuchenie koldogovorov i podniatie proizvoditel'nosti truda. Moscow: Profizdat, 1933.
The Reorganization of the Work of the Trade Unions. Moscow: Co-Operative Publishing Society of Foreign Workers in the USSR, 1934.
Stakhanovskoe dvizhenie i zadachi profsoiuzov. Moscow: Profizdat, 1935.
Stalin, J. V. *Works.* Moscow: Foreign Language Publishing House, 1952–6.
Tomskii, M. P. *Izbrannye stat'i i rechi, 1917–1927.* Moscow: VTsSPS, 1928.
Professional'nye soiuzy na novykh putiakh. Moscow: VTsSPS, 1926.
Profsoiuzy SSSR i ikh otnoshenie k kompartii i sovetskomu gosudarstvu. Moscow: VTsSPS, 1928.

B. *Published documents*

Biulleten' Verkhovnogo suda RSFSR.
Biulleten' Verkhovnogo suda SSSR.
Biulleten' VTsSPS.
Instruktsiia o provedenii vyborov profsoiuznykh organov (utverzhdena prezidiumom VTsSPS 17 ianvariia 1964 goda, chastichnye izmeniia vneseny 5 iiulia 1968 goda). Moscow: Profizdat, 1968.
Instruktsiia o provedenii vyborov profsoiuznykh organov (utverzhdena prezidiumom VTsSPS 17 ianvariia 1964 g., chastichnaia izmeniia vneseny 5 iiulia 1968g., i 11 maia 1973 goda. Leningrad: No. 6 upravlenie izdatel'stva Lengorispolkoma, 1973.
Kamskii kabel'nyi zavod imeni 50-letiia SSSR. *Kollektivnyi dogovor na 1974 god.* Kudymkar: Kudymkarskaia tipografiia, 1974.
Kommunisticheskaia partiia Sovetskogo soiuza. *X s"ezd RKP(b): Stenograficheskii otchet.* Moscow: KPSS–Partizdat, 1963.
XI s"ezd RKP(b): Stenograficheskii otchet. Moscow: Gosizdat Poliliteratura, 1961.
XII s"ezd RKP(b): Stenograficheskii otchet. Moscow: Poliliteratura, 1968.
XIII s"ezd RKP(b): Stenograficheskii otchet. Moscow: Poliliteratura, 1963.
XV s"ezd RKP(b): Stenografisheskii otchet. Moscow: Gosizdat Poliliteratura, 1961.
XVI s"ezd RKP(b): Stenograficheskii otchet. Moscow: Partizdat TsK VKP(b), 1935.
XXV s"ezd KPSS: Stenograficheskii otchet. Moscow: Poliliteratura, 1976.
Kommunisticheskaia partiia Sovetskogo soiuza v rezoliutsiiakh i resheniiakh s"ezdov, konferentsii i plenumov TsK. Moscow: Gosizdat Poliliteratura, 1954.
KPSS o profsoiuzakh. Moscow: Profizdat, 1957.
KPSS o profsoiuzakh. Moscow: Profizdat, 1963.
KPSS o profsoiuzakh. Moscow: Profizdat, 1967.
KPSS o profsoiuzakh. Moscow: Profizdat, 1974.
Spravochnik partiinogo rabotnika. Moscow: Poliliteratura, 1974.

Profsoiuz rabochikh kozhevnikov SSSR. *II-i Leningradskii oblastnoi s"ezd: Rezoliutsii s"ezda.* Leningrad: LOPS kozhevnikov SSSR, 1929.
Sbornik zakonodatel'nykh aktov o trude. Moscow: Iuridicheskaia literatura, 1974.
Sbornik zakonodatel'nykh aktov o trude. Moscow: Iuridicheckaia literatura, 1977.
Sobranie postanovlenii pravitel'stva RSFSR.
Sobranie postanovlenii pravitel'stva SSSR.
Tsentral'noe statisticheskoe upravlenie SSSR, *Narodnoe khoziaistvo SSSR v 1978 g.* Moscow: Statistika, 1979.
Tsentral'noe upravlenie narodno-khoziaistvennogo ucheta Gosplana SSSR. *Sostav rukovodiashchikh rabotnikov i spetsialistov Soiuza SSSR.* Moscow: Soiuzorguchet, 1936.
Vedomosti Verkhovnogo soveta RSFSR.
Vedomosti Verkhovnogo soveta SSSR.
Verkhovnyi sovet SSSR. *Zasedaniia Verkhovnogo soveta SSSR, chetvertogo sozyva (7–10 maia, 1957): Stenograficheskii otchet.* Moscow: Izdatel'stuo Verkhovnogo soveta SSSR, 1957.
Vologodskii oblastnoi sovet professional'nykh soiuzov. Uchebnometodicheskii kabinet profsoiuznykh kursov. *Metodicheskoe pis'mo po organizatsii shkol i postoianno-deistvuiushchikh seminarov po obucheniiu profsoiuznogo aktiva.* Vologda: Oblastnaia tipografiia, 1972.
Vsesoiuznyi tsentral'nyi sovet professional'nykh soiuzov. *Profsoiuzy SSSR; Dokumenty i materialy.* Moscow: Profizdat, 1963, 1974.
Sbornik postanovlenii VTsSPS. Moscow: Profizdat, 1960–79.
Spravochnik profsoiuznogo rabotnika. Moscow: Profizdat, 1971.
Spravochnik profsoiuznogo rabotnika. Moscow: Profizdat, 1974.
Statotdel. *Profsoiuznaia perepis', 1932–1933gg.* Moscow: Profizdat, 1934.

C. Dissertations

Babaeva, M. "Fabrichno-zavodskie komitety professional'nykh soiuzov i ikh rol' v regulirovanii uslovii truda rabochikh i sluzhashchikh (po materialam predpriiatii Uzbekskoi SSR)." Candidate's dissertation, Institute of Philosophy and Law, Academy of Sciences of the Uzbek Republic, Tashkent, 1967.
Borodina, N. N. "Gosudarstvenno-pravovye i obshchestvennye mery ukrepleniia distsiplina truda rabochikh i sluzhashchikh v SSSR." Candidate's dissertation, Institute of State and Law, Academy of Sciences of the USSR, Moscow, 1966.

D. Periodical publications and newspapers

Eko
Ekonomicheskaia gazeta

Istoriia SSSR
Izvestiia
Kommunist (Moscow)
Kommunist (Vilnius)
Kommunist Uzbekistana
Leningradskaia pravda
Literaturnaia gazeta
Moscow Daily News
Moskovskaia pravda
Narody Azii i Afriki
Nedelia
Novaia i noveishaia istoriia
Novgorodskaia pravda
Novyi mir
Okhrana truda i sotsial'noe strakhovanie
Partiinaia zhizn'
Pravda
Pravovedenie
Professional'nye soiuzy
Profsoiuzy SSSR
Promyshlenno-ekonomicheskaia gazeta
Rabochii klass i sovremennyi mir
Sotsialisticheskaia zakonnost'
Sotsialisticheskii trud
Sovetskaia iustitsiia
Sovetskie profsoiuzy
Sovetskii shakhter
Sovetskoe gosudarstvo i pravo
Soviet Union
Stroitel'stvo i arkhitektura Leningrada
Trud
Uchenye zapiski Vsesoiuznogo nauchno-issledovatel'skogo instituta sovetskogo
     zakonodatel'stva
Uchenye zapiski Vysshei shkoly profdvizheniia
Udarnik
V pomoshch' VZMK
V pomoshch' profsoiuznomu aktivu
Vecherniaia Moskva
Vechernii Leningrad
Vestnik Leningradskogo gosudarstvennogo universiteta
Vestnik Moskovskogo gosudarstvennogo universiteta
Voprosy ekonomiki
Voprosy istorii
Voprosy profdvizheniia
Vsemirnoe profsoiuznoe dvizhenie
World Trade Union Movement

E. *Other works*

Abramova, A. A. *Distsiplina truda v SSSR.* Moscow: Iuridicheskaia literatura, 1969.

Akademiia nauk SSSR. Institut gosudarstva i prava. *Pravo i sotsiologiia.* Moscow: Nauka, 1973.

Pravovye aspekty deiatel'nosti profsoiuzov SSSR. Moscow: Nauka, 1973.

Akademiia obshchestvennykh nauk pri TsK KPSS. Kafedra filosofii. *Kollektiv i lichnost'.* Moscow: Mysl', 1968.

Akapova, E. M. *Okhrana trudovykh prav rabochikh i sluzhashchikh fab-zavmestkomami profsoiuzov.* Rostov-na-Donu: Rostovskii gosudarstvennyi universitet, 1964.

Aleksandrov, N. G. *Novoe v razvitii trudovogo prava v period mezhdu XX i XXI s"ezdami KPSS.* Moscow: Moskovskii gosudarstvennyi universitet, 1961.

Sotsialisticheskaia distsiplina truda. Moscow: Pravda, 1949.

Sovetskoe gosudarstvo i obshchestvennost' v usloviiakh razvernutogo stroitel'stva kommunizma. Moscow: Moskovskii gosudarstvennyi universitet, 1962.

Sovetskoe trudovoe pravo. Moscow: Iuridicheskoe izdatel'stvo, 1946.

Sovetskoe trudovoe pravo. Moscow: Iuridicheskaia literatura, 1972.

Voprosy trudovogo prava na sovremennom etape. Moscow: Moskovskii gosudarstvennyi universitet, 1964.

Aleksandrov, N. G. and Mutsinkov, G. B. *Trudovoe pravo.* Moscow: Znanie, 1967.

Alekseev, G. and Ivanov, E. *Profsoiuzy v period stroitel'stva kommunizma.* Moscow: Profizdat, 1968.

Aluf, A. S. *The Development of Socialist Methods and Forms of Labour.* Moscow: Co-Operative Publishing Society of Foreign Workers in the USSR, 1932.

Arkhipov, V. D.; Koniaev, N. I.; and Khoren, P. S. *Kommentarii k polozheniiu o poriadke rassmotreniia trudovykh sporov.* Moscow: Iuridicheskaia literatura, 1976.

Baglaia, M. V. (ed.). *Klassovaia bor'ba i profsoiuzy.* Moscow: Profizdat, 1971.

Balabanov, M. *Istoriia rabochei kooperatsii v Rossii.* Moscow: Tsentrosoiuz, 1928.

Berezanskii, L. *Proizvodstvennoe soveshchanie: Chto takoe proizvodstvennoe soveshchanie i kak v nem rabotat'.* Moscow: Doloi negramotnost', 1927.

Bezina, A. K. and Shchelyvanova, Zh. V. *Sovetskoe trudovoe pravo: Ukazatel' literatury, 1917–1969.* Kazan: Kazanskii universitet, 1971.

Boiarskii, I. I. *Profsoiuzy ot XVI k XVII s"ezdu VKP(b): Dlia nizovogo profaktiva.* Moscow: Profizdat, 1934.

Bol'shaia sovetskaia entsiklopediia. 3rd Ed. Moscow: Sovetskaia entsiklopediia 1970–8.

Bor, M. Z. *Aims and Methods of Soviet Planning.* New York: International Publishers, 1967.

Bukhalovskii, O. N. *Pravovoe polozhenie predpriiatiia po trudovomu zakon-odatel'stvu.* Voronezh: Voronezhskii universitet, 1974.

Burov, V. P. *Rabota profsoiuzov po organizatsii sotsialisticheskogo sorevno-vaniia i razvitiia dvizheniia za kommunisticheskii trud.* Perm: Profkursy Permskogo oblastnogo soveta profsoiuzov, Permskoe obshchestvo znanie, 1970.
Rabota profsoiuzov po zakliucheniiu i proverke vypolneniia kollektivnykh dogovorov. Perm: Profkursy Permskogo oblastnogo soveta prof-soiuzov. Permskoe obshchestvo znanie, 1971.

Chavpilo, L.; Shimko, I.; and Ivashkin, B. *Finansovaia rabota profsoiuzov.* Moscow: Profizdat, 1975.

D''iakov, S. *Profsoiuznye komitety v bor'be za ukreplenie trudovoi distsipliny.* Moscow: Profizdat, 1974.

Dogodov, A. *Sostoianie professional'nogo dvizheniia v SSSR, 1924–1926gg.* Moscow: VTsSPS, 1927.

Dvornikov, I. *How Labour Disputes Are Settled in the USSR.* Moscow: Novosti Press, 1974.

Dvornikov, I.; Livshits, R.; and Rumiantseva, M. *Trudovoe zakonodatel'stvo.* Moscow: Profizdat, 1971.

Dzelomanov, V. *USSR Working People in Production Management.* Moscow: Novosti Press, 197?.

Fedinin, V. K. *Sotsialisticheskoe sorevnovanie na sovremennom etape.* Moscow: Ekonomika, 1974.

Fedosov, A. D., *Kommunisty i ekonomicheskaia reforma.* Moscow: Mysl', 1972.

Gershanov, V. and Shelomov, V. *Prava fabrichnogo, zavodskogo, mestnogo komiteta profsoiuza.* Riga: Mezhotraslevoi institut povysheniia kval-ifikatsii spetsialistov narodnogo khoziaistva Latviiskoi SSR, 1973.

Gershanov, V.; Shelomov, B. A.; and Snigireva, I. *The Rights of Trade Unions in the USSR.* Moscow: Profizdat, 1973.

Govorushin, K. V. *Za narvskoi zastavoi.* Moscow: Politizdat, 1975.

Grinevich, V. *Professional'noe dvizhenie rabochikh v Rossii.* Moscow: Kras-naia nov'. 1923.

Guseinov, K. A. *Trade Union Association: USSR, Asia and Africa.* Moscow: Nauka, 1967.

Iakovlev, P. I. *Ocherki po istorii mezhdunarodnoi solidarnosti trudiashchikhsia.* Moscow: Nauka, 1974.

Iampol'skaia, Ts. A. and Tsepin, A. I. (eds.). *Pravovye aspekty deiatel'nosti profsoiuzov SSSR.* Moscow: Nauka, 1973.

Iavich, L. S. and Snigireva, I. O. *Gosudarstvo i profsoiuzy.* Moscow: Profizdat, 1967.

Kaliakin, P. V.; Kovalerchuk, Ia. N.; and Masevich, M. G. *Povyshenie effektivnosti promyshlennogo proizvodstva.* Moscow: Iuridicheskaia lit-eratura, 1972.

Kamalov, U. Kh.; Muzafarov, A. A.; and Saakov, V. G. *Bukhara: Putevoditel'.* Tashkent: TsK KP Uzbekistana, 1973.

Kanayev, G. *Soviet Trade Unions and the International Trade Union Move-ment.* Moscow: Novosti Press, 1971.

Kantorovich, V. *Ty i vy.* Moscow: Sovetskaia Rossiia, 1974.

Khakimova, R. and Bushkina, A. *Sovetskaia Bashkiriia.* Moscow: Sovetskaia Rossiia, 1969.

Khoziaistvennaia reforma, trud i pravo. Moscow: Moskovskii gosudarstvennyi universitet, 1969.

Kliuev, A. *Kak reshaiutsia trudovye spory.* Moscow: Profizdat, 1960.

Kliuev, A. and Lapai, A. *O pravakh komiteta profsoiuza.* Stalino-Donbass: Knizhnoe izdatel'stvo, 1960.

Kliuev, A. and Mavrin, A. V. *Rukovoditeliu predpriiatiia o trudovom zakonodatel'stve.* Moscow: Iuridicheskaia literatura, 1973.

Kogan, N., Pavlov, B. S. *Molodoi rabochii: Vchera, segodnia.* Sverdlovsk: Sredno-Ural'skoe knizhnoe izdatel'stvo, 1976.

Kondrat'ev, R. I. *Lokal'nye normy trudovogo prava i material'noe stimulirovanie.* Lvov: Vishcha shkola, 1973.

Sochetanie tsentralizovannogo i lokal'nogo pravovogo regulirovaniia trudovykh otnoshenii. Lvov: Vishcha shkola, 1977.

Kornikova, M. I. *Vospitatel'naia rabota v trudovom kollektive.* Moscow: Profizdat, 1975.

Lasker, I. B. and Scott, H. *The Soviet Trade Unions on the Threshold of the Second Five Year Plan.* Moscow: Co-Operative Publishing Society of Foreign Workers in the USSR, 1933.

Leningrad. Institut istorii partii. *Istoriia Kirovskogo (byv. Putilovskogo) metallurgicheskogo i mashinostroitel'nogo zavoda v Leningrade.* Moscow: Sotsial'no-ekonomicheskaia literatura, 1961–6.

Mezhvuzovskaia nauchnaia konferentsiia 'Sovetskoe gosudarstvo i pravo v period razvernutogo stroitel'stva kommunizma.' *Doklady.* Leningrad: Leningradskii gosudarstvennyi universitet, 1961.

Mikul'skii, K. I. (ed.). *Effektivnost' sotsialisticheskogo proizvodstva i khoziaistvennyi mekhanism.* Moscow: Nauka, 1979.

Mineev, V. N. *Upravlenie sotsialisticheskim proizvodstvom.* Moscow: Profizdat, 1973.

Ministerstvo vysshego i srednego spetsial'nogo obrazovaniia Ukrainskoi SSR. L'vov gosudarstvennyi universitet. Iuridicheskii fakul'tet. Respublikanskaia mezhvuzovskaia nauchnaia konferentsiia na teme 'Rol' pravovoi nauki v sovershenstvovanii prakticheskoi deiatel'nosti gosudarstvennykh organov, khoziaistvennykh i obshchestvennykh organizatsii.' *Tezisy dokladov i nauchnykh soobshchenii.* Lvov: L'vovskii gosudarstvennyi universitet, 1967.

Mordkovich, V. G. *Obshchestvenno-politicheskaia aktivnost' trudiashchikhsia.* Sverdlovsk: Akademiia nauk SSSR, Ural'skii filial, 1970.

Mozhayev, V. *True to the Ideals of Brotherhood and Solidarity.* Moscow: Profizdat, 1974.

Mukhtasipov, M. *Sovetskie profsoiuzy v bor'be za mezhdunarodnoe edinstvo rabochego klassa, 1918–1939gg.* Moscow: Mysl', 1966.

Nikitinskii, V. I. *Effektivnost' norm trudovogo prava.* Moscow: Iuridicheskaia literatura, 1971.

Polozhenie o pravakh fabrichnogo, zavodskogo, mestnogo komiteta professional'nogo soiuza. Moscow: Profizdat, 1974.

Nikitinsky, V. *The Rights of the Factory (Office) Trade Union Committee in the U.S.S.R.* Moscow: Profizdat, 1961.

Okun', S. B. *Putilovets v trekh revoliutsiiakh.* Leningrad: Istoriia zavoda, 1933.

Pasherstnik, A. E. *Distsiplina truda v SSSR.* Moscow: Iuridicheskaia literatura, 1950.

Pashkov, A. S. (ed.). *Sovetskoe trudovoe pravo.* Moscow: Iuridicheskaia literatura, 1976.

Petrovichev, N. A. *Partiinoe stroitel'stvo.* Moscow: Politizdat, 1976.

Piatakov, A. V. *Profsoiuzy i sovetskoe gosudarstvo: Ocherki ob uchastii profsoiuzov v khoziaistvenno-organizatorskoi i kul'turno-vospitatel'noi deiatel'nosti sovetskogo gosudarstva.* Moscow: Gosiurizdat, 1960.

Podorov, G. *O distsipline truda.* Moscow: Politizdat, 1972.

Postoianno-deistvuiushchie proizvodstvennye soveshchaniia na predpriiatiiakh: Sbornik stat'ei. Moscow: Profizdat, 1960.

Razmologin, B. *Ukreplenie trudovoi distsipliny.* Moscow: Profizdat, 1973.

Rebrov, Iu. V. *Problemy ispol'zovaniia osnovnykh proizvodstvennykh fondov.* Moscow: Ekonomika, 1974.

Rozhdestvenskii, A. P. *Bashkiriia: Putevoditel'.* Ufa: Bashkirskoe knizhnoe izdatel'stvo, 1970.

Savinov, N. *V pomoshch' revizionnym komissiiam FZMK.* Moscow: Profizdat, 1974.

Sharapov, G. V. (ed.). *Istoriia profsoiuzov SSSR chast' 1 (1905–1937 gody).* Moscow: Profizdat, 1977.

Istoriia profsoiuzov SSSR chast' 2 (1938–1978 gody). Moscow: Profizdat, 1979.

Shulikov, M. I. *Fabrichno-zavodskie komitety i rastsenichno-konfliktnye kommissii: Ikh stroenie, zadachi i funktsii.* Moscow: VTsSPS, 1926.

Smirnov, I. *Profsoiuzy SSSR: 100 voprosov – 100 otvetov.* Moscow: Profizdat, 1972.

Smirnov, V. N. *Distsiplina truda v SSSR.* Leningrad: Leningradskii gosudarstvennyi universitet, 1972.

Smoliarchuk, V. I. *Prava profsoiuzov v regulirovanii trudovykh otnoshenii rabochikh i sluzhashchikh.* Moscow: Profizdat, 1973.

Snigireva, I. O. and Iavich, L. S. *Gosudarstvo i profsoiuzy.* Moscow: Profizdat, 1967.

Tolstoi, Iu. K. *Pravovye voprosy upravleniia promyshlennost'iu i stroitel'stvom.* Leningrad: Leningradskii gosudarstvennyi universitet, 1959.

Tsepin, A. I. *Kontrol' FZMK za sobliudeniem zakonodatel'stva o trude.* Moscow: Profizdat, 1975.

Priem, perevod i uvol'nenie s raboty. Moscow: Moskovskii rabochii, 1973.

L'Université de l'amité des peuples, Patrice Lumumba. Moscow, 1970.

Vasil'ev, V. G. *Problemy povysheniia proizvoditel'nosti truda na predpriiatiiakh promyshlennosti i transporta.* Moscow: Nauka, 1974.

Vladycheno, I. *Soviet Trade Unions Ensure the Workers' Participation in Socialist Production Management.* Moscow: Novosti Press, 1972.

Uchastie rabochikh i sluzhashchikh v upravlenii proizvodstvom. Moscow: Profizdat, 1967.

Voprosy gosudarstva i prava. Alma-Ata: Kazakhskii gosudarstvennyi universitet, 1963.
Voskresenskaia, M. and Kuznetsov, S. *Voprosy profsoiuznoi raboty.* Moscow: Profizdat, 1953.
Vyrypaev, A. and Kuznetsov, S. *Voprosy profsoiuznoi raboty.* Moscow: Profizdat, 1953.
Zagliadin, V. V. (ed.). *The World Communist Movement.* Moscow: Progress, 1973.
Zagorul'kin, V. A. *Postoianno-deistvuiushchie proizvodstvennye soveshchaniia.* Moscow: Profizdat, 1963.

II. Non-Soviet works

A. Reports

Congress of Industrial Organizations. *Report of the CIO Delegation to the Soviet Union.* Washington, D.C.: CIO, 1945.
Dunn, R.; Chase S.; Tugwell, R. G.; and Douglas, P. *Soviet Russia in the Second Decade: Report of the First American Trade Union Delegation to the Soviet Union.* New York: John Day, 1928.
Institute for the Study of the USSR (Munich). *Prominent Personalities in the USSR.* Metuchen, N.J.: Scarecrow Press, 1968.
International Labour Office. *Labour Conditions in Soviet Russia.* London: Harrison, 1920.
Industrial Life in Soviet Russia: Studies and Reports. Series B, No. 14. Geneva: ILO, 1924.
The Trade Union Movement in Soviet Russia: Studies and Reports. Series A, No. 26. Geneva: ILO, 1927.
Trade Union Rights in the USSR: Studies and Reports. New Series, No. 49. Geneva: ILO, 1959.
U.S. Congress. Joint Economic Committee. *The Soviet Economy in a Time of Change (Vols. 1 & 2).* Washington, D.C.: Government Printing Office, 1979.
U.S. Department of Labor. Bureau of Labor Standards. "Wartime Activities of Soviet Trade Unions." Unpublished report prepared by E. Nash. Washington, D.C., 1944.
U.S. Department of State. *Soviet World Outlook.* Washington, D.C.: Government Printing Office, 1959.

B. Dissertations

Langsam, D. "Pressure Group Politics in NEP Russia: The Case of the Trade Unions." Ph.D. dissertation, Princeton University, Princeton, New Jersey, 1974.
Morrell, E. "Communist Unionism: Organized Labor and the Soviet State." Ph.D. dissertation, Harvard University, Cambridge, Massachusetts, 1965.

Ruble, B. A. "Soviet Trade Unions: Changing Balances and Their Functions." Ph.D. dissertation, University of Toronto, Toronto, Ontario, 1977.

Schwartz, M. "Soviet Policy and the World Federation of Trade Unions, 1945–1949." Ph.D. dissertation, Columbia University, New York, 1963.

C. *Periodical publications and newspapers*

ACES Bulletin
AFL-CIO Free Trade Union News
American Journal of International Law
American Political Science Review
British Journal of Industrial Relations
British Journal of Sociology
Comparative Labor Law
Current Digest of the Soviet Press
Foreign Affairs
Freedom Appeals
Industrial and Labor Relations Review
International Labour Review
International Organization
Journal of Contemporary History
Journal of Politics
Labour Focus on Eastern Europe
London Times
Monthly Labor Review
New York Review of Books
New York Times
Orbis
Policy Review
Posev
Problems of Communism
Slavic Review
Sotsialisticheskii vestnik
Soviet Studies
Washington Post
World Politics

D. *Other works*

Anweiler, O. *The Soviets: The Russian Workers', Peasants' and Soldiers' Councils: 1905–1921*. Translated by R. Hein. New York: Random House–Pantheon, 1974.

Azrael, J. *Managerial Power and Soviet Politics*. Cambridge, Mass.: Harvard University Press, 1966.

Bakke, E. W.; Ker, C.; and Anrod, C. W. *Unions, Management and the Public.* New York: Harcourt Brace, 1967.

Barabash, J. *The Practice of Unionism.* New York: Harper, 1956.

Barry, D. D.; Butler, W. E.; and Ginsburgs, G. *Contemporary Soviet Law: Essays in Honor of John N. Hazard.* The Hague: Martinus Nijhoff, 1974.

Bauer, R. A. *The New Man in Soviet Psychology.* Cambridge, Mass.: Harvard University Press, 1952.

Bergson, A. *The Structure of Soviet Wages.* Cambridge, Mass.: Harvard University Press, 1944.

Berliner, J. *The Innovation Decision in Soviet Industry.* Cambridge, Mass.: MIT Press, 1976.

Berman, H. J. *Justice in the USSR.* Cambridge, Mass.: Harvard University Press, 1963.

Broadersen, A. *The Soviet Worker.* New York: Random House, 1966.

Brown, E. C. *Soviet Trade Unions and Labor Relations.* Cambridge, Mass.: Harvard University Press, 1966.

Calhoun, D. F. *The United Front: The TUC and the Russians, 1923–1928.* Cambridge University Press, 1976.

Carr, E. H. *The Bolshevik Revolution.* Middlesex: Penguin, 1966.
The Interregnum. Middlesex: Penguin, 1969.
Socialism in One Country. Middlesex: Penguin, 1969.

Carr, E. H. and Davies, R. W. *Foundations of a Planned Economy.* Hammondsworth: Penguin, 1969.

Chapman, J. G. *Real Wages in Soviet Russia Since 1928.* Cambridge, Mass.: Harvard University Press, 1963.
Wage Variation in Soviet Industry: The Impact of the 1956–1960 Wage Reform. Santa Monica, Calif.: RAND, 1970.

Cohen, S. *Bukharin and the Bolshevik Revolution.* New York: Knopf, 1972.

Conquest, R. *Industrial Workers in the USSR.* London: Bodley Head, 1967.
Power and Policy in the USSR. New York: St. Martin's Press, 1962.

Cox, R. W. (ed.). *The Politics of International Organizations.* Washington, D.C.: Praeger, 1970.

Cox, R. W. and Jacobson, H. K. (eds.). *The Anatomy of Influence: Decision Making in International Organizations.* New Haven: Yale University Press, 1973.

Day, R. *Leon Trotsky and the Politics of Economic Isolation.* Cambridge University Press, 1973.

de Bellcombe, L. G. *Les Conventions collectives de travail en Union soviétique.* Paris: Mouton, 1958.

Deutscher, I. *Soviet Trade Unions.* New York: Oxford University Press, 1950.
Stalin. New York: Oxford University Press, 1966.

Dewar, M. *Labour Policy in the USSR.* London: Royal Institute of International Affairs, 1956.

Dore, R. *British Factory – Japanese Factory.* Berkeley: University of California Press, 1973.

Dunham, V. "The Worker and the Soviet System: A Literary Study (The Nineteen Sixties and Seventies)." Unpublished manuscript, 1980.

Dunn, R. W. *Soviet Trade Unions*. New York: Vanguard, 1928.

Fainsod, M. *How Russia Is Ruled*. Cambridge, Mass.: Harvard University Press, 1963.

Freeman, J. *The Soviet Worker*. New York: International, 1932.

Godson, R. *The Kremlin and Labor: A Study in National Security*. New York: Crane, Russak, 1977.

Gordon, M. *Workers Before and After Lenin*. New York: Dutton, 1941.

Granick, D. *Managerial Comparisons of Four Developed Countries: France, Britain, United States and Russia*. Cambridge, Mass.: MIT Press, 1972.

The Red Executive. Garden City, N.Y.: Doubleday, 1961.

Haber, W. (ed.). *Labor in a Changing America*. New York: Basic Books, 1966.

Hammer, D. P. *USSR: The Politics of Oligarchy*. Hinsdale, Ill.: Dryden Press, 1974.

Hammond, T. T. *Lenin on Trade Unions and Revolution: 1893–1917*. New York: Oxford University Press, 1957.

Haraszti, M. *A Worker in a Worker's State*. New York: Universe Books, 1977.

Haylenko, F. S. *Trade Unions and Labor in the Soviet Union*. Munich: Institute for the Study of the USSR, 1965.

Haynes, V. and Semyonova, O. (eds.). *Workers Against the GULAG*. London: Pluto Press, 1979.

Heldman, D. C. *Trade Unions and Labor Relations in the USSR*. Washington, D.C.: Council on American Affairs, 1977.

Hero, Jr., A. O. and Starr, E. *The Reuther–Meany Foreign Policy Dispute*. Dobbs Ferry, N.Y.: Oceana, 1970.

Hough, J. *The Soviet Prefects*. Cambridge, Mass.: Harvard University Press, 1969.

The Soviet Union and Social Science Theory. Cambridge, Mass.: Harvard University Press, 1977.

Hough, J. and Fainsod, M. *How the Soviet Union Is Governed*. Cambridge, Mass.: Harvard University Press, 1979.

Hutchings, R. *Soviet Economic Development*. New York: Barnes & Noble, 1971.

Kahan, A. and Ruble, B. A. (eds.). *Industrial Labor in the USSR*. Elmsford, N.Y.: Pergamon Press, 1979.

Kanter, R. M. *Social Science Frontiers No. 9: Work and Family in the United States: A Critical Review and Agenda for Research and Policy*. New York: Russell Sage Foundation, 1977.

Kaplan, F. *Bolshevik Ideology and the Ethics of Labor*. New York: Philosophical Library, 1968.

Katsenelinboigen, A. *Studies in Soviet Economic Planning*. White Plains, N.Y.: M.E. Sharpe, 1978.

Katz, A. *The Politics of Economic Reform in the Soviet Union.* New York: Praeger, 1972.

Keep, J. L. H. *The Russian Revolution.* New York: Norton, 1976.

Kirsch, L. J. *Soviet Wages: Changes in Structure and Administration Since 1956.* Cambridge, Mass.: MIT Press, 1972.

Kucherov, S. *The Organs of Soviet Administration of Justice: Their History of Operation.* Leiden: E.J. Brill, 1976.

Lane, D. and O'Dell, F. *The Soviet Industrial Worker.* New York: St. Martin's Press, 1978.

Leonhard, W. *The Kremlin Since Stalin.* New York: Oxford University Press, 1962.

Lewin, M. *Political Undercurrents in Soviet Economic Debates.* Princeton University Press, 1974.

Russian Peasants and Soviet Power. Evanston: University of Illinois Press, 1968.

Linden, C. A. *Khrushchev and the Soviet Leadership, 1957–1964.* Baltimore: Johns Hopkins University Press, 1966.

Lowit, T. *Le Syndicalism du type soviétique.* Paris: Colin, 1971.

Madison, B. *Social Welfare in the Soviet Union.* Stanford University Press, 1968.

"Soviet Income Maintenance Programs in the Struggle Against Poverty." Occasional Paper, No. 31, Washington, D.C.: Kennan Institute for Advanced Russian Studies, 1978.

Matthews, M. *Class and Society in Soviet Russia.* New York: Walker, 1972.

McAuley, A. *Economic Welfare in the Soviet Union.* Madison: University of Wisconsin Press, 1979.

McAuley, M. *Labour Disputes in Soviet Russia, 1957–1965.* Oxford: Clarendon, 1969.

Medvedev, R. A. *Let History Judge.* Translated by C. Taylor. New York: Knopf, 1972.

On Socialist Democracy. Translated by E. DeKadt. New York: Knopf, 1975.

Medvedev, R. A. and Medvedev, Zh. *Khrushchev: The Years in Power.* Translated by A. Durkin. New York: Columbia University Press, 1976.

Michels, R. *Political Parties.* Translated by E. Paul and C. Paul. New York: Dover, 1959.

Moore, B., Jr. *Terror and Progress – USSR.* Cambridge, Mass.: Harvard University Press, 1954.

Navarro, V. *Social Security and Medicine in the USSR.* Lexington, Mass.: Lexington Books, 1977.

Nove, A. *An Economic History of the USSR.* Middlesex: Penguin, 1972.

Osakwe, C. *The Participation of the Soviet Union in Universal International Organizations.* Leiden: Sijthoff, 1972.

Osborn, R. *Soviet Social Policy.* Georgetown, Ontario: Irwin-Dorsey, 1970.

Peterson, F. *American Labor Unions.* New York: Harper & Row, 1963.

Ploss, S. *Conflict and Decision-Making in Soviet Russia.* Princeton University Press, 1965.

Potichnyj, P. J. *Soviet Agricultural Trade Unions, 1917–1970.* University of Toronto Press, 1972.

Riasanovsky, N. *A History of Russia.* New York: Oxford University Press, 1963.

Richman, B. M. *Management Development and Education in the Soviet Union.* East Lansing: Michigan State University Press, 1967.

Soviet Management. Englewood Cliffs, N.J.: Prentice-Hall, 1965.

Rigby, T. H. *Communist Party Membership in the USSR.* Princeton University Press, 1968.

Ryavec, K. W. *Implementation of Soviet Economic Reforms.* New York: Praeger, 1975.

Schwartz, H. *Russia's Soviet Economy.* New York: Prentice-Hall, 1954.

Schwarz, S. *Labor in the Soviet Union.* New York: Praeger, 1952.

Scott, J. *Behind the Urals.* Bloomington: Indiana University Press, 1973.

Smith, G. B. *The Soviet Procuracy and the Supervision of Administration.* Leiden: Sijthoff & Noordhoff, 1978.

Solomon, P. H., Jr. *Soviet Criminologists and Criminal Policy.* New York: Columbia University Press, 1978.

Solzhenitsyn, A. *The GULAG Archipelago.* New York: Harper & Row, 1973–78.

Sorenson, J. B. *The Life and Death of Soviet Trade Unionism: 1917–1928.* New York: Atherton, 1969.

Taubman, W. *Governing Soviet Cities.* New York: Praeger, 1973.

Turin, S. P. *From Peter the Great to Lenin.* London: Frank Cass, 1935.

Tyler, G. *The Labor Revolution.* New York: Viking, 1966.

Ulam, A. *The Bolsheviks.* New York: Collier, 1965.

Vedel, G. *Les Organizations de masse en Union soviétique.* Paris: Cujas, 1965.

Venturi, F. *The Roots of Revolution.* Translated by F. Haskell. New York: Grossett & Dunlap, 1966.

Webb, B. and Webb, S. *Soviet Communism.* New York: Charles Scribner, 1936.

White, S. *Political Culture and Soviet Politics.* London: Macmillan, 1979.

Windmuller, J. P. *Labor Internationals.* Ithaca, N.Y.: Cornell University Press, 1969.

Yanowitch, M. (ed.). *Soviet Work Attitudes.* White Plains, N.Y.: M.E. Sharpe, 1979.

Zack, A. *Labor Training in Developing Countries.* New York: Praeger, 1964.

Index